The Expositor's Bible
The Book Of Genesis

by
Marcus Dods

The Expositor's Bible
The Book Of Genesis
by Marcus Dods

Copyright © 2024

All Rights reserved.

No part of this publication may be reproduced, stored in a retrieval system, or transmitted in any form or by any means, electronic, mechanical, photocopying or Otherwise, without the written permission of the publisher.
The author/editor asserts the moral right to be identified as the author/editor of this work.

ISBN: 978-93-61155-26-0

Published by
DOUBLE 9 BOOKS
2/13-B, Ansari Road
Daryaganj, New Delhi – 110002
info@double9books.com
www.double9books.com
Tel. 011-40042856

This book is under public domain

ABOUT THE AUTHOR

Marcus Dods was a Scottish divine and controversial biblical scholar. He was a minister for the Free Church of Scotland. He was Principal of New College, Edinburgh. He was born in Belford, Northumberland, the youngest son of Rev Marcus Dods, a Church of Scotland clergyman, and his wife, Sarah Pallister. He attended Edinburgh Academy before studying divinity at Edinburgh University, where he graduated in 1854 and received his licence in 1858. He had a terrible probationary period, being turned down by 23 congregations. In 1864, he was appointed preacher of Renfield Free Church in Glasgow, where he served for 25 years. He joined the United Free Church of Scotland when it was formed in 1900, and was chosen Moderator of its General Assembly in 1902. He declined the appointment, citing that "he cannot see his way to undertake the duties". It was expected that as a neutral moderator, he would be unable to convey his views on certain doctrinal issues that were to be examined. In later life, he lived with his children and grandchildren in a massive Georgian townhouse at 23 Great King Street in Edinburgh's Second New Town.

CONTENTS

I	THE CREATION	7
II	THE FALL	16
III	CAIN AND ABEL	24
IV	CAIN'S LINE, AND ENOCH	33
V	THE FLOOD	41
VI	NOAH'S FALL	49
VII	THE CALL OF ABRAHAM	57
VIII	ABRAM IN EGYPT	66
IX	LOT'S SEPARATION FROM ABRAM	74
X	ABRAM'S RESCUE OF LOT	82
XI	COVENANT WITH ABRAM	90
XII	BIRTH OF ISHMAEL	98
XIII	THE COVENANT SEALED	106
XIV	ABRAHAM'S INTERCESSION FOR SODOM	114
XV	DESTRUCTION OF THE CITIES OF THE PLAIN	123
XVI	SACRIFICE OF ISAAC	131
XVII	ISHMAEL AND ISAAC	140
XVIII	PURCHASE OF MACHPELAH	149
XIX	ISAAC'S MARRIAGE	158
XX	ESAU AND JACOB	167
XXI	JACOB'S FRAUD	175
XXII	JACOB'S FLIGHT AND DREAM	183
XXIII	JACOB AT PENIEL	192

XXIV	JACOB'S RETURN	201
XXV	JOSEPH'S DREAMS	210
XXVI	JOSEPH IN PRISON	221
XXVII	PHARAOH'S DREAMS	231
XXVIII	JOSEPH'S ADMINISTRATION	240
XXIX	VISITS OF JOSEPH'S BRETHREN	249
XXX	THE RECONCILIATION	257
XXXI	THE BLESSINGS OF THE TRIBES	268

I
THE CREATION

Genesis i. and ii.

If any one is in search of accurate information regarding the age of this earth, or its relation to the sun, moon, and stars, or regarding the order in which plants and animals have appeared upon it, he is referred to recent text-books in astronomy, geology, and palæontology. No one for a moment dreams of referring a serious student of these subjects to the Bible as a source of information. It is not the object of the writers of Scripture to impart physical instruction or to enlarge the bounds of scientific knowledge. But if any one wishes to know what connection the world has with God, if he seeks to trace back all that now is to the very fountain-head of life, if he desires to discover some unifying principle, some illuminating purpose in the history of this earth, then we confidently refer him to these and the subsequent chapters of Scripture as his safest, and indeed his only, guide to the information he seeks. Every writing must be judged by the object the writer has in view. If the object of the writer of these chapters was to convey physical information, then certainly it is imperfectly fulfilled. But if his object was to give an intelligible account of God's relation to the world and to man, then it must be owned that he has been successful in the highest degree.

It is therefore unreasonable to allow our reverence for this writing to be lessened because it does not anticipate the discoveries of physical science; or to repudiate its authority in its own department of truth because it does not give us information which it formed no part of the writer's object to give. As well might we deny to Shakespeare a masterly knowledge of human life, because his dramas are blotted by historical anachronisms. That the compiler of this book of Genesis did not aim at scientific accuracy in speaking of physical details is obvious, not merely from the general scope and purpose of the Biblical writers, but especially from this, that in these first two chapters of his book he lays side by side two accounts of man's creation which no ingenuity can reconcile. These two accounts, glaringly incompatible in details, but absolutely harmonious in their leading ideas, at once warn the reader that the writer's aim is rather to convey certain ideas regarding man's spiritual history and his connection with God, than to describe the process of creation. He does describe the process of creation, but he describes it only for the sake of the ideas regarding man's relation to God and God's relation to the world which he can thereby convey. Indeed what we mean by scientific knowledge was not in all the thoughts of the people for whom this book was written. The subject of creation, of the beginning of man upon earth, was not approached from that side at all; and if we are to understand what is here written we must burst the trammels of our own modes of thought and read these chapters not as a chronological, astronomical, geological, biological statement, but as a moral or spiritual conception.

It will, however, be said, and with much appearance of justice, that although the first object of the writer was not to convey scientific information, yet he might have been expected to be accurate in the information he did advance regarding the physical universe. This is an enormous assumption to make on *à priori* grounds, but it is an assumption worth seriously considering because it brings into view a real and important difficulty which every reader of Genesis must face. It brings into view the twofold character of this account of creation. On the one hand it is irreconcilable with the teachings of science. On the other hand it is in striking contrast to the other cosmogonies which have been handed down from pre-scientific ages. These are the two patent features of this record of creation and both require to be accounted for. Either feature alone would be easily accounted for; but the two co-existing in the same document are more baffling. We have to account at once for a want of perfect coincidence with the teachings of science, and for a singular freedom from those errors which disfigure all other primitive accounts of the creation of the world. The one feature of the document is as patent as the other and presses equally for explanation.

Now many persons cut the knot by simply denying that both these features exist. There is no disagreement with science, they say. I speak for many careful enquirers when I say that this cannot serve as a solution of the difficulty. I think it is to be freely admitted that, from whatever cause and however justifiably, the account of creation here given is not in strict and detailed accordance with the teaching of science. All attempts to force its statements into such accord are futile and mischievous. They are futile because they do not convince independent enquirers, but only those who are unduly anxious to be convinced. And they are mischievous because they unduly prolong the strife between Scripture and science, putting the question on a false issue. And above all, they are to be condemned because they do violence to Scripture, foster a style of interpretation by which the text is forced to say whatever the interpreter desires, and prevent us from recognising the real nature of these sacred writings. The Bible needs no defence such as false constructions of its language bring to its aid. They are its worst friends who distort its words that they may yield a meaning more in accordance with scientific truth. If, for example, the word 'day' in these chapters, does not mean a period of twenty-four hours, the interpretation of Scripture is hopeless. Indeed if we are to bring these chapters into any comparison at all with science, we find at once various discrepancies. Of a creation of sun, moon, and stars, subsequent to the creation of this earth, science can have but one thing to say. Of the existence of fruit trees prior to the existence of the sun, science knows nothing. But for a candid and unsophisticated reader without a special theory to maintain, details are needless.

Accepting this chapter then as it stands, and believing that only by looking at the Bible as it actually is can we hope to understand God's method of revealing Himself, we at once perceive that ignorance of some departments of truth does not disqualify a man for knowing and imparting truth about God. In order to be a medium of revelation a man does not need to be in advance of his age in secular learning. Intimate communion with God, a spirit trained to discern spiritual things, a perfect understanding of and zeal for God's purpose, these are qualities quite independent of a knowledge of the discoveries of science. The enlightenment which enables men to apprehend God and spiritual truth, has no necessary connection with scientific attainments. David's confidence in God and his declarations of His faithfulness are none the less valuable, because he was ignorant of a very great deal which every school-boy now knows. Had inspired men introduced into their writings information which anticipated the discoveries of science, their state of mind would be inconceivable, and revelation would be a source of confusion. God's methods are harmonious with one another, and as He has given men natural faculties to acquire scientific knowledge and historical information, He did not stultify this gift by imparting such knowledge in a miraculous and unintelligible manner. There is no evidence that inspired men were in advance of their age in the knowledge of physical facts and laws. And plainly, had they been supernaturally instructed in physical knowledge they would so far have been unintelligible to those to whom they spoke. Had the writer of this book mingled with his teaching regarding God, an explicit and exact account of how this world came into existence—had he spoken of millions of years instead of speaking of days— in all probability he would have been discredited, and what he had to say about God would have been rejected along with his premature science. But speaking from the point of view of his contemporaries, and accepting the current ideas regarding the formation of the world, he attached to these the views regarding God's connection with the world which are most necessary to be believed. What he had learned of God's unity and creative power and connection with man, by the inspiration of the Holy Ghost, he imparts to his contemporaries through the vehicle of an account of creation they could all understand. It is not in his knowledge of physical facts that he is elevated above his contemporaries, but in his knowledge of God's connection with all physical facts. No doubt, on the other hand, his knowledge of God reacts upon the entire contents of his mind and saves him from presenting such accounts of creation as have been common among polytheists. He presents an account purified by his conception of what was worthy of the supreme God he worshipped. His idea of God has given dignity and simplicity to all he says about creation, and there is an elevation and majesty about the whole conception, which we recognise as the reflex of his conception of God.

Here then instead of anything to discompose us or to excite unbelief, we recognise one great law or principle on which God proceeds in making Himself known to men. This has been called the Law of Accommodation. It is the law which requires that the condition and capacity of those to whom the revelation is made must be considered. If you wish to instruct a child, you must speak in language the child can understand. If you wish to elevate a savage, you must do it by degrees, accommodating yourself to his condition, and winking at much ignorance while you instil elementary knowledge. You must found all you teach on what is already understood by your pupil, and through that you must convey further knowledge and train his faculties to higher capacity. So was it with God's revelation. The Jews were children who had to be trained with what Paul somewhat contemptuously calls "weak and beggarly elements," the A B C of morals and religion. Not even in morals could the absolute truth be enforced. Accommodation had to be practised even here. Polygamy was allowed as a concession to their immature stage of development: and practices in war and in domestic law were permitted or enjoined which were inconsistent with absolute morality. Indeed the whole Jewish system was an adaptation to an immature state. The dwelling of God in the Temple as a man in his house, the propitiating of God with sacrifice as of an Eastern king with gifts; this was a teaching by picture, a teaching which had as much resemblance to the truth and as much mixture of truth as they were able then to receive. No doubt this teaching did actually mislead them in some of their ideas; but it kept them on the whole in a right attitude towards God, and prepared them for growing up to a fuller discernment of the truth.

Much more was this law observed in regard to such matters as are dealt with in these chapters. It was impossible that in their ignorance of the rudiments of scientific knowledge, the early Hebrews should understand an absolutely accurate account of how the world came into being; and if they could have understood it, it would have been useless, dissevered as it must have been from the steps of knowledge by which men have since arrived at it. Children ask us questions in answer to which we do not tell them the exact full truth, because we know they cannot possibly understand it. All that we can do is to give them some provisional answer which conveys to them some information they can understand, and which keeps them in a right state of mind, although this information often seems absurd enough when compared with the actual facts and truth of the matter. And if some solemn pedant accused us of supplying the child with false information, we would simply tell him he knew nothing about children. Accurate information on these matters will infallibly come to the child when he grows up; what is wanted meanwhile is to give him information which will help to form his conduct without gravely misleading him as to facts. Similarly, if any one tells me he cannot accept these chapters as inspired by God, because they do not convey scientifically accurate information regarding this earth, I can only say that he has yet to learn the first principles of revelation, and that he misunderstands the conditions on which all instruction must be given.

My belief then is, that in these chapters we have the ideas regarding the origin of the world and of man which were naturally attainable in the country where they were first composed, but with those important modifications which a monotheistic belief necessarily suggested. So far as merely physical knowledge went, there is probably little here that was new to the contemporaries of the writer; but this already familiar knowledge was used by him as the vehicle for conveying his faith in the unity, love and wisdom of God the creator. He laid a firm foundation for the history of God's relation to man. This was his object, and this he accomplished. The Bible is the book to which we turn for information regarding the history of God's revelation of Himself, and of His will towards men; and in these chapters we have the suitable introduction to this history. No changes in our knowledge of physical truth can at all affect the teaching of these chapters. What they teach regarding the relation of man to God is independent of the physical details in which this teaching is embodied, and can as easily be attached to the most modern statement of the physical origin of the world and of man.

What then are the truths taught us in these chapters? The first is that there has been a creation, that things now existing have not just grown of themselves, but have been called into being by a presiding intelligence and an originating will. No attempt to account for the existence of the world in any other way has been successful. A great deal has in this generation been added to our knowledge of the efficiency of material causes to produce what we see around us; but when we ask what gives harmony to these material causes, and what guides them to the production of certain ends, and what originally produced them, the answer must still be, not matter but intelligence and purpose. The best informed and most penetrating minds of our time affirm this. John Stuart Mill says: "It must be allowed that in the present state of our knowledge the adaptations in nature afford a large balance of probability in favour of creation by intelligence." Professor Tyndall adds his testimony and says: "I have noticed during years of self-observation that it is not in hours of clearness and vigour that [the doctrine of material atheism] commends itself to my mind—that in the hours of stronger and healthier thought it ever dissolves and disappears, as offering no solution of the mystery in which we dwell and of which we form a part."

There is indeed a prevalent suspicion, that in presence of the discoveries made by evolutionists the argument from design is no longer tenable. Evolution shows us that the correspondence of the structure of animals, with their modes of life, has been generated by the nature of the case; and it is concluded that a blind mechanical necessity and not an intelligent design rules all. But the discovery of the process by which the presently existing living forms have been evolved, and the perception that this process is governed by laws which have always been operating, do not make intelligence and design at all less necessary, but rather more so. As Professor Huxley himself says: "The teleological and mechanical views of nature are not necessarily exclusive. The teleologist can always defy the evolutionist to disprove that the primordial molecular arrangement was not intended to evolve the phenomena of the universe." Evolution, in short, by disclosing to us the marvellous power and accuracy of natural law, compels us more emphatically than ever to refer all law to a supreme, originating intelligence.

This then is the first lesson of the Bible; that at the root and origin of all this vast material universe, before whose laws we are crushed as the moth, there abides a living conscious Spirit, who wills and knows and fashions all things. The belief of this changes for us the whole face of nature, and instead of a chill, impersonal world of forces to which no appeal can be made, and in which matter is supreme, gives us the home of a Father. If you are yourself but a particle of a huge and unconscious universe—a particle which, like a flake of foam, or a drop of rain, or a gnat, or a beetle, lasts its brief space and then yields up its substance to be moulded into some new creature; if there is no power that understands you and sympathizes with you and makes provision for your instincts, your aspirations, your capabilities; if man is himself the highest intelligence, and if all things are the purposeless result of physical forces; if, in short, there is no God, no consciousness at the beginning as at the end of all things, then nothing can be more melancholy than our position. Our higher desires which seem to separate us so immeasurably from the brutes, we have, only that they may be cut down by the keen edge of time, and wither in barren disappointment; our reason we have, only to enable us to see and measure the brevity of our span, and so live our little day, not joyously as the unforeseeing beasts, but shadowed by the hastening gloom of anticipated, inevitable and everlasting night; our faculty for worshipping and for striving to serve and to resemble the perfect living One, that faculty which seems to be the thing of greatest promise and of finest quality in us, and to which is certainly due the largest part of what is admirable and profitable in human history, is the most mocking and foolishest of all our parts. But, God be thanked, He has revealed himself to us; has given us in the harmonious and progressive movement of all around us, sufficient indication that, even in the material world, intelligence and purpose reign; an indication which becomes immensely clearer as we pass into the world of man; and which, in presence of the person and life of Christ attains the brightness of a conviction which illuminates all besides.

The other great truth which this writer teaches is, that man was the chief work of God, for whose sake all else was brought into being. The work of creation was not finished till he appeared: all else was preparatory to this final product. That man is the crown and lord of this earth is obvious. Man instinctively assumes that all else has been made for him, and freely acts upon this assumption. But when our eyes are lifted from this little ball on which we are set and to which we are confined, and when we scan such other parts of the universe as are within our ken, a keen sense of littleness oppresses us; our earth is after all so minute and apparently inconsiderable a point when compared with the vast suns and planets that stretch system on system into illimitable space. When we read even the rudiments of what astronomers have discovered regarding the inconceivable vastness of the universe, the huge dimensions of the heavenly bodies, and the grand scale on which everything is framed, we find rising to our lips, and with tenfold reason, the words of David: "When I consider Thy heavens, the work of Thy fingers; the moon and the stars which Thou hast ordained; what is man that Thou art mindful of him, or the son of man that Thou visitest him?" Is it conceivable that on this scarcely discernible speck in the vastness of the universe, should be played out the chiefest act in the history of God? Is it credible that He whose care it is to uphold this illimitable universe, should be free to think of the wants and woes of the insignificant creatures who quickly spend their little lives in this inconsiderable earth?

But reason seems all on the side of Genesis. God must not be considered as sitting apart in a remote position of general superintendence, but as present with all that is. And to Him who maintains these systems in their respective relations and orbits, it can be no burden to relieve the needs of individuals. To think of ourselves as too insignificant to be attended to is to derogate from God's true majesty and to misunderstand His relation to the world. But it is also to misapprehend the real value of spirit as compared with matter. Man is dear to God because he is like Him. Vast and glorious as it is, the sun cannot think God's thoughts; can fulfil but cannot intelligently sympathize with God's purpose. Man, alone among God's works, can enter into and approve of God's purpose in the world and can intelligently fulfil it. Without man the whole material universe would have been dark and unintelligible, mechanical and apparently without any sufficient purpose. Matter, however fearfully and wonderfully wrought, is but the platform and material in which spirit, intelligence and will, may fulfil themselves and find development. Man is incommensurable with the rest of the universe. He is of a different kind and by his moral nature is more akin to God than to His works.

Here the beginning and the end of God's revelation join hands and throw light on one another. The nature of man was that in which God was at last to give His crowning revelation, and for that no preparation could seem extravagant. Fascinating and full of marvel as is the history of the past which science discloses to us; full as these slow-moving millions of years are in evidences of the exhaustless wealth of nature, and mysterious as the delay appears, all that expenditure of resources is eclipsed and all the delay justified when the whole work is crowned by the Incarnation, for in it we see that all that slow process was the preparation of a nature in which God could manifest Himself as a Person to persons. This is seen to be an end worthy of all that is contained in the physical history of the world: this gives completeness to the whole and makes it a unity. No higher, other end need be sought, none could be conceived. It is this which seems worthy of those tremendous and subtle forces which have been set at work in the physical world, this which justifies the long lapse of ages filled with wonders unobserved, and teeming with ever new life; this above all which justifies these latter ages in which all physical marvels have been outdone by the tragical history of man upon earth. Remove the Incarnation and all remains dark, purposeless, unintelligible: grant the Incarnation, believe that in Jesus Christ the Supreme manifested Himself personally, and light is shed upon all that has been and is.

Light is shed on the individual life. Are you living as if you were the product of blind mechanical laws, and as if there were no object worthy of your life and of all the force you can throw into your life? Consider the Incarnation of the Creator, and ask yourself if sufficient object is not given to you in His call that you be conformed to His image and become the intelligent executor of His purposes? Is life not worth having even on these terms? The man that can still sit down and bemoan himself as if there were no meaning in existence, or lounge languidly through life as if there were no zest or urgency in living, or try to satisfy himself with fleshly comforts, has surely need to turn to the opening page of Revelation and learn that God saw sufficient object in the life of man, enough to compensate for millions of ages of preparation. If it is possible that you should share in the character and destiny of Christ, can a healthy ambition crave anything more or higher? If the future is to be as momentous in results as the past has certainly been filled with preparation, have you no caring to share in these results? Believe that there is a purpose in things; that in Christ, the revelation of God, you can see what that purpose is, and that by wholly uniting yourself to Him and allowing yourself to be penetrated by His Spirit you can participate with Him in the working out of that purpose.

II
THE FALL

Genesis iii.

Profound as the teaching of this narrative is, its meaning does not lie on the surface. Literal interpretation will reach a measure of its significance, but plainly there is more here than appears in the letter. When we read that the serpent was more subtile than any beast of the field which the Lord God had made, and that he tempted the woman, we at once perceive that it is not with the outer husk of the story we are to concern ourselves, but with the kernel. The narrative throughout speaks of nothing but the brute serpent; not a word is said of the devil, not the slightest hint is given that the machinations of a fallen angel are signified. The serpent is compared to the other beasts of the field, showing that it is the brute serpent that is spoken of. The curse is pronounced on the beast, not on a fallen spirit summoned for the purpose before the Supreme; and not in terms which could apply to a fallen spirit, but in terms that are applicable only to the serpent that crawls. Yet every reader feels that this is not the whole mystery of the fall of man: moral evil cannot be accounted for by referring it to a brute source. No one, I suppose, believes that the whole tribe of serpents crawl as a punishment of an offence committed by one of their number, or that the whole iniquity and sorrow of the world are due to an actual serpent. Plainly this is merely a pictorial representation intended to convey some general impressions and ideas. Vitally important truths underlie the narrative and are bodied forth by it; but the way to reach these truths is not to adhere too rigidly to the literal meaning, but to catch the general impression which it seems fitted to make.

No doubt this opens the door to a great variety of interpretation. No two men will attach to it precisely the same meaning. One says, the serpent is a symbol for Satan, but Adam and Eve are historical persons. Another says, the tree of the knowledge of good and evil is a figure, but the driving out from the garden is real. Another maintains that the whole is a picture, putting in a visible, intelligible shape certain vitally important truths regarding the history of our race. So that every man is left very much to his own judgment, to read the narrative candidly and in such light from other sources as he has, and let it make its own impression upon him. This would be a sad result if the object of the Bible were to bring us all to a rigid uniformity of belief in all matters; but the object of the Bible is not that, but the far higher object of furnishing all varieties of men with sufficient light to lead them to God. And this being so, variety of interpretation in details is not to be lamented. The very purpose of such representations as are here given is to suit all stages of mental and spiritual advancement. Let the child read it and he will learn what will live in his mind and influence him all his life. Let the devout man who has ranged through all science and history and philosophy come back to this narrative, and he feels that he has here the essential truth regarding the beginnings of man's tragical career upon earth.

We should, in my opinion, be labouring under a misapprehension if we supposed that none even of the earliest readers of this account saw the deeper meaning of it. When men who felt the misery of sin and lifted up their hearts to God for deliverance, read the words addressed to the serpent, "I will put enmity between thee and the woman, and between thy seed and her seed; it shall bruise thy head, and thou shalt bruise his heel"—is it reasonable to suppose that such men would take these words in their literal sense, and satisfy themselves with the assurance that serpents, though dangerous, would be kept under, and would find in the words no assurance of that very thing they themselves were all their lifetime striving after, deliverance from the evil thing which lay at the root of all sin? No doubt some would accept the story in its literal meaning,—shallow and careless men whose own spiritual experience never urged them to see any spiritual significance in the words would do so; but even those who saw least in the story, and put a very shallow interpretation on its details, could scarcely fail to see its main teaching.

The reader of this perennially fresh story is first of all struck with the account given of man's primitive condition. Coming to this narrative with our minds coloured by the fancies of poets and philosophers, we are almost startled by the check which the plain and sober statements of this account give to an unpruned fancy. We have to read the words again and again to make sure we have not omitted something which gives support to those glowing descriptions of man's primitive condition. Certainly he is described as innocent and at peace with God, and in this respect no terms can exaggerate his happiness. But in other respects the language of the Bible is surprisingly moderate. Man is represented as living on fruit, and as going unclothed, and, so far as appears, without any artificial shelter either from the heat of the sun or the cold of night. None of the arts were as yet known. All working of metals had yet to be discovered, so that his tools must have been of the rudest possible description; and the arts, such as music, which adorn life and make leisure enjoyable, were also still in the future.

But the most significant elements in man's primitive condition are represented by the two trees of the garden; by trees, because with plants alone he had to do. In the centre of the garden stood the tree of life, the fruit of which bestowed immortality. Man was therefore naturally mortal, though apparently with a capacity for immortality. How this capacity would have actually carried man on to immortality had he not sinned, it is vain to conjecture. The mystical nature of the tree of life is fully recognised in the New Testament, by our Lord, when He says: "To him that overcometh will I give to eat of the tree of life, which is in the midst of the Paradise of God;" and by John, when he describes the new Jerusalem: "In the midst of the street of it, and on either side of the river, was there the tree of life, which bare twelve manner of fruits, and yielded her fruit every month: and the leaves of the tree were for the healing of the nations." Both these representations are intended to convey, in a striking and pictorial form, the promise of life everlasting.

And as of the tree of life which stands in the Paradise of the future it is said "Blessed are they that do His commandments, that they may have right to the tree of life;" so in Eden man's immortality was suspended on the condition of obedience. And the trial of man's obedience is imaged in the other tree, the tree of the knowledge of good and evil. From the child-like innocence in which man originally was, he was to pass forward into the condition of moral manhood, which consists not in mere innocence, but in innocence maintained in presence of temptation. The savage is innocent of many of the crimes of civilized men because he has no opportunity to commit them; the child is innocent of some of the vices of manhood because he has no temptation to them. But this innocence is the result of circumstance, not of character; and if savage or child is to become a mature moral being he must be tried by altered circumstances, by temptation and opportunity. To carry man forward to this higher stage trial is necessary, and this trial is indicated by the tree of knowledge. The fruit of this tree is prohibited, to indicate that it is only in presence of what is forbidden man can be morally tested, and that it is only by self-command and obedience to law, and not by the mere following of instincts, that man can attain to moral maturity. The prohibition is that which makes him recognise a distinction between good and evil. He is put in a position in which good is not the only thing he can do; an alternative is present to his mind, and the choice of good in preference to evil is made possible to him. In presence of this tree child-like innocence was no longer possible. The self-determination of manhood was constantly required. Conscience, hitherto latent, was now evoked and took its place as man's supreme faculty.

It is in vain to think of exhausting this narrative. We can, at the most, only remark upon some of the most salient points.

(1) Temptation comes like a serpent; like the most subtle beast of the field; like that one creature which is said to exert a fascinating influence on its victims, fastening them with its glittering eye, stealing upon them by its noiseless, low and unseen approach, perplexing them by its wide circling folds, seeming to come upon them from all sides at once, and armed not like the other beasts with one weapon of offence—horn, or hoof, or teeth—but capable of crushing its victim with every part of its sinuous length. It lies apparently dead for months together, but when roused it can, as the naturalist tells us, "outclimb the monkey, outswim the fish, outleap the zebra, outwrestle the athlete, and crush the tiger." How naturally in describing temptation do we borrow language from the aspect and movements of this creature. It does not need to hunt down its victims by long continued pursuit, its victims come and put themselves within its reach. Unseen, temptation lies by our path, and before we have time to think we are fascinated and bewildered, its coils rapidly gather round us and its stroke flashes poison through our blood. Against sin, when once it has wreathed itself around us, we seem helpless to contend; the very powers with which we could resist are benumbed or pinned useless to our side—our foe seems all round us, and to extricate one part is but to become entangled in another. As the serpent finds its way everywhere, over every fence or barrier, into every corner and recess, so it is impossible to keep temptation out of the life; it appears where least we expect it and when we think ourselves secure.

(2) Temptation succeeds at first by exciting our curiosity. It is a wise saying that "our great security against sin lies in being shocked at it. Eve gazed and reflected when she should have fled." The serpent created an interest, excited her curiosity about this forbidden fruit. And as this excited curiosity lies near the beginning of sin in the race, so does it in the individual. I suppose if you trace back the mystery of iniquity in your own life and seek to track it to its source, you will find it to have originated in this craving to taste evil. No man originally meant to become the sinner he has become. He only intended, like Eve, to taste. It was a voyage of discovery he meant to make; he did not think to get nipped and frozen up and never more return from the outer cold and darkness. He wished before finally giving himself to virtue, to see the real value of the other alternative.

This dangerous craving has many elements in it. There is in it the instinctive drawing towards what is mysterious. One veiled figure in an assembly will attract more scrutiny than the most admired beauty. An appearance in the heavens that no one can account for will nightly draw more eyes than the most wonderful sunset. To lift veils, to penetrate disguises, to unravel complicated plots, to solve mysteries, this is always inviting to the human mind. The tale which used to thrill us in childhood, of the one locked room, the one forbidden key, bears in it a truth for men as well as for children. What is hidden must, we conclude, have some interest for us—else why hide it from us? What is forbidden must have some important bearing upon us. Else why forbid it? Things which are indifferent to us are left in our way, obvious, and without concealment. But as action has been taken regarding the things that are forbidden, action in view of our relation to them, it is natural to us to desire to know what these things are and how they affect us.

There is added to this in young persons, a sense of incompleteness. They wish to be grown up. Few boys wish to be always boys. They long for the signs of manhood, and seek to possess that knowledge of life and its ways which they very much identify with manhood. But too commonly they mistake the path to manhood. They feel as if they had a wider range of liberty and were more thoroughly men when they transgress the limits assigned by conscience. They feel as if there were a new and brighter world outside that which is fenced round by strict morality, and they tremble with excitement on its borders. It is a fatal delusion. Only by choosing the good in presence of the evil are true manhood and real maturity gained. True manliness consists mainly in self control, in a patient waiting upon nature and God's law and when youth impatiently breaks through the protecting fence of God's law, and seeks growth by knowing evil, it misses that very advancement it seeks, and cheats itself out of the manhood it apes.

(3) Through this craving for an enlarged experience unbelief in God's goodness finds entrance. In the presence of forbidden pleasure we are tempted to feel as if God were grudging us enjoyment. The very arguments of the serpent occur to our mind. No harm will come of our indulging; the prohibition is needless, unreasonable and unkind; it is not based on any genuine desire for our welfare. This fence that shuts us out from knowing good and evil is erected by a timorous asceticism, by a ridiculous misconception of what truly enlarges human nature; it shuts us into a poor narrow life. And thus suspicions of God's perfect wisdom and goodness find entrance; we begin to think we know better than He what is good for us, and can contrive a richer, happier life than He has provided for us. Our loyalty to Him is loosened, and already we have lost hold of His strength and are launched on the current that leads to sin, misery, and shame. When we find ourselves saying Yes, where God has said No; when we see desirable things where God has said there is death; when we allow distrust of Him to rankle in our mind, when we chafe against the restrictions under which we live and seek liberty by breaking down the fence instead of by delighting in God, we are on the highway to all evil.

(4) If we know our own history we cannot be surprised to read that one taste of evil ruined our first parents. It is so always. The one taste alters our attitude towards God and conscience and life. It is a veritable Circe's cup. The actual experience of sin is like the one taste of alcohol to a reclaimed drunkard, like the first taste of blood to a young tiger, it calls out the latent devil and creates a new nature within us. At one brush it wipes out all the peace, and joy, and self-respect, and boldness of innocence, and numbers us among the transgressors, among the shame-faced, and self-despising, and hopeless. It leaves us possessed with unhappy thoughts which lead us away from what is bright, and honourable, and good, and like the letting out of water it seems to have tapped a spring of evil within us. It is but one step, but it is like the step over a precipice or down the shaft of a mine; it cannot be taken back, it commits to an altogether different state of things.

(5) The first result of sin is shame. The form in which the knowledge of good and evil comes to us is the knowing we are naked, the consciousness that we are stripped of all that made us walk unabashed before God and men. The promise of the serpent while broken in the sense is fulfilled to the ear; the eyes of Adam and Eve were opened and they knew that they were naked. Self-reflection begins, and the first movement of conscience produces shame. Had they resisted temptation, conscience would have been born but not in self-condemnation. Like children they had hitherto been conscious only of what was external to themselves, but now their consciousness of a power to choose good and evil is awakened and its first exercise is accompanied with shame. They feel that in themselves they are faulty, that they are not in themselves complete; that though created by God, they are not fit for His eye. The lower animals wear no clothes because they have no knowledge of good and evil; children feel no need of covering because as yet self-consciousness is latent, and their conduct is determined for them; those who are re-made in the image of God and glorified as Christ is, cannot be thought of as clothed, for in them there is no sense of sin. But Adam's clothing himself and hiding himself were the helpless attempts of a guilty conscience to evade the judgment of truth.

(6) But when Adam found he was no longer fit for God's eye, God provided a covering which might enable him again to live in His presence without dismay. Man had exhausted his own ingenuity and resources, and exhausted them without finding relief to his shame. If his shame was to be effectually removed, God must do it. And the clothing in coats of skins indicates the restoration of man, not indeed to pristine innocence, but to peace with God. Adam felt that God did not wish to banish him lastingly from His presence, nor to see him always a trembling and confused penitent. The self-respect and progressiveness, the reverence for law and order and

God, which came in with clothes, and which we associate with the civilised races, were accepted as tokens that God was desirous to co-operate with man, to forward and further him in all good.

It is also to be remarked that the clothing which God provided was in itself different from what man had thought of. Adam took leaves from an inanimate, unfeeling tree; God deprived an animal of life, that the shame of His creature might be relieved. This was the last thing Adam would have thought of doing. To us life is cheap and death familiar, but Adam recognised death as the punishment of sin. Death was to early man a sign of God's anger. And he had to learn that sin could be covered not by a bunch of leaves snatched from a bush as he passed by and that would grow again next year, but only by pain and blood. Sin cannot be atoned for by any mechanical action nor without expenditure of feeling. Suffering must ever follow wrong-doing. From the first sin to the last, the track of the sinner is marked with blood. Once we have sinned we cannot regain permanent peace of conscience save through pain, and this not only pain of our own. The first hint of this was given as soon as conscience was aroused in man. It was made apparent that sin was a real and deep evil, and that by no easy and cheap process could the sinner be restored. The same lesson has been written on millions of consciences since. Men have found that their sin reaches beyond their own life and person, that it inflicts injury and involves disturbance and distress, that it changes utterly our relation to life and to God, and that we cannot rise above its consequences save by the intervention of God Himself, by an intervention which tells us of the sorrow He suffers on our account.

For the chief point is that it is God who relieves man's shame. Until we are certified that God desires our peace of mind we cannot be at peace. The cross of Christ is the permanent witness to this desire on God's part. No one can read what Christ has done for us without feeling sure that for himself there is a way back to God from all sin—that it is God's desire that his sin should be covered, his iniquity forgiven. Too often that which seems of prime importance to God seems of very slight importance to us. To have our life founded solidly in harmony with the Supreme, seems often to excite no desire within us. It is about sin we find man first dealing with God, and until you have satisfied God and yourself regarding this prime and fundamental matter of your own transgression and wrong-doing you look in vain for any deep and lasting growth and satisfaction. Have you no reason to be ashamed before God? Have you loved Him in any proportion to His worthiness to be loved? Have you cordially and habitually fallen in with His will? Have you zealously done His work in the world? Have you fallen short of no good He intended you should do and gave you opportunity to do? Is there no reason for shame on your part before God? Has His desire to cover sin no application to you? Can you not understand His meaning when He comes to you with offers of pardon and acts of oblivion? Surely the candid mind, the clear-judging conscience can be at no loss to explain God's solicitous concern for the sinner; and must humbly own that even that unfathomable Divine emotion which is exhibited in the cross of Christ, is no exaggerated and theatrical demonstration, but the actual carrying through of what was really needed for the restoration of the sinner. Do not live as if the cross of Christ had never been, or as if you had never sinned and had no connection with it. Strive to learn what it means; strive to deal fairly with it and fairly with your own transgressions and with your present actual relation to God and His will.

III
CAIN AND ABEL

Genesis iv.

It is not the purpose of this narrator to write the history of the world. It is not his purpose to write even the history of mankind. His object is to write the history of redemption. Starting from the broad fact of man's alienation from God, he means to trace that element in human history which results in the perfect re-union of God and man. The key-note has been struck in the promise already given that the seed of the woman should prevail over the seed of the serpent, that the effects of man's voluntary dissociation from God should be removed. It is the fulfilment of this promise which is traced by this writer. He steadily pursues that one line of history which runs directly towards this fulfilment; turning aside now and again to pursue, to a greater or less distance, diverging lines, but always returning to the grand highway on which the promise travels. His method is first to dispose of collateral matter and then to proceed with his main theme. As here, he first disposes of the line of Cain and then returns to Seth through whom the line of promise is maintained.

The first thing we have to do with outside the garden is death—the curse of sin speedily manifests itself in its most terrible form. But the sinner executes it himself. The first death is a murder. As if to show that all death is a wrong inflicted on us and proceeds not from God but from sin, it is inflicted by sin and by the hand of man. Man becomes his own executioner, and takes part with Satan, the murderer from the beginning. But certainly the first feeling produced by these events must have been one of bitter disappointment, as if the promise were to be lost in the curse.

The story of Cain and Abel was to all appearance told in order to point out that from the very first men have been divided into two great classes, viewed in connection with God's promise and presence in the world. Always there have been those who believed in God's love and waited for it, and those who believed more in their own force and energy. Always there have been the humble and self-diffident who hoped in God, and the proud and self-reliant who felt themselves equal to all the occasions of life.

And this story of Cain and Abel and the succeeding generations does not conceal the fact, that for the purposes of this world there has been visible an element of weakness in the godly line, and that it is to the self-reliant and God-defying energy of the descendants of Cain that we owe much of the external civilisation of the world. While the descendants of Seth pass away and leave only this record, that they "walked with God," there are found among Cain's descendants, builders of cities, inventors of tools and weapons, music and poetry and the beginnings of culture.

These two opposed lines are in the first instance represented by Cain and Abel. With each child that comes into the world some fresh hope is brought; and the name of Cain points to the expectation of his parents that in him a fresh start would be made. Alas! as the boy grew they saw how vain such expectation was and how truly their nature had passed into his, and how no imparted experience of theirs, taught him from without, could countervail the strong propensities to evil which impelled him from within. They experienced that bitterest punishment which parents undergo, when they see their own defects and infirmities and evil passions repeated in their children and leading them astray as they once led themselves; when in those who are to perpetuate their name and remembrance on earth they see evidence that their faults also will be perpetuated; when in those whom they chiefly love they have a mirror ceaselessly held up to them forcing them to remember the follies and sins of their own youth. Certainly in the proud, self-willed, sullen Cain no redemption was to be found.

Both sons own the necessity of labour. Man is no longer in the primitive condition, in which he had only to stretch out his hand when hungry, and satisfy his appetite. There are still some regions of the earth in which the trees shower fruit, nutritious and easily preserved, on men who shun labour. Were this the case throughout the world, the whole of life would be changed. Had we been created self-sufficing or in such conditions as involved no necessity of toil, nothing would be as it now is. It is the need of labour that implies occasional starvation and frequent poverty, and gives occasion to charity. It is the need of labour which involves commerce and thereby sows the seed of greed, worldliness, ambition, drudgery. The ultimate physical wants of men, food and clothes, are the motive of the greater part of all human activity. Trace to their causes the various industries of men, the wars, the great social movements, all that constitutes history, and you find that the bulk of all that is done upon earth is done because men must have food and wish to have it as good and with as little labour as possible. The broad facts of human life are in many respects humiliating.

The disposition of men is consequently shown in the occupations they choose and the idea of life they carry into them. Some, like Abel, choose peaceful callings that draw out feeling and sympathy; others prefer pursuits which are stirring and active. Cain chose the tillage of the ground, partly no doubt from the necessity of the case, but probably also with the feeling that he could subdue nature to his own purposes notwithstanding the curse that lay upon it. Do we not all sometimes feel a desire to take the world as it is, curse and all, and make the most of it; to face its disease with human skill, its disturbing and destructive elements with human forethought and courage, its sterility and stubbornness with human energy and patience? What is stimulating men still to all discovery and invention, to forewarn seamen of coming storms, to break a precarious passage for commerce through eternal ice or through malarious swamps, to make life at all points easier and more secure? Is it not the energy which opposition excites? We know that it will be hard work; we expect to have thorns and thistles everywhere, but let us see whether this may not after all be a thoroughly happy world, whether we cannot cultivate the curse altogether out of it. This is indeed the very work God has given man to do—to subdue the earth and make the desert blossom as the rose. God is with us in this work, and he who believes in God's purpose and strives to reclaim nature and compel it to some better products than it naturally yields, is doing God's work in the world. The misery is that so many do it in the spirit of Cain, in a spirit of self-confident or sullen alienation from God, willing to endure all hardship but unable to lay themselves at God's feet with every capacity for work and every field He has given them to till for Him and in a spirit of humble love to co-operate with Him. To this spirit of godless energy, of merely selfish or worldly ambition and enterprise, the world owes not only much of its poverty and many of its greatest disasters, but also the greater part of its present advantages in external civilisation. But from this spirit can never arise the meekness, the patience, the tenderness, the charity which sweeten the life of society and are more to be desired than gold; from this spirit and all its achievements the natural outcome is the proud, vindictive, self-glorifying war-song of a Lamech.

The incompatibility of the two lines and the persecuting spirit of the godless are set forth by the after history of Cain and Abel. The one line is represented in Cain, who with all his energy and indomitable courage, is depicted as of a dark, morose, suspicious, jealous, violent temper; a man born under the shadow of the fall. Abel is described in contrast as guileless and sunny, free from harshness and resentment. What was in Cain was shown by what came out of him, murder. The reason of the rejection of his offering was his own evil condition of heart. "If thou doest well, shalt not thou also be accepted;" implying that he was not accepted because he was not doing well. His offering was a mere form; he complied with the fashion of the family; but in spirit he was alienated from God, cherishing thoughts which the rejection of his offering brings to a head. He may have seen that the younger son won more of the parents' affection, that his company was more welcome. Jealousy had been produced, that deep jealousy of the humble and godly which proud men of the world cannot help betraying and which has so very often in the world's history produced persecution.

This cannot be considered too weak a motive to carry so enormous a crime. Even in a highly civilised age we find an English statesman saying: "Pique is one of the strongest motives in the human mind. Fear is strong but transient. Interest is more lasting, perhaps, and steady, but weaker; I will ever back pique against them both. It is the spur the devil rides the noblest tempers with, and will do more work with them in a week, than with other poor jades in a twelve-month." And the age of Cain and Abel was an age in which impulse and action lay close together, and in which jealousy is notoriously strong. To this motive John ascribes the act: "Wherefore slew he him? Because his own works were evil, and his brother's righteous."

We have now learned better how to disguise our feelings; and we are compelled to control them better; but now and again we meet with a deep-seated hatred of goodness which might give rise to almost any crime. Few of us can say that for our own part we have extinguished within us the spirit that disparages and depreciates and fixes the charge of hypocrisy or refers good actions to interested motives, searches out failings and watches for haltings and is glad when a blot is found. Few are filled with unalloyed grief when the man who has borne an extraordinary reputation turns out to be just like the rest of us. Many of us have a true delight in goodness and humble ourselves before it when we see it, and yet we know also what it is to be exasperated by the presence of superiority. I have seen a schoolboy interrupt his brother's prayers, and gird at him for his piety, and strive to draw him into sin, and do the devil's work with zest and diligence. And where goodness is manifestly in the minority how constantly does it excite hatred that pours itself out in sneers and ridicule and ignorant calumny.

But this narrative significantly refers this early quarrel to religion. There is no bitterness to compare with that which worldly men who profess religion, feel towards those who cultivate a spiritual religion. They can never really grasp the distinction between external worship and real godliness. They make their offerings, they attend to the rites of the religion to which they belong and are beside themselves with indignation if any person or event suggests to them that they might have saved themselves all their trouble, because these do not at all constitute religion. They uphold the Church, they admire and praise her beautiful services, they use strong but meaningless language about infidelity, and yet when brought in contact with spirituality and assured that regeneration and penitent humility are required above all else in the kingdom of God, they betray an utter inability to comprehend the very rudiments of the Christian religion. Abel has always to go to the wall because he is always the weaker party, always in the minority. Spiritual religion, from the very nature of the case, must always be in the minority; and must be prepared to suffer loss, calumny, and violence, at the hands of the worldly religious, who have contrived for themselves a worship that calls for no humiliation before God and no complete surrender of heart and will to Him. Cain is the type of the ignorant religious, of the unregenerate man who thinks he merits God's favour as much as any one else; and Cain's conduct is the type of the treatment which the Christ-like and intelligent godly are always likely to receive at such hands.

We never know where we may be led by jealousy and malice. One of the striking features of this incident is the rapidity with which small sins generate great ones. When Cain went in the joy of harvest and offered his first fruits no thought could be further from his mind than murder. It may have come as suddenly on himself as on the unsuspecting Abel, but the germ was in him. Great sins are not so sudden as they seem. Familiarity with evil thought ripens us for evil action; and a moment of passion, an hour's loss of self-control, a tempting occasion, may hurry us into irremediable evil. And even though this does not happen, envious, uncharitable, and malicious thoughts make our offerings as distasteful as Cain's. He that loveth not his brother knoweth not God. First be reconciled to thy brother, says our Lord, and then come and offer thy gift.

Other truths are incidentally taught in this narrative.

(1) The acceptance of the offering depends on the acceptance of the offerer. God had respect to Abel and his offering—the man first and then the offering. God looks through the offering to the state of soul from which it proceeds; or even, as the words would indicate, sees the soul first and judges and treats the offering according to the inward disposition. God does not judge of what you are by what you say to Him or do for Him, but He judges what you say to Him and do for Him by what you are. "By *faith*" says a New Testament writer, "Abel offered a more acceptable sacrifice than Cain." He had the faith which enabled him to believe that God is, and that

He is a rewarder of them that diligently seek Him. His attitude towards God was sound; his life was a diligent seeking to please God; and from all such persons God gladly receives acknowledgment. When the offering is the true expression of the soul's gratitude, love, devotedness, then it is acceptable. When it is a merely external offering, that rather veils than expresses the real feeling; when it is not vivified and rendered significant by any spiritual act on the part of the worshipper, it is plainly of no effect.

What is true of all sacrifices is true of the sacrifice of Christ. It remains invalid and of none effect to those who do not through it yield themselves to God. Sacrifices were intended to be the embodiment and expression of a state of feeling towards God, of a submission or offering of men's selves to God; of a return to that right relation which ought ever to subsist between creature and Creator. Christ's sacrifice is valid for us when it is that outward thing which best expresses our feeling towards God and through which we offer or yield ourselves to God. His sacrifice is the open door through which God freely admits all who aim at a consecration and obedience like to His. It is valid for us when through it we sacrifice ourselves. Whatever His sacrifice expresses we desire to take and use as the only satisfactory expression of our own aims and desires. Did Christ perfectly submit to and fulfil the will of God? So would we. Did He acknowledge the infinite evil of sin and patiently bear its penalties, still loving the Holy and Righteous God? So would we endure all chastening, and still resist unto blood striving against sin.

(2) Again, we here find a very sharp and clear statement of the welcome truth, that continuance in sin is never a necessity, that God points the way out of sin, and that from the first He has been on man's side and has done all that could be done to keep men from sinning. Observe how He expostulates with Cain. Take note of the plain, explicit fairness of the words in which He expostulates with him—instance, as it is, of how absolutely in the right God always is, and how abundantly He can justify all His dealings with us. God says as it were to Cain; Come now: and let us reason together. All God wants of any man is to be reasonable; to look at the facts of the case. "If thou doest well, shalt thou not (as well as Abel) be accepted? and if thou doest not well, sin lieth at the door," that is, if thou doest not well, the sin is not Abel's nor any one's but thine own, and therefore anger at another is not the proper remedy, but anger at yourself, and repentance.

No language could more forcibly exhibit the unreasonableness of not meeting God with penitent and humble acknowledgment. God has fully met our case, and has satisfied all its demands, has set Himself to serve us and laid Himself out to save us pain and misery, and has so entirely succeeded in making salvation and blessedness possible to us, that if we continue in sin we must trample not only upon God's love and our own reason, but on the very means of salvation. State your case at the worst, bring forward every reason why your countenance should be fallen as Cain's and why your face should lower with the gloom of eternal despair—say that you have as clear evidence as Cain had that your offerings are displeasing to God, and that while others are accepted you receive no token from Him,—in answer to all your arguments, these words addressed to Cain rise up. If not accepted already you have the means of being so. If you do well to be hardened in sin it is not because it is necessary, nor because God desires it. If you are to continue in sin you must put aside His hand. It can only be *sin* which causes you either to despair of salvation or keeps you any way separate from God—there is no other thing worse than sin, and for sin there is an offering provided. You have not fallen into some lower grade of beings than that which is designated sinners, and it is sinners that God in His mercy hems in with this inevitable dilemma He presented to Cain.

If, therefore, you continue at war with God it is not because you must not do otherwise: if you go forward to any new thought, plan, or action unpardoned; if acceptance of God's forgiveness and entrance into a state of reconciliation with Him be not your first action, then you must thrust aside His counsel, backed though it is with every utterance of your own reason. Some of us may be this day or this week in as critical a position as Cain, having as truly as he the making or marring of our future in our hands, seeing clearly the right course, and all that is good, humble, penitent and wise in us urging us to follow that course, but our pride and self-will holding us back. How often do men thus barter a future of blessing for some mean gratification of temper or lust or pride; how often by a reckless, almost listless and indifferent continuance in sin do they let themselves be carried on to a future as woful as Cain's; how often when God expostulates with them do they make no answer and take no action, as if there were nothing to be gained by listening to God—as if it were a matter of no importance what future I go to—as if in the whole eternity that lies in reserve there were nothing worth making a choice about—nothing about which it is worth my while to rouse the whole energy of which I am capable, and to make, by God's grace, the determination which shall alter my whole future—to choose for myself and assert myself.

(3) The writer to the Hebrews makes a very striking use of this event. He borrows from it language in which to magnify the efficacy of Christ's

sacrifice, and affirms that the blood of Christ speaketh better things, or, as it must rather be rendered, crieth louder than the blood of Abel. Abel's blood, we see, cried for vengeance, for evil things for Cain, called God to make inquisition for blood, and so pled as to secure the banishment of the murderer. The Arabs have a belief that over the grave of a murdered man his spirit hovers in the form of a bird that cries "Give me drink, give me drink," and only ceases when the blood of the murderer is shed. Cain's conscience told him the same thing; there was no criminal law threatening death to the murderer, but he felt that men would kill him if they could. He heard the blood of Abel crying from the earth. The blood of Christ also cries to God, but cries not for vengeance but for pardon. And as surely as the one cry was heard and answered in very substantial results; so surely does the other cry call down from heaven its proper and beneficent effects. It is as if the earth would not receive and cover the blood of Christ, but ever exposes it before God and cries to Him to be faithful and just to forgive us our sins. This blood cries louder than the other. If God could not overlook the blood of one of His servants, but adjudged to it its proper consequences, neither is it possible that He should overlook the blood of His Son and not give to it its proper result.

If then you feel in your conscience that you are as guilty as Cain, and if sins clamour around you which are as dangerous as his, and which cry out for judgment upon you, accept the assurance that the blood of Christ has a yet louder cry for mercy. If you had been Abel's murderer, would you have been justly afraid of God's anger? Be as sure of God's mercy now. If you had stood over his lifeless body and seen the earth refusing to cover his blood, if you felt the stain of it crimson on your conscience and if by night you started from your sleep striving vainly to wash it from your hands, if by every token you felt yourself exposed to a just punishment, your fear would be just and reasonable were nothing else revealed to you. But there is another blood equally indelible, equally clamorous. In it you have in reality what is elsewhere pretended in fable, that the blood of the murdered man will not wash out, but through every cleansing oozes up again a dark stain on the oaken floor. This blood can really not be washed out, it cannot be covered up and hid from God's eye, its voice cannot be stifled, and its cry is all for mercy.

With how different a meaning then comes now to us this question of God's: "Where is thy brother?" Our Brother also is slain. Him Whom God sent among us to reverse the curse, to lighten the burden of this life, to be the loving member of the family on Whom each leans for help and looks to for counsel and comfort—Him Who was by His goodness to be as the dayspring from on high in our darkness, we found *too* good for our endurance and dealt with as Cain dealt with his more righteous brother. But He Whom we slew God has raised again to give repentance and remission of sins, and assures us that His blood cleanseth from all sin. To every one therefore He repeats this question, "Where is thy brother?" He repeats it to every one who is living with a conscience stained with sin; to every one that knows remorse and walks with the hanging head of shame; to every one whose whole life is saddened by the consciousness that all is not settled between God and himself; to every one who is sinning recklessly as if Christ's blood had never been shed for sin; and to every one who, though seeking to be at peace with God, is troubled and downcast—to all God says, "Where is thy brother?" tenderly reminding us of the absolute satisfaction for sin that has been made, and of the hope towards God we have through the blood of His Son.

IV
CAIN'S LINE, AND ENOCH

Genesis iv. 12–24.

"My punishment is greater than I can bear," so felt Cain as soon as his passion had spent itself and the consequences of his wickedness became apparent—and so feels every one who finds he has now to live in the presence of the irrevocable deed he has done. It seems too heavy a penalty to endure for the one hour of passion; and yet as little as Cain could rouse the dead Abel so little can we revive the past we have destroyed. Thoughtlessness has set in motion agencies we are powerless to control; the whole world is changed to us. One can fancy Cain turning to see if his victim gave no sign of life, striving to reanimate the dead body, calling the familiar name, but only to see with growing dismay that the one blow had finished all with which that name was associated, and that he had made himself a new world. So are we drawn back and back in thought to that which has for ever changed life to us, striving to see if there is no possibility of altering the past, but only to find we might quite as well try to raise the dead. No voice responds to our cries of grief and dismay and too late repentance. All life now seems but a reaping of the consequences of the past. We have put ourselves in every respect at a disadvantage. The earth seems cursed so that we are hampered in our employments and cannot make as much of them as we would had we been innocent. We have got out of right relations to our fellow-men and cannot feel the same to them as we ought to feel; and the face of God is hid from us, so that now and again as time after time our hopes are blighted, our life darkened and disturbed by the obvious results of our own past deeds, we are tempted to cry out with Cain: "My punishment is greater than I can bear."

Yet Cain's punishment was less than he expected. He was not put to death as he would have been at any later period of the world's history, but was banished. And even this punishment was lightened by his having a token from God, that he would not be put to death by any zealous avenger of Abel. He would experience the hardships of a man entering unexplored territory, but to an enterprising spirit this would not be without its charms. As the fresh beauties of the world's youth were disclosed to him and by their bright and peaceful friendliness allayed the bitterness of his spirit, and as the mysteries and dangers of the new regions excited him and called his thoughts from the past, some of the old delight in life may have been recovered by him. Probably in many a lonely hour the recollection of his crime would return and with it all the horrors of a remorse which would drive rest and peace from his soul, and render him the most wretched of men. But busied as he was with his new enterprises, there is little doubt that he would find it, as it is still found, not impossible to banish such dreary thoughts and live in the measure of contentment which many enjoy who are as far from God as Cain.

It is not difficult to detect the spirit he carried with him, and the tone he gave to his line of the race. The facts recorded are few but significant. He begat a son, he built a city; and he gave to both the name Enoch, that is "initiation," or "beginning," as if he were saying in his heart, "What so great harm after all in cutting short one line in Abel? I can begin another and find a new starting point for the race. I am driven forth cursed as a vagabond, but a vagabond I will not be; I will make for myself a settled abode, and I will fence it round with knife-blade thorns so that no man will be able to assault me."

In this settling of Cain, however, we see not any symptom of his ceasing to be a vagabond, but the surest evidence that now he was content to be a fugitive from God and had cut himself off from hope. His heart had found rest and had found it apart from God. *Here*, in this city he would make a fresh beginning for himself and for men. Here he abandoned all clinging memories of former things, of his old home and of the God there worshipped. He had wisdom enough not to call his city by his own name, and so invite men to consider his former career or trace back anything to his old life. He cut it all off from him; his crime, his God also, all that was in it was to be no more to him and his comrades. He would make a clean start, and that men might be led to expect a great future he called his city, Enoch, a Beginning.

But it is one thing to forgive ourselves, another thing to have God's forgiveness. It is one thing to reconcile ourselves to the curse that runs through our life, another thing to be reconciled to God and so defeat the curse. It is sometimes, though by no means always, possible to escape some of the consequences of sin: we can change our front so as to lessen the breadth of life that is exposed to them, or we can accustom and harden ourselves to a very second-rate kind of life. We can teach ourselves to live without much love in our homes or in our connections with those outside; we can learn to be satisfied if we can pay our way and make the time pass and be outwardly like other people; we can build a little city, and be content to be on no very friendly terms with any but the select few inside the trench, and actually be quite satisfied if we can *defend ourselves against* the rest of men; we can forget the one commandment, that we should love one another. We can all find much in the world to comfort, to lull, to soothe sorrowful but wholesome remembrances; much to aid us in an easy treatment of the curse; much to shed superficial brightness on a life darkened and debased by sin, much to hush up the sad echoes that mutter from the dark mountains of vanity we have left behind us, much that assures us we have nothing to do but forget our old sins and busily occupy ourselves with new duties. But no David will say, nor will any man of true spiritual discernment say, "Blessed is the man whose transgression is *forgotten;*" but only, "Blessed is the man whose transgression is forgiven." By all means make a fresh start, a new beginning, but let it be in your own broken heart, in a spirit humble and contrite, frankly acknowledging your guilt and finding rest and settlement for your soul in reconciliation with God.

It is in the family of Lamech the characteristics of Cain's line are most distinctly seen, and the significance of their tendencies becomes apparent. As Cain had set himself to cultivate the curse out of the world, so have his children derived from him the self-reliant hardiness and hardihood which are resolute to make of this world as bright and happy a home as may be. They make it their task to subdue the world and compel it to yield them a life in which they can delight. They are so far successful that in a few generations they have formed a home in which all the essentials of civilized life are found—the arts are cultivated and female society is appreciated.

Of his three sons, Jabal—or "Increase"—was "the father of such as dwell in tents and of such as have cattle." He had originality enough to step beyond all traditional habits and to invent a new mode of life. Hitherto men had been tied to one spot by their fixed habitations, or found shelter when overtaken by storm in caves or trees. To Jabal the idea first occurs, I can carry my house about with me and regulate its movements and not it mine. I need not return every night this long weary way from the pastures, but may go wherever grass is green and streams run cool. He and his comrades would thus become aware of the vast resources of other lands, and would unconsciously lay the foundations both of commerce and of wars of conquest. For both in ancient and more modern times the most formidable armies have been those vast moving shepherd races bred outside the borders of civilization and flooding as with an irresistible tide the territories of more settled and less hardy tribes.

Jubal again was, as his name denotes, the reputed father of all such as handle the harp and the organ, stringed and wind instruments. The stops of the reed or flute and the divisions of the string being once discovered, all else necessarily followed. The twanging of a bow-string in a musical ear was enough to give the suggestion to an observant mind; the varying notes of the birds; the winds expressing at one time unbridled fury and at another a breathing benediction, could not fail to move and stir the susceptible spirit. The spontaneous though untuned singing of children, that follows no mere melody made by another to express *his* joy, but is the instinctive expression of their own joy, could not but give however meagrely the first rudiments of music. But here was the man who first made a piece of wood help him; who out of the commonest material of the physical world found for himself a means of expressing the most impalpable moods of his spirit. Once the idea was caught that matter inanimate as well as animate was man's servant and could do his finest work for him, Jabal and his brother Jubal would make rapid work between them. If the rude matter of the world could *sing* for them, what might it not do for them? They would see that there was a precision in machine-work which man's hand could not rival—a regularity which no nervous throb could throw out and no feeling interrupt, and yet at the same time when they found how these rude instruments responded to every finest shade of feeling, and how all external nature seemed able to express what was in man, must it not have been the birth of poetry as well as of music? Jubal in short originates what we now compendiously describe as the Fine Arts.

The third brother again may be taken as the originator of the Useful Arts—though not exclusively—for being the instructor of every artificer in brass and iron, having something of his brother's genius for invention and more than his brother's handiness and practical faculty for embodying his ideas in material forms, he must have promoted all arts which require tools for their culture.

Thus among these three brothers we find distributed the various kinds of genius and faculty which ever since have enriched the world. Here in germ was really all that the world can do. The great lines in which individual and social activity have since run were then laid down.

This notable family circle was completed by Naamah, the sister of Tubal-Cain. The strength of female influence began to be felt contemporaneously with the cultivation of the arts. Very early in the world's history it was perceived that although debarred from the rougher activities of life, women have an empire of their own. Men have the making of civilisation, but women have the making of men. It is they who form the character of the individual and give its tone to the society in which they live. It is natural to men to consider the feelings and tastes of women and to adapt their manners and conversation to them; and it is for women to exercise worthily the sway they thus possess. Practically and to a large extent women settle what subjects shall be spoken of, and in what tone, trifling or serious; and each ought therefore to recognise her own burden of responsibility, and see to it that the deference paid to her shall not lower him who pays it, and that the respect shown to her shall help him who shows it to respect what is pure and true, charitable, just, and worthy. Let women show that it is worldly trifling or slanderous malignity or empty tittle-tattle that delights them, then they act the part of Eve and tempt to sin; let them show that they prize most highly the mirth that is innocent and the conversation that is elevating and helpful, and while they win admiration for themselves they win it also for what is healthy and purifying. No woman can renounce her influence; helpful or hurtful she certainly is and must be in proportion as she is pleasing and attractive.

Thus early did it appear how much of what is admirable and serviceable clung to human nature apart from any recognition of God. The worldly life was then what it is now, a life not wholly and obviously polluted by excess, nor destroyed by violence, but displaying features which appeal to our sensibilities and provoke applause; a life of manifold beauty, of great power and resource, of abundant promise. There is abundant material in the world for beautifying and elevating human life, and this material may be used and is used by men who acknowledge neither its origin in God nor the ends He would serve by it. The interests of men may be advanced and the best work of the world done by three distinct classes of men—by those who work as God's children in thorough sympathy with His purposes; by those who do not know God but who are humble in heart and would sympathise with God's purposes, did they become acquainted with them; and by those who are proud and self-willed, positively alienated from God, and who do the world's work for their own ends. And so far as the external work goes the last-named class of men may be most efficient. In mental endowment, social and political wisdom, scientific aptitude, and all that tends to substantial utility, it is quite possible they may excel the godly, for "not many noble, not many wise are called." But we have nothing to measure permanent success by, save conformity with God's will; and we have nothing by which we can estimate how character will endure and how deeply it is rooted save conformity with the nature of God. If a man believes in God, in one Supreme Who rules and orders all things for just, holy and wise ends; if he is in sympathy with the nature and will of God and finds his truest satisfaction in forwarding the purposes of God, then you have a guarantee for this man's continuance in good and for his ultimate success.

The precarious nature of all godless civilisation and the real tendency of self-sufficing pride are shown in Lamech.

It is in Lamech the tendency culminates and in him the issue of all this brilliant but godless life is seen. Therefore though he is the father, the historian speaks of him *after* his children. In his one recorded utterance his character leaps to view definite and complete—a character of boundless force, self-reliance and godlessness. It is a little uncertain whether he means that he has actually slain a man, or whether he is putting a hypothetical case—the character of his speech is the same whichever view is taken.

> "I have slain," he says, or suppose I slay, "a man for wounding me,
> A young man for hurting me:
> But if Cain shall be avenged seven-fold—then Lamech seventy and seven-fold."

That is, I take vengeance for myself with those good weapons my son has forged for me. He has furnished me with a means of defence many times more effectual than God's avenging of Cain. This is the climax of the self-sufficiency to which the line of Cain has been tending. Cain besought God's protection; he needed God for at least one purpose, this one thread bound him yet to God. Lamech has no need of God for any purpose; what his sons can make and his own right hand do is enough for him. This is what comes of finding enough in the world without God—a boastful, self-sufficient man, dangerous to society, the incarnation of the pride of life. In the long run separation from God becomes isolation from man and cruel self-sufficiency.

The line of Seth is followed from father to son, for the sake of showing that the promise of a seed which should be victorious over evil was being fulfilled. Apparently it is also meant that during this uneventful period long ages elapsed. Nothing can be told of these old world people but that they lived and died, leaving behind them heirs to transmit the promise.

Only once is the monotony broken; but this in so striking a manner as to rescue us from the idea that the historian is mechanically copying a barren list of names. For in the seventh generation, contemporaneous with the culmination of Cain's line in the family of Lamech, we come upon the simple but anything but mechanical statement: "Enoch walked with God and he was not; for God took him." The phrase is full of meaning. Enoch walked with God because he was His friend and liked His company, because he was going in the same direction as God, and had no desire for anything but what lay in God's path. We walk with God when He is in all our thoughts; not because we consciously think of Him at all times, but because He is naturally suggested to us by all we think of; as when any person or plan or idea has become important to us, no matter what we think of, our thought is always found recurring to this favourite object, so with the godly man everything has a connection with God and must be ruled by that connection. When some change in his circumstances is thought of, he has first of all to determine how the proposed change will affect his connection with God—will his conscience be equally clear, will he be able to live on the same friendly terms with God and so forth. When he falls into sin he cannot rest till he has resumed his place at God's side and walks again with Him. This is the general nature of walking with God; it is a persistent endeavour to hold all our life open to God's inspection and in conformity to His will; a readiness to give up what we find does cause any misunderstanding between us and God; a feeling of loneliness if we have not some satisfaction in our efforts at holding fellowship with God, a cold and desolate feeling when we are conscious of doing something that displeases Him. This walking with God necessarily tells on the whole life and character. As you instinctively avoid subjects which you know will jar upon the feelings of your friend, as you naturally endeavour to suit yourself to your company, so when the consciousness of God's presence begins to have some weight with you, you are found instinctively endeavouring to please Him, repressing the thoughts you know He disapproves, and endeavouring to educate such dispositions as reflect His own nature.

It is easy then to understand how we may practically walk with God—it is to open to Him all our purposes and hopes, to seek His judgment on our scheme of life and idea of happiness—it is to be on thoroughly friendly terms with God. Why then do any not walk with God? Because they seek what is wrong. You would walk with Him if the same idea of good possessed you as possesses Him; if you were as ready as He to make no deflexion from the straight path. Is not the very crown of life depicted in the testimony given to Enoch, that "he pleased God"? Cannot you take your way through life with a resolute and joyous spirit if you are conscious that you please Him Who judges not by appearances, not by your manners, but by your real state, by your actual character and the eternal promise it bears? Things were not made easy to Enoch. In evil days, with much to mislead him, with everything to oppose him, he had by faith and diligent seeking, as the Epistle to the Hebrews says, to cleave to the path on which God walked, often left in darkness, often thrown off the track, often listening but unable to hear the footfall of God or to hear his own name called upon, receiving no sign but still diligently seeking the God he knew would lead him only to good. Be it yours to give such diligence. Do not accept it as a thing fixed that you are to be one of the graceless and ungodly, always feeble, always vacillating, always without a character, always in doubt about your state, and whether life might not be some other and better thing to you.

"Enoch was not, for God took him." Suddenly his place on earth was empty and men drew their own conclusions. He had been known as the Friend of God, where could he be but in God's dwelling-place? No sickness had slowly worn him to the grave, no mark of decay had been visible in his unabated vigour. His departure was a favour conferred and as such men recognised it. "God has taken him," they said, and their thoughts followed upward, and essayed to conceive the finished bliss of the man whom God has taken away where blessing may be more fully conferred. His age corresponded to our thirty-three, the age when the world has usually got fair hold of a man, when a man has found his place in life and means to live and see good days. The awkward, unfamiliar ways of youth that keep him outside of much of life are past, and the satiety of age is not yet reached; a man has begun to learn there is something he can do, and has not yet learned how little. It is an age at which it is most painful to relinquish life, but it was at this age God took him away, and men knew it was in kindness. Others had begun to gather round him, and depend upon him, hopes were resting in him, great things were expected of him, life was strong in him. But let life dress itself in its most attractive guise, let it shine on a man with its most fascinating smile, let him be happy at home and the pleasing centre of a pleasing circle of friends, let him be in that bright summer of life when a man begins to fear he is too prosperous and happy, and yet there is for man a better thing than all this, a thing so immeasurably and independently superior to it that all this may be taken away and yet the man be far more blessed. If God would confer His highest favours, He must take a man out of all this and bring him closer to Himself.

V
THE FLOOD

Genesis v.–ix.

The first great event which indelibly impressed itself on the memory of the primeval world was the Flood. There is every reason to believe that this catastrophe was co-extensive with the human population of the world. In every branch of the human family traditions of the event are found. These traditions need not be recited, though some of them bear a remarkable likeness to the Biblical story, while others are very beautiful in their construction, and significant in individual points. Local floods happening at various times in different countries could not have given birth to the minute coincidences found in these traditions, such as the sending out of the birds, and the number of persons saved. But we have as yet no material for calculating how far human population had spread from the original centre. It might apparently be argued that it could not have spread to the sea-coast, or that at any rate no ships had as yet been built large enough to weather a severe storm; for a thoroughly nautical population could have had little difficulty in surviving such a catastrophe as is here described. But all that can be affirmed is that there is no evidence that the waters extended beyond the inhabited part of the earth; and from certain details of the narrative, this part of the earth may be identified as the great plain of the Euphrates and Tigris.

Some of the expressions used in the narrative might indeed lead us to suppose that the writer understood the catastrophe to have extended over the whole globe; but expressions of similar largeness elsewhere occur in passages where their meaning must be restricted. Probably the most convincing evidence of the limited extent of the Flood is furnished by the animals of Australia. The animals that abound in that island are different from those found in other parts of the world, but are similar to the species which are found fossilized in the island itself, and which therefore must have inhabited these same regions long anterior to the Flood. If then the Flood extended to Australia and destroyed all animal life there, what are we compelled to suppose as the order of events? We must suppose that the creatures, visited by some presentiment of what was to happen many months after, selected specimens of their number, and that these specimens by some unknown and quite inconceivable means crossed thousands of miles of sea, found their way through all kinds of perils from unaccustomed climate, food, and beasts of prey; singled out Noah by some inscrutable instinct, and surrendered themselves to his keeping. And after the year in the ark expired, they turned their faces homewards, leaving behind them no progeny, again preserving themselves intact, and transporting themselves by some unknown means to their island home. This, if the Deluge was universal, must have been going on with thousands of animals from all parts of the globe; and not only were these animals a stupendous miracle in themselves, but wherever they went they were the occasion of miracle in others, all the beasts of prey refraining from their natural food. The fact is, the thing will not bear stating.

But it is not the physical but the moral aspects of the Flood with which we have here to do. And, first, this narrator explains its cause. He ascribes it to the abnormal wickedness of the antediluvians. To describe the demoralised condition of society before the Flood, the strongest language is used. "God saw that the wickedness of man was great," monstrous in acts of violence, and in habitual courses and established usages. "Every imagination of the thoughts of his heart was only evil continually,"—there was no mixture of good, no relentings, no repentances, no visitings of compunction, no hesitations and debatings. It was a world of men fierce and energetic, violent and lawless, in perpetual war and turmoil; in which if a man sought to live a righteous life, he had to conceive it of his own mind and to follow it out unaided and without the countenance of any.

This abnormal wickedness again is accounted for by the abnormal marriages from which the leaders of these ages sprang. Everything seemed abnormal, huge, inhuman. As there are laid bare to the eye of the geologist in those archaic times vast forms bearing a likeness to forms we are now familiar with, but of gigantic proportions and wallowing in dim, mist-covered regions; so to the eye of the historian there loom through the obscurity colossal forms perpetrating deeds of more than human savagery, and strength, and daring; heroes that seem formed in a different mould from common men.

However we interpret the narrative, its significance for us is plain. There is nothing prudish in the Bible. It speaks with a manly frankness of the beauty of women and its ensnaring power. The Mosaic law was stringent against intermarriage with idolatresses, and still in the New Testament something more than an echo of the old denunciation of such marriages is heard. Those who were most concerned about preserving a pure morality and a high tone in society were keenly alive to the dangers that threatened from this quarter.

It is a permanent danger to character because it is to a permanent element in human nature that the temptation appeals. To many in every generation, perhaps to the majority, this is the most dangerous form in which worldliness presents itself; and to resist this the most painful test of principle. With natures keenly sensitive to beauty and superficial attractiveness, some are called upon to make their choice between a conscientious cleaving to God and an attachment to that which in the form is perfect but at heart is defective, depraved, godless. Where there is great outward attraction a man fights against the growing sense of inward uncongeniality, and persuades himself he is too scrupulous and uncharitable, or that he is a bad reader of character. There may be an undercurrent of warning; he may be sensible that his whole nature is not satisfied and it may seem to him ominous that what is best within him does not flourish in his new attachment, but rather what is inferior, if not what is worst. But all such omens and warnings are disregarded and stifled by some such silly thought as that consideration and calculation are out of place in such matters. And what is the result? The result is the same as it ever was. Instead of the ungodly rising to the level of the godly, he sinks to hers. The worldly style, the amusements, the fashions once distasteful to him, but allowed for her sake, become familiar, and at last wholly displace the old and godly ways, the arrangements that left room for acknowledging God in the family; and there is one household less as a point of resistance to the incursion of an ungodly tone in society, one deserter more added to the already too crowded ranks of the ungodly, and the life-time if not the eternity of one soul embittered. Not without a consideration of the temptations that do actually lead men astray did the law enjoin: "Thou shalt not make a covenant with the inhabitants of the land, nor take of their daughters unto thy sons."

It seems like a truism to say that a greater amount of unhappiness has been produced by mismanagement, folly, and wickedness in the relation subsisting between men and women than by any other cause. God has given us the capacity of love to regulate this relation and be our safe guide in all matters connected with it. But frequently, from one cause or another, the government and direction of this relation are taken out of the hands of love and put into the thoroughly incompetent hands of convenience, or fancy, or selfish lust. A marriage contracted from any such motive is sure to bring unhappiness of a long-continued, wearing and often heart-breaking kind. Such a marriage is often the form in which retribution comes for youthful selfishness and youthful licentiousness. You cannot cheat nature. Just in so far as you allow yourself to be ruled in youth by a selfish love of pleasure, in so far do you incapacitate yourself for love. You sacrifice what is genuine and satisfying, because provided by nature, to what is spurious, unsatisfying, and shameful. You cannot afterwards, unless by a long and bitter discipline, restore the capacity of warm and pure love in your heart. Every indulgence in which true love is absent is another blow given to the faculty of love within you—you make yourself in that capacity decrepit, paralyzed, dead. You have lost, you have killed the faculty that should be your guide in all these matters, and so you are at last precipitated without this guidance into a marriage formed from some other motive, formed therefore against nature, and in which you are the everlasting victim of nature's relentless justice. Remember that you cannot have both things, a youth of loveless pleasure and a loving marriage—you must make your choice. For as surely as genuine love kills all evil desire; so surely does evil desire kill the very capacity of love, and blind utterly its wretched victim to the qualities that ought to excite love.

The language used of God in relation to this universal corruption strikes every one as remarkable. "It repented the Lord that He had made man on the earth, and it grieved Him at His heart." This is what is usually termed anthropomorphism, *i.e.* the presenting of God in terms applicable only to man; it is an instance of the same mode of speaking as is used when we speak of God's hand or eye or heart. These expressions are not absolutely true, but they are useful and convey to us a meaning which could scarcely otherwise be expressed. Some persons think that the use of these expressions proves that in early times God was thought of as wearing a body and as being very like ourselves in His inward nature. And even in our day we have been ridiculed for speaking of God as a magnified man. Now in the first place the use of such expressions does not prove that even the earliest worshippers of God believed Him to have eyes and hands and a body. We freely use the same expressions though we have no such belief. We use them because our language is formed for human uses and on a human level, and we have no capacity to frame a better. And in the second place, though not absolutely true they do help us towards the truth. We are told that it degrades God to think of Him as hearing prayer and accepting praise; nay, that to think of Him as a Person at all, is to degrade Him. We ought to think of Him as the Absolutely Unknowable. But which degrades God most, and which exalts Him most? If we find that it is impossible to worship an absolutely unknowable, if we find that practically such an idea is a mere nonentity to us, and that we cannot in point of fact pay any homage or show any consideration to such an empty abstraction, is not this really to lower God? And if we find that when we think of Him as a Person, and ascribe to Him all human virtue in an infinite degree, we can rejoice in Him and worship Him with true adoration, is not this to exalt Him? While we call Him our Father we know that this title is inadequate, while we speak of

God as planning and decreeing we know that we are merely making shift to express what is inexpressible by us—we know that our thoughts of Him are never adequate and that to think of Him at all is to lower Him, is to think of Him inadequately; but when the practical alternative is such as it is, we find we do well to think of Him with the highest personal attributes we can conceive. For to refuse to ascribe such attributes to Him because this is degrading Him, is to empty our minds of any idea of Him which can stimulate either to worship or to duty. If by ridding our minds of all anthropomorphic ideas and refusing to think of God as feeling, thinking, acting as men do, we could thereby get to a really higher conception of Him, a conception which would practically make us worship Him more devotedly and serve Him more faithfully, then by all means let us do so. But if the result of refusing to think of Him as in many ways like ourselves, is that we cease to think of Him at all or only as a dead impersonal force, then this certainly is not to reach a higher but a lower conception of Him. And until we see our way to some truly higher conception than that which we have of a Personal God, we had better be content with it.

In short, we do well to be humble, and considering that we know very little about existence of any kind, and least of all about God's, and that our God has been presented to us in human form, we do well to accept Christ as our God, to worship, love, and serve Him, finding Him sufficient for all our wants of this life, and leaving it to other times to get the solution of anything that is not made plain to us in Him. This is one boon that the science and philosophy of our day have unintentionally conferred upon us. They have laboured to make us feel how remote and inaccessible God is, how little we can know Him, how truly He is past finding out; they have laboured to make us feel how intangible and invisible and incomprehensible God is, but the result of this is that we turn with all the stronger longing to Him who is the Image of the Invisible God, and on whom a voice has fallen from the excellent glory, "This is My beloved Son, hear Him."

The Flood itself we need not attempt to describe. It has been remarked that though the narrative is vivid and forcible, it is entirely wanting in that sort of description which in a modern historian or poet would have occupied the largest space. "We see nothing of the death-struggle; we hear not the cry of despair; we are not called upon to witness the frantic agony of husband and wife, and parent and child, as they fled in terror before the rising waters. Nor is a word said of the sadness of the one righteous man, who, safe himself, looked upon the destruction which he could not avert." The Chaldean tradition which is the most closely allied to the Biblical account is not so reticent. Tears are shed in heaven over the catastrophe, and even consternation affected its inhabitants, while within the ark itself the Chaldean Noah says, "When the storm came to an end and the terrible water-spout ceased, I opened the window and the light smote upon my face. I looked at the sea attentively observing, and the whole of humanity had returned to mud, like seaweed the corpses floated. I was seized with sadness; I sat down and wept and my tears fell upon my face."

There can be little question that this is a true description of Noah's feeling. And the sense of desolation and constraint would rather increase in Noah's mind than diminish. Month after month elapsed; he was coming daily nearer the end of his food, and yet the waters were unabated. He did not know how long he was to be kept in this dark, disagreeable place. He was left to do his daily work without any supernatural signs to help him against his natural anxieties. The floating of the ark and all that went on in it had no mark of God's hand upon it. He was indeed *safe* while others had been destroyed. But of what good was this safety to be? Was he ever to get out of this prison-house? To what straits was he to be first reduced? So it is often with ourselves. We are left to fulfil God's will without any sensible tokens to set over against natural difficulties, painful and pinching circumstances, ill health, low spirits, failure of favourite projects and old hopes—so that at last we come to think that perhaps safety is all we are to have in Christ, a mere exemption from suffering of one kind purchased by the endurance of much suffering of another kind; that we are to be thankful for pardon on any terms; and escaping with our *life*, must be content though it be bare. Why, how often does a Christian wonder whether, after all, he has chosen a life that he can endure, whether the monotony and the restraints of the Christian life are not inconsistent with true enjoyment?

This strife between the felt restriction of the Christian life and the natural craving for abundant life, for entrance into all that the world can show us, and experience of all forms of enjoyment—this strife goes on unceasingly in the heart of many of us as it goes on from age to age in the world. Which is the true view of life, which is the view to guide *us* in choosing and refusing the enjoyments and pursuits that are presented to us? Are we to believe that the ideal man for this life is he who has tasted all culture and delight, who believes in nature, recognising no fall and seeking for no redemption, and makes enjoyment his end; or he who sees that all enjoyment is deceptive till man is set right morally, and who spends himself on this, knowing that blood and misery must come before peace and rest, and crowned as our King and Leader, not with a garland of roses, but with the crown of Him Who is greatest of all, because servant of all—to Whom the most sunken is not repulsive, and Who will not abandon the most hopeless? This comes to be very much the question, whether this life is final or preparatory?—whether, therefore, our work in it should be to check lower propensities and develop and train all that is best in character, so as to be fit for highest life and enjoyment in a world to come—or should take ourselves as we find ourselves, and delight in this present world? whether this is a placid eternal state, in which things are very much as they should be, and in which therefore we can live freely and enjoy freely; or whether it is a disordered, initial condition in which our main task should be to do a little towards putting things on a better rail and getting at least the germ and small beginnings of future good planted in one another? So that in the midst of all felt restriction, there is the highest hope, that one day we shall go forth from the narrow precincts of our ark, and step out into the free bright sunshine, in a world where there is nothing to offend, and that the time of our deprivation will seem to have been well spent indeed, if it has left within us a capacity permanently to enjoy love, holiness, justice, and all that is delighted in by God Himself.

The use made of this event in the New Testament is remarkable. It is compared by Peter to baptism, and both are viewed as illustrations of salvation by destruction. The eight souls, he says, who were in the ark, "were saved by water." The water which destroyed the rest saved them. When there seemed little hope of the godly line being able to withstand the influence of the ungodly, the Flood came and left Noah's family in a new world, with freedom to order all things according to their own ideas. In this Peter sees some analogy to baptism. In baptism, the penitent who believes in the efficacy of Christ's blood to purge away sin, lets his defilement be washed away and rises new and clean to the life Christ gives. In Christ the sinner finds shelter for himself and destruction for his sins. It is God's wrath against sin that saves us by destroying our sins; just as it was the Flood which devastated the world, that at the same time, and thereby, saved Noah and his family.

In this event, too, we see the completeness of God's work. Often we feel reluctant to surrender our sinful habits to so final a destruction as is implied in being one with Christ. The expense at which holiness is to be bought seems almost too great. So much that has given us pleasure must be parted with; so many old ties sundered, a condition of holiness presents an aspect of dreariness and hopelessness; like the world after the flood, not a moving thing on the surface of the earth, everything levelled, prostrate, and washed even with the ground; here the corpse of a man, there the carcase of a beast; here mighty forest timber swept prone like the rushes on the banks of a flooded stream, and there a city without inhabitants, everything dank, dismal and repellent. But this is only one aspect of the work; the beginning, necessary if the work is to be thorough. If any part of the sinful life remain it will spring up to mar what God means to introduce us to. Only that is to be preserved which we can take with us into our ark. Only that is to pass on into our life which we can retain while we are in true connection with Christ, and which we think can help us to live as His friends, and to serve Him zealously.

This event then gives us some measure by which we can know how much God will do to maintain holiness upon earth. In this catastrophe every one who strives after godliness may find encouragement, seeing in it the Divine earnestness of God for good and against evil. There is only one other event in history that so conspicuously shows that holiness among men is the object for which God will sacrifice everything else. There is no need now of any further demonstration of God's purpose in this world and His zeal for carrying it out. And may it not be expected of us His children, that we stand in presence of the cross until our cold and frivolous hearts catch something of the earnestness, the "resisting unto blood striving against sin," which is exhibited there? The Flood has not been forgotten by almost any people under heaven, but its moral result is *nil*. But he whose memory is haunted by a dying Redeemer, by the thought of One Whose love found its most appropriate and practical result in dying for him, *is* prevented from much sin, and finds in that love the spring of eternal hope, that which his soul in the deep privacy of his most sacred thoughts can feed upon with joy, that which he builds himself round and broods over as his inalienable possession.

VI
NOAH'S FALL

Genesis ix. 20–27.

Noah in the ark was in a position of present safety but of much anxiety. No sign of any special protection on God's part was given. The waters seem to stand at their highest level still; and probably the risk of the ark's grounding on some impracticable peak, or precipitous hill-side, would seem as great a danger as the water itself. Five months had elapsed, and though the rain had ceased the sky was heavy and threatening, and every day now was worth many measures of corn in the coming harvest. A reflection of the anxiety within the ark is seen in the expression, "And God remembered Noah." It was needful to say so, for there was as yet no outward sign of this.

To such anxieties all are subject who have availed themselves of the salvation God provides. At the first there is an easy faith in God's aid; there are many signs of His presence; the subjects in whom salvation operates have no disposition or temptation to doubt that God is with them and is working for them. But this initial stage is succeeded by a very different state of things. We seem to be left to ourselves to cope with the world and all its difficulties and temptations in our own strength. Much as we crave some sign that God remembers us, no sign is given. We no longer receive the same urgent impulses to holiness of life; we have no longer the same freshness in devotion as if speaking to a God at hand. There is nothing which of itself and without reasoning about it says to us, Here is God's hand upon me.

In fact, the great part of our life has to be spent under these conditions, and we need to hold some well-ascertained principle regarding God's dealings, if our faith is to survive. And here in God's treatment of Noah we see that God may as certainly be working for us when not working directly upon us, as when His presence is palpable. His absence from us is as needful as His presence. The clouds are as requisite for our salvation as the sunny sky. When therefore we find that salvation from sin is a much slower and more anxious matter than we once expected it to be, we are not to suppose that God is not hearing our prayers. When Noah day by day cried to God for relief, and yet night after night found himself "cribb'd, cabin'd, and confined," with no sign from God but such as faith could apprehend, depend upon it he had very different feelings from those with which he first stepped into the ark. And when we are left to one monotonous rut of duty and to an unchanging and dry form of devotion, when we are called to learn to live by faith not by sight, to learn that God's purposes with us are spiritual, and that slow and difficult growth in self-command and holiness is the best proof that He hears our prayers, we must strive to believe that this also is a needful part of our salvation; and we must especially be on our guard against supposing that as God has ceased to disclose Himself to us, and so to make faith easy, we may cease to disclose ourselves to Him.

For this is the natural and very frequent result of such an experience. Discouraged by the obscurity of God's ways and the difficulty of believing when the mind is not sustained by success or by new thoughts or manifest tokens of God's presence, we naturally cease to look for any clear signs of God's concernment about our state, and rest from all anxious craving to know God's will about us. To this temptation the majority of Christian people yield, and allow themselves to become indifferent to spiritual truth and increasingly interested in the non-mysterious facts of the present world, attending to present duties in a mechanical way, seeing that their families have enough to eat and that all in their little ark are provided for. But to this temptation Noah did not yield. Though to all appearance abandoned by God, he did what he could to ascertain what was beyond his immediate sight and present experience. He sent out his raven and his dove. Not satisfied with his first enquiry by the raven, which could flit from one piece of floating garbage to another, he sent out the dove, and continued to do so at intervals of seven days.

Noah sent out the raven first, probably because it had been the most companionable bird and seemed the wisest, preferable to "the silly dove;" but it never came back with God's message. And so has one often found that an enquiry into God's will, the examination, for example, of some portion of Scripture, undertaken with a prospect of success and with good human helps, has failed, and has failed in this peculiar ravenlike way; the enquiry has settled down on some worthless point, on some rotting carcase, on some subject of passing interest or worldly learning, and brings back no message of God to us. On the other hand, the continued use, Sabbath after Sabbath, of God's appointed means, and the patient waiting for some message of God to come to us through what seems a most unlikely messenger, will often be rewarded. It may be but a single leaf plucked off that we get, but enough to convince us that God has been mindful of our need, and is preparing for us a habitable world.

Many a man is like the raven, feeding himself on the destruction of others, satisfied with knowing how God has dealt with others. He thinks he has done his part when he has found out who has been sinning and what has been the result. But the dove will not settle on any such resting-place, and is dissatisfied until for herself she can pluck off some token that God's anger is turned away and that now there is peace on earth. And if only you wait God's time and renew your endeavours to find such tokens, some assurance will be given you, some green and growing thing, some living part, however small, of the new creation which will certify you of your hope.

On the first day of the first month, New Year's day, Noah removed the covering of the ark, which seems to have stranded on the Armenian tableland, and looked out upon the new world. He cannot but have felt his responsibility, as a kind of second Adam. And many questionings must have arisen in his mind regarding the relation of the new to the old. Was there to be any connection with the old world at all, or was all to begin afresh? Were the promises, the traditions, the events, the genealogies of the old world of any significance now? The Flood distinctly marked the going out of one order of things and the establishment of another. Man's career and development, or what we call history, had not before the Flood attained its goal. If this development was not to be broken short off, and if God's purpose in creation was to be fulfilled, then the world must still go on. Some worlds may perhaps die young, as individuals die young. Others endure through hair-breadth escapes and constant dangers, find their way like our planet through showers of fire, and pass without collision the orbits of huge bodies, carrying with them always, as our world does, the materials of their destruction within themselves. But catastrophes do not cut short, but evolve God's purposes. The Flood came that God's purpose might be fulfilled. The course of nature was interrupted, the arrangements of social and domestic life were overturned, all the works of men were swept away that this purpose might be fulfilled. It was expedient that one generation should die for all generations; and this generation having been taken out of the way, fresh provision is made for the co-operation of man with God. On man's part there is an emphatic acknowledgment of God by sacrifice; on God's part there is a renewed grant to man of the world and its fulness, a renewed assurance of His favour.

This covenant with Noah was on the plane of nature. It is man's natural life in the world which is the subject of it. The sacredness of life is its great lesson. Men might well wonder whether God did not hold life cheap. In the old world violence had prevailed. But while Lamech's sword may have slain its thousands, God had in the Flood slain tens of thousands. The covenant, therefore, directs that human life must be reverenced. The primal blessing is renewed. Men are to multiply and replenish the earth; and the slaughter of a man was to be reckoned a capital crime; and the maintenance of life was guaranteed by a special clause, securing the regularity of the seasons. If, then, you ask, Was this just a beginning again where Adam began? Did God just wipe out man as a boy wipes his slate clean, when he finds his calculation is turning out wrong? Had all these generations learned nothing; had the world not grown at all since its birth?—the answer is, it had grown, and in two most important respects,—it had come to the knowledge of the uniformity of nature, and the necessity of human law. This great departure from the uniformity of nature brought into strong relief its normal uniformity, and gave men their first lesson in the recognition of a God who governs by fixed laws. And they learned also from the Flood that wickedness must not be allowed to grow unchecked and attain dimensions which nothing short of a flood can cope with.

Fit symbol of this covenant was the rainbow. Seeming to unite heaven and earth, it pictured to those primitive people the friendliness existing between God and man. Many nations have looked upon it as not merely one of the most beautiful and striking objects in nature, but as the messenger of heaven to men. And arching over the whole horizon, it exhibits the all-embracing universality of the promise. They accepted it as a sign that God has no pleasure in destruction, that He does not give way to moods, that He does not always chide, that if weeping may endure for a night joy is sure to follow. If any one is under a cloud, leading a joyless, hopeless, heartless life, if any one has much apparent reason to suppose that God has given him up to catastrophe, and lets things run as they may, there is some satisfaction in reading this natural emblem and recognising that without the cloud, nay, without the cloud breaking into heavy sweeping rains, there cannot be the bow, and that no cloud of God's sending is permanent, but will one day give place to unclouded joy. Let the prayer of David be yours, "I know, O Lord, that Thy judgments are right, and that Thou in faithfulness hast afflicted me. Let, I pray Thee, Thy merciful kindness be for my comfort according to Thy word unto Thy servant."

It may be felt that the matters about which God spoke to Noah were barely religious, certainly not spiritual. But to take God as our God in any one particular is to take Him as our God for all. If we can eat our daily bread as given to us by our Father in heaven, then we are heirs of the righteousness which is by faith. It is because we wait for some wonderful and out-of-the-way proofs that God is keeping faith with us that we so much lack a real and living faith. If you think of God only in connection with some spiritual difficulty, or if you are waiting for some critical spiritual experience about which you may deal with God,—if you are not transacting with Him about your daily work, about your temporal wants and difficulties, about your friendships and your tastes, about that which makes up the bulk of your thought, feeling, and action, then you have yet to learn what living with God means. You have yet to learn that God the Infinite Creator of all is present in all your life. We are not in advance of Noah, but behind him, if we cannot speak to God about common things.

Besides, the relation of man to God was sufficiently determined by this covenant. When any man in that age began to ask himself the question which all men in all ages ask, How shall I win the favour of God? it must, or it might, at once have struck him, Why, God has already favoured me and has bound Himself to me by express and solemn pledges. And radically this is all that any one needs to know. It is not a change in God's attitude towards you that is required. What is required is that you believe what is actually the case, that the Holy God loves you already and is already seeking to bless you by making you like Himself. Believe that, and let the faith of it sink more and more deeply into your spirit, and you will find that you are saved from your sin.

What remains to be told of Noah is full of moral significance. Rare indeed is a *wholly* good man; and happy indeed is he who throughout his youth, his manhood, and his age lets principle govern all his actions. The righteous and rescued Noah lying drunk on his tent-floor is a sorrowful spectacle. God had given him the earth, and this was the use he made of the gift; melancholy presage of the fashion of his posterity. He had God to help him to bear his responsibilities, to refresh and gladden him; but he preferred the fruit of his vineyard. Can the most sacred or impressive memories secure a man against sin? Noah had the memory of a race drowned for sin and of a year in solitude with God. Can the dignity and weight of responsibility steady a man? This man knew that to him God had declared His purpose and that he only could carry it forward to fulfilment. In that heavy helpless figure, fallen insensible in his tent, is as significant a warning as in the Flood.

Noah's sin brings before us two facts about sin. First, that the smaller temptations are often the most effectual. The man who is invulnerable on the field of battle amidst declared and strong enemies falls an easy prey to the assassin in his own home. When all the world was against him, Noah was able to face single-handed both scorn and violence, but in the midst of his vineyard, among his own people who understood him and needed no preaching or proof of his virtue, he relaxed.

He was no longer in circumstances so difficult as to force him to watch and pray, as to drive him to God's side. The temptations Noah had before known were mainly from without; he now learnt that those from within are more serious. Many of us find it comparatively easy to carry clean hands before the public, or to demean ourselves with tolerable seemliness in circumstances where the temptation may be very strong but is also very patent; but how careless are we often in our domestic life, and how little strain do we put upon ourselves in the company of those whom we can trust. What petulance and irritability, what angry and slanderous words, what sensuality and indolence could our own homes witness to! Noah is not the only man who has walked uprightly and kept his garment unspotted from the world so long as the eye of man was on him, but who has lain uncovered on his own tent-floor.

Secondly, we see here how a man may fall into new forms of sin, and are reminded especially of one of the most distressing facts to be observed in the world, viz., that men in their prime and even in their old age are sometimes overtaken in sins of sensuality from which hitherto they have kept themselves pure. We are very ready to think we know the full extent of wickedness to which we may go; that by certain sins *we* shall never be much tempted. And in some of our predictions we may be correct; our temperament or our circumstances may absolutely preclude some sins from mastering us. Yet who has made but a slight alteration in his circumstances, added a little to his business, made some new family arrangements, or changed his residence, without being astonished to find how many new sources of evil seem to have been opened within him? While therefore you rejoice over sins defeated, beware of thinking your work is nearly done. Especially let those of us who have for years been fighting mainly against one sin beware of thinking that if only *that* were defeated we should be free from sin. As a man who has long suffered from one bodily disease congratulates himself that at least he knows what he may expect in the way of pain, and will not suffer as some other man he has heard of does suffer; whereas though one disease may kill others, yet some diseases only prepare the body for the assault of worse ailments than themselves, and the constitution at last breaks up under a combination of ills that make the sufferer a pity to his friends and a perplexity to his physicians. And so is it in the spirit; you cannot say that because you are so consumed by one infirmity, others can find no room in you. In short, there is nothing that can secure us against the unspeakable calamity of falling into new sins, except the direction given by our Lord, "Watch and pray, lest ye enter into temptation." There *is need* of watching, else this precept had never been uttered; too many things absolutely needful for us to do have to be enjoined upon us to leave any room for the injunction of precepts that are unnecessary, and he who is not watching has no security that he shall not sin so as to be a scandal to his friends and a shame to himself.

Noah's sin brought to light the character of his three sons—the coarse irreverence of Ham, the dignified delicacy and honour of Shem and Japheth. The bearing of men towards the sins of others is always a touchstone of character. The full exposure of sin where good is expected to come of the exposure and when it is done with sorrow and with shame is one thing, and the exposure of sin to create a laugh and merely to amuse is another. They are the true descendants of Ham, whether their faces be black or white, and whether they go with no clothes or with clothes that are the product of much thought and anxiety, who find pleasure in the mere contemplation of deeds of shame, in real life, on the boards of the theatre, in daily journals, or in works of fiction. Extremes meet, and the savage grossness of Ham is found in many who count themselves the last and finest product of culture. It is found also in the harder and narrower set of modern investigators, who glory in exposing the scientific weakness of our forefathers, and make a jest of the mistakes of men to whom they owe much of their freedom, and whose shoe latchet they are not worthy to tie, so far as the deeper moral qualities go.

But neither is religious society free from this same sin. The faults and mistakes and sins of others are talked over, possibly with some show of regret, but with, as we know, very little real shame and sadness, for these feelings prompt us, not to talk them over in companies where no good can be done in the way of remedy, but to cover them as these sorrowing sons of Noah, with averted eye and humbled head. Charity is the prime grace enjoined upon us and charity *covers* a multitude of sins. And whatever excuses for exposing others we may make, however we may say it is only a love of truth and fair play that makes us drag to light the infirmities of a man whom others are praising, we may be very sure that if all *evil* motives were absent this kind of evil speaking would cease among us. But there is a malignity in sin that leaves its bitter root in us all, and causes us to be glad when those whom we have been regarding as our superiors are reduced to our poor level. And there is a cowardliness in sin which cannot bear to be alone, and eagerly hails every symptom of others being in the same condemnation.

Before exposing another, think first whether your own conduct could bear a similar treatment, whether you have never done the thing you desire to conceal, said the thing you would blush to hear repeated, or thought the thought you could not bear another to read. And if you be a Christian, does it not become you to remember what you yourself have learnt of the slipperiness of this world's ways, of your liability to fall, of your sudden exposure to sin from some physical disorder, or some slight mistake which greatly extenuates your sin, but which you could not plead before another?

And do you know nothing of the difficulty of conquering one sin that is rooted in your constitution, and the strife that goes on in a man's own soul and in secret though he show little immediate fruit of it in his life before men? Surely it becomes us to give a man credit for much good resolution and much sore self-denial and endeavour, even when he fails and sins still, because such we know to be our own case, and if we disbelieve in others until they can walk with perfect rectitude, if we condemn them for one or two flaws and blemishes, we shall be tempted to show the same want of charity towards ourselves, and fall at length into that miserable and hopeless condition that believes in no regenerating spirit nor in any holiness attainable by us.

VII
THE CALL OF ABRAHAM

Genesis xi. 27–xii. 5.

With Abraham there opens a new chapter in the history of the race; a chapter of the profoundest significance. The consequences of Abraham's movements and beliefs have been limitless and enduring. All succeeding time has been influenced by him. And yet there is in his life a remarkable simplicity, and an entire absence of such events as impress contemporaries. Among all the forgotten millions of his own time he stands alone a recognisable and memorable figure. But around his figure there gathers no throng of armed followers; with his name, no vast territorial dominion, no new legislation, not even any work of literature or art is associated. The significance of his life was not military, nor legislative, nor literary, but religious. To him must be carried back the belief in one God. We find him born and brought up among idolaters; and although it is certain there were others besides himself who here and there upon earth had dimly arrived at the same belief as he, yet it is certainly from him the Monotheistic belief has been diffused. Since his day the world has never been without its explicit advocacy. It is his belief in the true God, in a God who manifested His existence and His nature by responding to this belief, it is this belief and the place he gave it as the regulating principle of all his movements and thoughts, that have given him his everlasting influence.

With Abraham there is also introduced the first step in a new method adopted by God in the training of men. The dispersion of men and the divergence of their languages are now seen to have been the necessary preliminary to this new step in the education of the world—the fencing round of one people till they should learn to know God and understand and exemplify His government. It is true, God reveals Himself to all men and governs all; but by selecting one race with special adaptations, and by giving to it a special training, God might more securely and more rapidly reveal Himself to all. Each nation has certain characteristics, a national character which grows by seclusion from the influences which are forming other races. There is a certain mental and moral individuality stamped upon every separate people. Nothing is more certainly retained; nothing more certainly handed down from generation to generation. It would therefore be a good practical means of conserving and deepening the knowledge of God, if it were made the national interest of a people to preserve it, and if it were closely identified with the national characteristics. This was the method adopted by God. He meant to combine allegiance to Himself with national advantages, and spiritual with national character, and separation in belief with a distinctly outlined and defensible territory.

This method, in common with all Divine methods, was in strict keeping with the natural evolution of history. The migration of Abraham occurred in the epoch of migrations. But although for centuries before Abraham new nations had been forming, none of them had belief in God as its formative principle. Wave upon wave of warriors, shepherds, colonists have left the prolific plains of Mesopotamia. Swarm after swarm has left that busy hive, pushing one another further and further west and east, but all have been urged by natural impulses, by hunger, commerce, love of adventure and conquest. By natural likings and dislikings, by policy, and by dint of force the multitudinous tribes of men were finding their places in the world, the weaker being driven to the hills, and being schooled there by hard living till their descendants came down and conquered their conquerors. All this went on without regard to any very high motives. As it was with the Goths who invaded Italy for her wealth, as it is now with those who people America and Africa because there is land or room enough, so it was then. But at last God selects one man and says, "*I* will make of thee a great nation." The origin of this nation is not facile love of change nor lust of territory, but belief in God. Without this belief this people had not been. No other account can be given of its origin. Abraham is himself already the member of a tribe, well-off and likely to be well-off; he has no large family to provide for, but he is separated from his kindred and country, and led out to be himself a new beginning, and this because, as he himself throughout his life said, he heard God's call and responded to it.

The city which claims the distinction of being Abraham's birthplace, or at least of giving its name to the district where he was born, is now represented by a few mounds of ruins rising out of the flat marshy ground on the western bank of the Euphrates, not far above the point where it joins its waters to those of the Tigris and glides on to the Persian gulf. In the time of Abraham, Ur was the capital city which gave its name to one of the most populous and fertile regions of the earth. The whole land of Accad which ran up from the sea-coast to Upper Mesopotamia (or Shinar) seems to have been known as Ur-ma, the land of Ur. This land was of no great extent, being little if at all larger than Scotland, but it was the richest of Asia. The high civilisation which this land enjoyed even in the time of Abraham has been disclosed in the abundant and multifarious Babylonian remains which have recently been brought to light.

What induced Terah to abandon so prosperous a land can only be conjectured. It is possible that the idolatrous customs of the inhabitants may have had something to do with his movements. For while the ancient Babylonian records reveal a civilisation surprisingly advanced, and a social order in some respects admirable, they also make disclosures regarding the worship of the gods which must shock even those who are familiar with the immoralities frequently fostered by heathen religions. The city of Ur was not only the capital, it was the holy city of the Chaldeans. In its northern quarter rose high above the surrounding buildings the successive stages of the temple of the moon-god, culminating in a platform on which the priests could both accurately observe the motions of the stars and hold their night-watches in honour of their god. In the courts of this temple might be heard breaking the silence of midnight, one of those magnificent hymns, still preserved, in which idolatry is seen in its most attractive dress, and in which the Lord of Ur is invoked in terms not unworthy of the living God. But in these same temple-courts Abraham may have seen the firstborn led to the altar, the fruit of the body sacrificed to atone for the sin of the soul; and here too he must have seen other sights even more shocking and repulsive. Here he was no doubt taught that strangely mixed religion which clung for generations to some members of his family. Certainly he was taught in common with the whole community to rest on the seventh day; as he was trained to look to the stars with reverence and to the moon as something more than the light which was set to rule the night.

Possibly then Terah may have been induced to move northwards by a desire to shake himself free from customs he disapproved. The Hebrews themselves seem always to have considered that his migration had a religious motive. "This people," says one of their old writings, "is descended from the Chaldeans, and they sojourned heretofore in Mesopotamia because they would not follow the gods of their fathers which were in the land of Chaldea. For they left the way of their ancestors and worshipped the God of heaven, the God whom they knew; so they cast them out from the face of their gods, and they fled into Mesopotamia and sojourned there many days. Then their God commanded them to depart from the place where they sojourned and to go into the land of Canaan." But if this is a true account of the origin of the movement northwards, it must have been Abraham rather than his father who was the moving spirit of it; for it is certainly Abraham and not Terah who stands as the significant figure inaugurating the new era.

If doubt rests on the moving cause of the migration from Ur, none rests on that which prompted Abraham to leave Charran and journey towards Canaan. He did so in obedience to what he believed to be a Divine command, and in faith on what he understood to be a Divine promise. How he became aware that a Divine command thus lay upon him we do not know. Nothing could persuade him that he was not commanded. Day by day he heard in his soul what he recognised as a Divine voice, saying: "Get thee out of thy country and from thy kindred and from thy father's house, unto a land that I will show thee!" This was God's first revelation of Himself to Abraham. Up to this time Abraham to all appearance had no knowledge of any God but the deities worshipped by his fathers in Chaldea. Now, he finds within himself impulses which he cannot resist and which he is conscious he ought not to resist. He believes it to be his duty to adopt a course which may look foolish and which he can justify only by saying that his conscience bids him. He recognises, apparently for the first time, that through his conscience there speaks to him a God Who is supreme. In dependence on this God he gathered his possessions together and departed.

So far, one may be tempted to say, no very unusual faith was required. Many a poor girl has followed a weakly brother or a dissipated father to Australia or the wild west of America; many a lad has gone to the deadly west coast of Africa with no such prospects as Abraham. For Abraham had the double prospect which makes migration desirable. Assure the colonist that he will find land and have strong sons to till and hold and leave it to, and you give him all the motive he requires. These were the promises made to Abraham—a land and a seed. Neither was there at this period much difficulty in believing that both promises would be fulfilled. The land he no doubt expected to find in some unoccupied territory. And as regards the children, he had not yet faced the condition that only through Sarah was this part of the promise to be fulfilled.

But the peculiarity in Abraham's abandonment of present certainties for the sake of a future and unseen good is, that it was prompted not by family affection or greed or an adventurous disposition, but by faith in a God Whom no one but himself recognised. It was the first step in a life-long adherence to an Invisible, Spiritual Supreme. It was that first step which committed him to life-long dependence upon and intercourse with One Who had authority to regulate his movements and power to bless him. From this time forth all that he sought in life was the fulfilment of God's promise. He staked his future upon God's existence and faithfulness. Had Abraham abandoned Charran at the command of a widely ruling monarch who promised him ample compensation, no record would have been made of so ordinary a transaction. But this was an entirely new thing and well worth recording, that a man should leave country and kindred and seek an unknown land under the impression that thus he was obeying the command of the unseen God. While others worshipped sun, moon, and stars, and recognised the Divine in their brilliance and power, in their exaltation above earth and control of earth and its life, Abraham saw that there was something greater than the order of nature and more worthy of worship, even the still small voice that spoke within his own conscience of right and wrong in human conduct, and that told him how his own life must be ordered. While all around him were bowing down to the heavenly host and sacrificing to them the highest things in human nature, he heard a voice falling from these shining ministers of God's will, which said to him, "See thou do it not, for we are thy fellow-servants; worship thou God!" This was the triumph of the spiritual over the material; the acknowledgment that in God there is something greater than can be found in nature; that man finds his true affinity not in the things that are seen but in the unseen Spirit that is over all. It is this that gives to the figure of Abraham its simple grandeur and its permanent significance.

Under the simple statement "The Lord said unto Abram, Get thee out of thy country," there are probably hidden years of questioning and meditation. God's revelation of Himself to Abram in all probability did not take the determinate form of articulate command without having passed through many preliminary stages of surmise and doubt and mental conflict. But once assured that God is calling him, Abraham responds quickly and resolutely. The revelation has come to a mind in which it will not be lost. As one of the few theologians who have paid attention to the method of revelation has said: "A Divine revelation does not dispense with a certain character and certain qualities of mind in the person who is the instrument of it. A man who throws off the chains of authority and association must be a man of extraordinary independence and strength of mind, although he does so in obedience to a Divine revelation; because no miracle, no sign or wonder which accompanies a revelation can by its simple stroke force human nature from the innate hold of custom and the adhesion to and fear of established opinion; can enable it to confront the frowns of men, and take up truth opposed to general prejudice, except there is in the man himself, who is the recipient of the revelation, a certain strength of mind and independence which concurs with the Divine intention."

That Abraham's faith triumphed over exceptional difficulties and enabled him to do what no other motive would have been strong enough to accomplish, there is therefore no call to assert. During his after-life his faith was severely tried, but the mere abandonment of his country in the hope of gaining a better was the ordinary motive of his day. It was the *ground* of this hope, the belief in God, which made Abraham's conduct original and fruitful. That sufficient inducement was presented to him is only to say that God is reasonable. There is always sufficient inducement to obey God; because life is reasonable. No man was ever commanded or required to do anything which it was not for his advantage to do. Sin is a mistake. But so weak are we, so liable to be moved by the things present to us and by the desire for immediate gratification, that it never ceases to be wonderful and admirable when a sense of duty enables a man to forego present advantage and to believe that present loss is the needful preliminary of eternal gain.

Abraham's faith is chosen by the author of the Epistle to the Hebrews as an apt illustration of his definition of Faith, that it is "the substance of things hoped for, the evidence of things not seen." One property of faith is that it gives to things future and which are as yet only hoped for all the reality of actual present existence. Future things may be said to have no existence for those who do not believe in them. They are not taken into account. Men do not shape their conduct with any reference to them. But when a man believes in certain events that are to be, this faith of his lends to these future things the reality, the "substance" which things actually existing in the present have. They have the same weight with him, the same influence upon his conduct.

Without some power to realize the future and to take account of what is to be as well as of what already is, we could not carry on the common affairs of life. And success in life very greatly depends on foresight, or the power to see clearly what is to be and give it due weight. The man who has no foresight makes his plans, but being unable to apprehend the future his plans are disconcerted. Indeed it is one of the most valuable gifts a man can have, to be able to say with tolerable accuracy what is to happen and what is not; to be able to sift rumours, common talk, popular impressions, probabilities, chances, and to be able to feel sure what the future will really be; to be able to weigh the character and commercial prospects of the men he deals with, so as to see what must be the issue of their operations and whom he may trust. Many of our most serious mistakes in life arise from our inability to imagine the consequences of our actions and to forefeel how these consequences will affect us.

Now faith largely supplies the want of this imaginative foresight. It lends substance to things future. It believes the account given of the future by a trustworthy authority. In many ordinary matters all men are dependent on the testimony of others for their knowledge of the result of certain operations. The astronomer, the physiologist, the navigator, each has his department within which his predictions are accepted as authoritative. But for what is beyond the ken of science no faith in our fellow-men avails. Feeling that if there is a life beyond the grave, it must have important bearings on the present, we have yet no data by which to calculate what will then be, or only data so difficult to use that our calculations are but guesswork. But faith accepts the testimony of God as unhesitatingly as that of man and gives reality to the future He describes and promises. It believes that the life God calls us to is a better life, and it enters upon it. It believes that there is a world to come in which all things are new and all things eternal; and, so believing, it cannot but feel less anxious to cling to this world's goods. That which embitters all loss and deepens sorrow is the feeling that this world is all; but faith makes eternity as real as time and gives substantial existence to that new and limitless future in which we shall have time to forget the sorrows and live past the losses of this present world.

The radical elements of greatness are identical from age to age, and the primal duties which no good man can evade do not vary as the world grows older. What we admire in Abraham we feel to be incumbent on ourselves. Indeed the uniform call of Christ to all His followers is even in form almost identical with that which stirred Abraham, and made him the father of the faithful. "Follow Me," says our Lord, "and every one that forsaketh houses, or brethren, or sisters, or father, or mother, or wife, or children, or lands, for My name's sake, shall receive an hundredfold, and shall inherit everlasting life." And there is something perennially edifying in the spectacle of a man who believes that God has a place and a use for him in the world, and who puts himself at God's disposal; who enters upon life refusing to be bound by the circumstances of his upbringing, by the expectations of his friends, by prevailing customs, by prospect of gain and advancement among men; and resolved to listen to the highest voice of all, to discover what God has for him to do upon earth and where he is likely to find most of God; who virtually and with deepest sincerity says, Let God choose my destination: I have good land here, but if God wishes me elsewhere, elsewhere I go: who, in one word, believes in the call of God to himself, who admits it into the springs of his conduct, and recognises that for him also the highest life his conscience can suggest is the only life he can live, no matter how cumbrous and troublesome and expensive be the changes involved in entering it. Let the spectacle take hold of your imagination—the spectacle of a man believing that there is something more akin to himself and higher than the material life and the great laws that govern it, and going calmly and hopefully forward into the unknown, because he knows that God is with him, that in God is our true life, that man liveth not by bread only, but by every word that cometh out of the mouth of God.

Even thus then may we bring our faith to a true and reliable test. All men who have a confident expectation of future good make sacrifices or run risks to obtain it. Mercantile life proceeds on the understanding that such ventures are reasonable and will always be made. Men might if they liked spend their money on present pleasure, but they rarely do so. They prefer to put it into concerns or transactions from which they expect to reap large returns. They have faith and as a necessary consequence they make ventures. So did these Hebrews—they ran a great risk, they gave up the sole means of livelihood they had any experience of and entered what they knew to be a bare desert, because they believed in the land that lay beyond and in God's promise. What then has your faith done? What have you ventured that you would not have ventured but for God's promise? Suppose Christ's promise failed, in what would you be the losers? Of course you would lose what you call your hope of heaven—but what would you find you had lost in this world? When a merchant's ships are wrecked or when his investment turns out bad, he loses not only the gain he hoped for, but the means he risked. Suppose then Christ were declared bankrupt, unable to fulfil your expectations, would you really find that you had ventured so much upon His promise that you are deeply involved in His bankruptcy, and are much worse off in this world and now than you would otherwise have been? Or may I not use the words of one of the most cautious and charitable of men, and say, "I really fear, when we come to examine, it will be found that there is nothing we resolve, nothing we do, nothing we do not do, nothing we avoid, nothing we choose, nothing we give up, nothing we pursue, which we should not resolve, and do, and not do, and avoid, and choose, and give up, and pursue, if Christ had not died and heaven were not promised us." If this be the case—if you would be neither much better nor much worse though Christianity were a fable—if you have in nothing become poorer in this world that your reward in heaven may be greater, if you have made no investments and run no risks, then really the natural inference is that your faith in the future inheritance is small. Barnabas sold his Cyprus property because he believed heaven was his, and his bit of land suddenly became a small consideration; useful only in so far as he could with the mammon of unrighteousness make himself a mansion in heaven. Paul gave up his prospects of advancement in the nation, of which he would of course as certainly have become the leader and first man as he took that position in the Church, and plainly tells us that having made so large a venture on Christ's word, he would if this word failed be a great loser, of all men most miserable because he had risked his all *in this life* on it. People sometimes take offence at Paul's plain way of speaking of the sacrifices he had made, and of Peter's plain way of saying "we have left all and followed Thee, what shall we have therefore?" but when people have made sacrifices they know it and can specify them, and a faith that makes no sacrifices is no good either in this world's affairs or in religion. Self-consciousness may not be a very good thing: but self-deception is a worse.

Here as elsewhere a clear hope sprang from faith. Recognising God, Abraham knew that there was for men a great future. He looked forward to a time when all men should believe as he did, and in him all families of the earth be blessed. No doubt in these early days when all men were on the move and striving to make a name and a place for themselves, an onward look might be common. But the far-reaching extent, the certainty, and the definiteness of Abraham's view of the future were unexampled. There far back in the hazy dawn he stood while the morning mists hid the horizon from every other eye, and he alone discerns what is to be. One clear voice and one only rings out in unfaltering tones and from amidst the babel of voices that utter either amazing follies or misdirected yearnings, gives the one true forecast and direction—the one living word which has separated itself from and survived all the prognostications of Chaldean sooth-sayers and priests of Ur, because it has never ceased to give life to men. It has created for itself a channel and you can trace it through the centuries by the living green of its banks and the life it gives as it goes. For this hope of Abraham has been fulfilled; the creed and its accompanying blessing which that day lived in the heart of one man only has brought blessing to all the families of the earth.

VIII
ABRAM IN EGYPT

Genesis xii. 6–20.

Abram still journeying southward and not as yet knowing where his shifting camp was finally to be pitched, came at last to what may be called the heart of Palestine, the rich district of Shechem. Here stood the oak of Moreh, a well-known landmark and favourite meeting-place. In after years every meadow in this plain was owned and occupied, every vineyard on the slopes of Ebal fenced off, every square yard specified in some title-deed. But as yet the country seems not to have been densely populated. There was room for a caravan like Abram's to move freely through the country, liberty for a far-stretching encampment such as his to occupy the lovely vale that lies between Ebal and Gerizim. As he rested here and enjoyed the abundant pasture, or as he viewed the land from one of the neighbouring hills, the Lord appeared to him and made him aware that this was the land designed for him. Here accordingly under the spreading oak round whose boughs had often clung the smoke of idolatrous sacrifice, Abram erects an altar to the living God in devout acceptance of the gift, taking possession as it were of the land jointly for God and for himself. Little harm will come of worldly possessions so taken and so held.

As Abram traversed the land, wondering what were the limits of his inheritance, it may have seemed far too large for his household. Soon he experiences a difficulty of quite the opposite kind; he is unable to find in it sustenance for his followers. Any notion that God's friendship would raise him above the touch of such troubles as were incident to the times, places, and circumstances in which his life was to be spent, is quickly dispelled. The children of God are not exempt from any of the common calamities; they are only expected and aided to be calmer and wiser in their endurance and use of them. That we suffer the same hardships as all other men is no proof that we are not eternally associated with God, and ought never to persuade us our faith has been in vain.

Abram, as he looked at the bare, brown, cracked pastures and at the dry watercourses filled only with stones, thought of the ever-fresh plains of Mesopotamia, the lovely gardens of Damascus, the rich pasturage of the northern borders of Canaan; but he knew enough of his own heart to make him very careful lest these remembrances should make him turn back. No doubt he had come to the promised land expecting it to be the real Utopia, the Paradise which had haunted his thoughts as he lay among the hills of Ur watching his flocks under the brilliant midnight sky. No doubt he expected that here all would be easy and bright, peaceful and luxurious. His first experience is of famine. He has to look on his herd melting away, his favourite cattle losing their appearance, his servants murmuring and obliged to scatter. In his dreams he must have night after night seen the old country, the green breadth of the land that Euphrates watered, the heavy headed corn bending before the warm airs of his native land; but morning by morning he wakes to the same anxieties, to the sad reality of parched and burnt-up pastures, shepherds hanging about with gloomy looks, his own heart distressed and failing. He was also a stranger here who could not look for the help an old resident might have counted on. It was probably years since God had made any sign to him. Was the promised land worth having after all? Might he not be better off among his old friends in Charran? Should he not brave their ridicule and return? He will not so much as make it possible to return. He will not even for temporary relief go north towards his old country, but will go to Egypt, where he cannot stay, and from which he must return to Canaan.

Here, then, is a man who plainly believes that God's promise cannot fail; that God will magnify His promise, and that it above all else is worth waiting for. He believes that the man who seeks without flinching and through all disappointment and bareness to do God's will, shall one day have an abundantly satisfying reward, and that meanwhile association with God in carrying forward His abiding purposes with men is more for a man to live upon than the cattle upon a thousand hills. And thus famine rendered to Abram no small service if it quickened within him the consciousness that the call of God was not to ease and prosperity, to land-owning and cattle-breeding, but to be God's agent on earth for the fulfilment of remote but magnificent purposes. His life might seem to be down among the commonplace vicissitudes, pasture might fail, and his well-stocked camp melt away, but out of his mind there could not fade the future God had revealed to him. If it had been his ambition to give his name to a tribe and be known as a wide-ruling chief, that ambition is now eclipsed by his desire to be a step towards the fulfilment of that real end for which the whole world is. The belief that God has called him to do His work has lifted him above concern about personal matters; life has taken a new meaning in his eyes by its connection with the Eternal.

The extraordinary country to which Abram betook himself, and which was destined to exercise so profound an influence on his descendants, had even at this early date attained a high degree of civilisation. The origin of this civilisation is shrouded in obscurity, as the source of the great river to which the country owes its prosperity for many centuries kept the secret of its birth. As yet scholars are unable to tell us with certainty what Pharaoh was on the throne when Abram went down into Egypt. The monuments have preserved the effigies of two distinct types of rulers; the one simple, kindly, sensible, stately, handsome, fearless, as of men long accustomed to the throne. These are the faces of the native Egyptian rulers. The other type of face is heavy and massive, proud and strong but full of care, with neither the handsome features nor the look of kindliness and culture which belong to the other. These are the faces of the famous Shepherd kings who held Egypt in subjection, probably at the very time when Abram was in the land.

For our purposes it matters little whether Abram's visit occurred while the country was under native or under foreign rule, for long before the Shepherd kings entered Egypt it enjoyed a complete and stable civilisation. Whatever dynasty Abram found on the throne, he certainly found among the people a more refined social life than he had seen in his native city, a much purer religion, and a much more highly developed moral code. He must have kept himself entirely aloof from Egyptian society if he failed to discover that they believed in a judgment after death, and that this judgment proceeded upon a severe moral code. Before admission into the Egyptian heaven the deceased must swear that "he has not stolen nor slain any one intentionally; that he has not allowed his devotions to be seen; that he has not been guilty of hypocrisy or lying; that he has not calumniated any one nor fallen into drunkenness or adultery; that he has not turned away his ear from the words of truth; that he has been no idle talker; that he has not slighted the king or his father." To a man in Abram's state of mind the Egyptian creed and customs must have conveyed many valuable suggestions.

But virtuous as in many respects the Egyptians were, Abram's fears as he approached their country were by no means groundless. The event proved that whatever Sarah's age and appearance at this time were, his fears were something more than the fruit of a husband's partiality. Possibly he may have heard the ugly story which has recently been deciphered from an old papyrus, and which tells how one of the Pharaohs, acting on the advice of his princes, sent armed men to fetch a beautiful woman and make away with her husband. But knowing the risk he ran, why did he go? He contemplated the possibility of Sarah's being taken from him; but, if this should happen, what became of the promised seed? We cannot suppose that, driven by famine from the promised land, he had lost all hope regarding the fulfilment of the other part of the promise. Probably his idea was that some of the great men might take a fancy to Sarah, and that he would so temporise with them and ask for her such large gifts as would hold them off for a while until he could provide for his people and get clear out of the land. It had not occurred to him that she might be taken to the palace. Whatever his idea of the probable course of events was, his proposal to guide them by disguising his true relationship to Sarah was unjustifiable. And his feelings during these weeks in Egypt must have been far from enviable as he learned that of all virtues the Egyptians set greatest store by truth, and that lying was the vice they held in greatest abhorrence.

Here then was the whole promise and purpose of God in a most precarious position; the land abandoned, the mother of the promised seed in a harem through whose guards no force on earth could penetrate. Abram could do nothing but go helplessly about, thinking what a fool he had been, and wishing himself well back among the parched hills of Bethel. Suddenly there is a panic in the royal household; and Pharaoh is made aware that he was on the brink of what he himself considered a great sin. Besides effecting its immediate purpose, this visitation might have taught Pharaoh that a man cannot safely sin within limits prescribed by himself. He had not intended such evil as he found himself just saved from committing. But had he lived with perfect purity, this liability to fall into transgression, shocking to himself, could not have existed. Many sins of most painful consequence we commit, not of deliberate purpose, but because our previous life has been careless and lacking in moral tone. We are mistaken if we suppose that we can sin within a certain safe circle and never go beyond it.

By this intervention on God's part Abram was saved from the consequences of his own scheme, but he was not saved from the indignant rebuke of the Egyptian monarch. This rebuke indeed did not prevent him from a repetition of the same conduct in another country, conduct which was met with similar indignation: "What have I offended thee, that thou hast brought on me and on my kingdom this great sin? Thou hast done deeds unto me that ought not to be done. What sawest thou that thou hast done this thing?" This rebuke did not seem to sink deeply into the conscience of Abram's descendants, for the Jewish history is full of instances in which leading men do not shrink from manœuvre, deceit and lying. Yet it is impossible to suppose that Abram's conception of God was not vastly enlarged by this incident, and this especially in two particulars.

(1) Abram must have received a new impression regarding God's truth. It would seem that as yet he had no very clear idea of God's holiness. He had the idea of God which Mohammedans entertain, and past which they seem

unable to get. He conceived of God as the Supreme Ruler; he had a firm belief in the unity of God and probably a hatred of idolatry and a profound contempt for idolaters. He believed that this Supreme God could always and easily accomplish His will, and that the voice that inwardly guided him was the voice of God. His own character had not yet been deepened and dignified by prolonged intercourse with God and by close observation of His actual ways; and so as yet he knows little of what constitutes the true glory of God.

For learning that truth is an essential attribute of God he could not have gone to a better school than Egypt. His own reliance on God's promise might have been expected to produce in him a high esteem for truth and a clear recognition of its essential place in the Divine character. Apparently it had only partially had this effect. The heathen, therefore, must teach him. Had not Abram seen the look of indignation and injury on the face of Pharaoh, he might have left the land feeling that his scheme had succeeded admirably. But as he went at the head of his vastly increased household, the envy of many who saw his long train of camels and cattle, he would have given up all could he have blotted from his mind's eye the reproachful face of Pharaoh and nipped out this entire episode from his life. He was humbled both by his falseness and his foolishness. He had told a lie, and told it when truth would have served him better. For the very precaution he took in passing off Sarai as his sister was precisely what encouraged Pharaoh to take her, and produced the whole misadventure. It was the heathen monarch who taught the father of the faithful his first lesson in God's holiness.

What he so painfully learned we must all learn, that God does not need lying for the attainment of His ends, and that double-dealing is always shortsighted and the proper precursor of shame. Frequently men are tempted like Abram to seek a God-protected and God-prospered life by conduct that is not thoroughly straightforward. Some of us who statedly ask God to bless our endeavours, and who have no doubt that God approves the ends we seek to accomplish, do yet adopt such means of attaining our ends as not even men with any high sense of honour would countenance. To save ourselves from trouble, inconvenience, or danger, we are tempted to evasions and shifts which are not free from guilt. The more one sees of life, the higher value does he set on truth. Let lying be called by whatever flattering title men please—let it pass for diplomacy, smartness, self-defence, policy, or civility—it remains the device of the coward, the absolute bar to free and healthy intercourse, a vice which diffuses itself through the whole character and makes growth impossible. Trade and commerce are always hampered and retarded, and often overwhelmed in disaster, by the determined and deliberate doubleness of those who engage in them; charity is minimised and withheld from its proper objects by the suspiciousness engendered in us by the almost universal falseness of men; and the habit of making things seem to others what they are not, reacts upon the man himself and makes it difficult for him to feel the abiding effective reality of anything he has to do with or even of his own soul. If then we are to know the living and true God we must ourselves be true, transparent, and living in the light as He is the Light. If we are to reach His ends we must adopt His means and abjure all crafty contrivances of our own. If we are to be His heirs and partners in the work of the world, we must first be His children, and show that we have attained our majority by manifesting an indubitable resemblance to His own clear truth.

(2) But whether Abram fully learned this lesson or not, there can be little doubt that at this time he did receive fresh and abiding impressions of God's faithfulness and sufficiency. In Abram's first response to God's call he exhibited a remarkable independence and strength of character. His abandonment of home and kindred on account of a religious faith which he alone possessed, was the act of a man who relied much more on himself than on others and who had the courage of his convictions. This qualification for playing a great part in human affairs he undoubtedly had. But he had also the defects of his qualities. A weaker man would have shrunk from going into Egypt and would have preferred to see his flocks dwindle rather than take so venturesome a step. No such hesitations could trammel Abram's movements. He felt himself equal to all occasions. That part of his character which was reproduced in his grandson Jacob, a readiness to rise to every emergency that called for management and diplomacy, an aptitude for dealing with men and using them for his purposes—this came to the front now! To all the timorous suggestions of his household he had one reply: Leave it all to me; I will bring you through. So he entered Egypt confident that single-handed he could cope with their Pharaohs, priests, magicians, guards, judges, warriors; and find his way through the finely-meshed net that held and examined every person and action in the land.

He left Egypt in a much more healthy state of mind, practically convinced of his own inability to work his way to the happiness God had promised him, and equally convinced of God's faithfulness and power to bring him through all the embarrassments and disasters into which his own folly and sin might bring him. His own confidence and management had placed God's promise in a position of extreme hazard; and without the intervention of God Abram saw that he could neither recover the mother of the promised seed nor return to the land of promise. Abram is put to shame even in the eyes of his household slaves; and with what burning shame must he have stood before Sarai and Pharaoh, and received back his wife from him whose wickedness he had feared, but who so far from meaning to sin as Abram suspected, was indignant that Abram should have made it even possible. He returned to Canaan humbled and very little disposed to feel confident in his own powers of managing in emergencies; but quite assured that God might at all times be relied on. He was convinced that God was not depending upon him, but he upon God. He saw that God did not trust to his cleverness and craft, no, nor even to his willingness to do and endure God's will, but that He was trusting in Himself, and that by His faithfulness to His own promise, by His watchfulness and providence, He would bring Abram through all the entanglements caused by his own poor ideas of the best way to work out God's ends and attain to His blessing. He saw, in a word, that the future of the world lay not with Abram but with God.

This certainly was a great and needful step in the knowledge of God. Thus early and thus unmistakably was man taught in how profound and comprehensive a sense God is his Saviour. Commonly it takes a man a long time to learn that it is God who is saving him, but one day he learns it. He learns that it is not his own faith but God's faithfulness that saves him. He perceives that he needs God throughout, from first to last; not only to make him offers, but to enable him to accept them; not only to incline him to accept them to-day, but to maintain within him at all times this same inclination. He learns that God not only makes him a promise and leaves him to find his own way to what is promised; but that He is with him always, disentangling him day by day from the results of his own folly and securing for him not only possible but actual blessedness.

Few discoveries are so welcome and gladdening to the soul. Few give us the same sense of God's nearness and sovereignty; few make us feel so deeply the dignity and importance of our own salvation and career. This is God's affair; a matter in which are involved not merely our personal interests, but God's responsibility and purposes. God calls us to be His, and He does not send us a-warring on our own charges, but throughout furnishes us with *everything* we need. When we go down to Egypt, when we quite diverge from the path that leads to the promised land and worldly straits tempt us to turn our back upon God's altar and seek relief by our own arrangements and devices, when we forget for a while how God has identified our interests with His own and tacitly abjure the vows we have silently registered before Him, even then He follows us and watches over us and lays His hand upon us and bids us back. And this only is our hope. Not in any determination of our own to cleave to Him and to live in faith on His promise can we trust. If we have this determination, let us cherish it, for this is God's present means of leading us onwards. But should this determination fail, the shame with which you recognise your want of steadfastness may prove a stronger bond to hold you to Him than the bold confidence with which to-day you view the future. The waywardness, the foolishness, the obstinate depravity that cause you to despair, God will conquer. With untiring patience, with all-foreseeing love, He stands by you and will bring you through. His gifts and calling are without repentance.

IX
LOT'S SEPARATION FROM ABRAM

Genesis xiii.

Abram left Egypt thinking meanly of himself, highly of God. This humble frame of mind is disclosed in the route he chooses; he went straight back "unto the place where his tent had been at the beginning, unto the altar which he had made there at the first." With a childlike simplicity he seems to own that his visit to Egypt had been a mistake. He had gone there supposing that he was thrown upon his own resources, and that in order to keep himself and his dependants alive he must have recourse to craft and dishonesty. By retracing his steps and returning to the altar at Bethel, he seems to acknowledge that he should have remained there through the famine in dependence on God.

Whoever has attempted a similar practical repentance, visible to his own household and affecting their place of abode or daily occupations, will know how to estimate the candour and courage of Abram. To own that some distinctly marked portion of our life, upon which we entered with great confidence in our own wisdom and capacity, has come to nothing and has betrayed us into reprehensible conduct, is mortifying indeed. To admit that we have erred and to repair our error by returning to our old way and practice, is what few of us have the courage to do. If we have entered on some branch of business or gone into some attractive speculation, or if we have altered our demeanour towards some friend, and if we are finding that we are thereby tempted to doubleness, to equivocation, to injustice, our only hope lies in a candid and straightforward repentance, in a manly and open return to the state of things that existed in happier days and which we should never have abandoned. Sometimes we are aware that a blight began to fall on our spiritual life from a particular date, and we can easily and distinctly trace an unhealthy habit of spirit to a well-marked passage in our outward career; but we shrink from the sacrifice and shame involved in a thoroughgoing restoration of the old state of things. We are always so ready to fancy we have done enough, if we get one heartfelt word of confession uttered; so ready, if we merely turn our faces towards God, to think our restoration complete. Let us make a point of getting through mere beginnings of repentance, mere intention to recover God's favour and a sound condition of life, and let us return and return till we bow at God's very altar again, and know that His hand is laid upon us in blessing as at the first.

Out of Egypt Abram brought vastly increased wealth. Each time he encamped, quite a town of black tents quickly rose round the spot where his fixed spear gave the signal for halting. And along with him there journeyed his nephew, apparently of almost equal, or at least considerable wealth; not dependent on Abram, nor even a partner with him, for "Lot also had flocks and herds and tents." So rapidly was their substance increasing that no sooner did they become stationary than they found that the land was not able to furnish them with sufficient pasture. The Canaanite and the Perizzite would not allow them unlimited pasture in the neighbourhood of Bethel; and as the inevitable result of this the rival shepherds, eager to secure the best pasture for their own flocks and the best wells for their own cattle and camels, came to high words and probably to blows about their respective rights.

To both Abram and Lot it must have occurred that this competition between relatives was unseemly, and that some arrangement must be come to. And when at last some unusually blunt quarrel took place in presence of the chiefs, Abram divulges to Lot the scheme which had suggested itself to him. This state of things, he says, must come to an end; it is unseemly, unwise, and unrighteous. And as they walk on out of the circle of tents to discuss the matter without interruption, they come to a rising ground where the wide prospect brings them naturally to a pause. Abram looking north and south and seeing with the trained eye of a large flock-master that there was abundant pasture for both, turns to Lot with a final proposal: "Is not the whole land before thee? Separate thyself, I pray thee, from me: if thou wilt take the left hand, then I will go to the right; or if thou depart to the right hand, then I will go to the left."

Thus early did wealth produce quarrelling among relatives. The men who had shared one another's fortunes while comparatively poor, no sooner become wealthy than they have to separate. Abram prevented quarrel by separation. "Let us," he says, "come to an understanding. And rather than be separate in heart, let us be separate in habitation." It is always a sorrowful time in family history when it comes to this, that those who have had a common purse and have not been careful to know what exactly is theirs and what belongs to the other members of the family, have at last to make a division and to be as precise and documentary as if dealing with strangers. It is always painful to be compelled to own that law can be more trusted than love, and that legal forms are a surer barrier against quarrelling than brotherly kindness. It is a confession we are sometimes compelled to make, but never without a mixture of regret and shame.

As yet the character of Lot has not been exhibited, and we can only calculate from the relation he bears to Abram what his answer to the proposal will probably be. We know that Abram has been the making of his nephew, and that the land belongs to Abram; and we should expect that in common decency Lot would set aside the generous offer of his uncle and demand that he only should determine the matter. "It is not for me to make choice in a land which is wholly yours. My future does not carry in it the import of yours. It is a small matter what kind of subsistence I secure or where I find it. Choose for yourself, and allot to me what is right." We see here what a safeguard of happiness in life right feeling is. To be in right and pleasant relations with the persons around us will save us from error and sin even when conscience and judgment give no certain decision. The heart which feels gratitude is beyond the need of being schooled and compelled to do justly. To the man who is affectionately disposed it is superfluous to insist upon the rights of other persons. The instinct which tells a man what is due to others and makes him sensitive to their wrongs will preserve him from many an ignominious action which would degrade his whole life. But such instinct was awanting in Lot. His character though in some respects admirable had none of the generosity of Abram's in it. He had allowed himself on countless previous occasions to take advantage of Abram's unselfishness. Generosity is not always infectious; often it encourages selfishness in child, relative, or neighbour. And so Lot instead of rivalling, traded on his uncle's magnanimity; and chose him all the plains of Jordan because in his eye it was the richest part of the land.

This choice of Sodom as a dwelling-place was the great mistake of Lot's life. He is the type of that very large class of men who have but one rule for determining them at the turning points of life. He was swayed solely by the consideration of worldly advantage. He has nothing deep, nothing high in him. He recognises no duty to Abram, no gratitude, no modesty; he has no perception of spiritual relations, no sense that God should have something to say in the partition of the land. Lot may be acquitted of a good deal which at first sight one is prompted to lay to his charge, but he cannot be acquitted of showing an eagerness to better himself, regardless of all considerations but the promise of wealth afforded by the fertility of the Jordan valley. He saw a quick though dangerous road to wealth. There seemed a certainty of success in his earthly calling, a risk only of moral disaster. He shut his eyes to the risk that he might grasp the wealth; and so doing, ruined both himself and his family.

The situation is one which is ceaselessly repeated. To men in business or in the cultivation of literature or art, or in one of the professions, there are presented opportunities of attaining a better position by cultivating the friendship or identifying oneself with the practice of men whose society is not in itself desirable. Society is made up of little circles, each of which has its own monopoly of some social or commercial or political advantage, and its own characteristic tone and enjoyments and customs. And if a man will not join one of these circles and accommodate himself to the mode of carrying on business and to the style of living it has identified with itself, he must forego the advantages which entrance to that circle would secure for him. As clearly as Lot saw that the well-watered plain stretching away under the sunshine was the right place to exercise his vocation as a flock-master, so do we see that associated with such and such persons and recognised as one of them, we shall be able more effectively than in any other position to use whatever natural gifts we have, and win the recognition and the profit these gifts seem to warrant. There is but one drawback. "The men of Sodom were wicked and sinners before the Lord exceedingly." There is a tone you do not like; you hesitate to identify yourself with men who live solely and with cynical frankness only for gain; whose every sentence betrays the contemptible narrowness of soul to which worldliness condemns men; who live for money and who glory in their shame.

The very nature of the world in which we live makes such temptation universal. And to yield is common and fatal. We persuade ourselves we need not enter into close relations with the persons we propose to have business connections with. Lot would have been horrified, that day he made his choice, had it been told him his daughters would marry men of Sodom. But the swimmer who ventures into the outer circle of the whirlpool finds that his own resolve not to go further presents a very weak resistance to the water's inevitable suction. We fancy perhaps that to refuse the companionship of any class of men is pharisaic; that we have no business to condemn the attitude towards the Church, or the morality, or the style of living adopted by any class of men among us. This is the mere cant of liberalism. We do not condemn persons who suffer from smallpox, but a smallpox hospital would be about the last place we should choose for a residence. Or possibly we imagine we shall be able to carry some better influences into the society we enter. A vain imagination; the motive for choosing the society has already sapped our power for good.

Many of the errors of worldly men only reveal their most disastrous consequences in the second generation. Like some virulent diseases they have a period of incubation. Lot's family grew up in a very different atmosphere from that which had nourished his own youth in Abram's tents.

An adult and robust Englishman can withstand the climate of India; but his children who are born in it cannot. And the position in society which has been gained in middle life by the carefully and hardily trained child of a God-fearing household, may not very visibly damage his own character, but may yet be absolutely fatal to the morality of his children. Lot may have persuaded himself he chose the dangerous prosperity of Sodom mainly for the sake of his children; but in point of fact he had better have seen them die of starvation in the most barren and parched desolation. And the parent who disregards conscience and chooses wealth or position, fancying that thus he benefits his children, will find to his life-long sorrow that he has entangled them in unimagined temptations.

But the man who makes Lot's choice not only does a great injury to his children, but cuts himself off from all that is best in life. We are safe to say that after leaving Abram's tents Lot never again enjoyed unconstrainedly happy days. The men born and brought up in Sodom were possibly happy after their kind and in their fashion; but Lot was not. His soul was daily vexed. Many a time while hearing the talk of the men his daughters had married, must Lot have gone out with a sore heart, and looked to the distant hills that hid the tents of Abram, and longed for an hour of the company he used to enjoy. And the society to which you are tempted to join yourself may not be unhappy, but you can take no surer means of beclouding, embittering, and ruining your whole life than by joining it. You cannot forget the thoughts you once had, the friendships you once delighted in, the hopes that shed brightness through all your life. You cannot blot out the ideal that once you cherished as the most animating element of your life. Every day there will be that rising in your mind which is in the sharpest contrast to the thoughts of those with whom you are associated. You will despise them for their shallow, worldly ideas and ways; but you will despise yourself still more, being conscious that what they are through ignorance and upbringing, you are in virtue of your own foolish and mean choice. There is that in you which rebels against the superficial and external measure by which they judge things, and yet you have deliberately chosen these as your associates, and can only think with heart-broken regret of the high thoughts that once visited you and the hopes you have now no means of fulfilling. Your life is taken out of your own hands; you find yourself in bondage to the circumstances you have chosen; and you are learning in bitterness, disappointment, and shame, that indeed "a man's life consisteth not in the abundance of the things which he possesseth." To determine your life solely by the prospect of worldly success is to risk the loss of the best things in life. To sacrifice friendship or conscience to success in your calling is to sacrifice what is best to what is lowest, and to blind yourself to the highest human happiness. For happily the essential elements of the highest happiness are as open to the poor as to the rich, to the unsuccessful as to the successful—love of wife and children, congenial and educating friendships, the knowledge of what the best men have done and the wisest men have said; the pleasure and impulse, the sentiments and beliefs which result from our knowledge of the heroic deeds done from year to year among men; the enlivening influence of examples that tell on all men alike, young and old, rich and poor; the insight and strength of character that are won in the hard wrestle with life; the growing consciousness that God is in human life, that He is ours and that we are His—these things and all that makes human life of value are universal as air and sunshine, but must be missed by those who make the world their object.

Though in point of fact Lot cut himself off by his choice from direct participation in the special inheritance to which Abram was called by God, it might perhaps be too much to say that his choice of the valley of Jordan was an explicit renunciation of the special blessedness of those who find their joy in responding to God's call and doing His work in the world. It might also be extravagant to say that his choice of the richest land was prompted by the feeling that he was not included in the promise to Abram, and might as well make the most of his present opportunities. But it is certain that Abram's generosity to Lot arose out of his sense that in God he himself had abundant possession. In Egypt he had learned that in order to secure all that is worth having a man need never resort to duplicity, trickery, bold lying. He now learns that in order to enter on his own God-provided lot, he need shut no other man out of his. He is taught that to acknowledge amply the rights of other men is the surest road to the enjoyment of his own rights. He is taught that there is room in God's plan for every man to follow his most generous impulses and the highest views of life that visit him.

It was Abram's simple belief that God's promise was meant and was substantial, that made him indifferent as to what Lot might choose. His faith was judged in this scene, and was proved to be sound. This man whose very calling it was to own this land, could freely allow Lot to choose the best of it. Why? Because he has learned that it is not by any plan of his own he is to come into possession; that God Who promised is to give him the land in His own way, and that his part is to act uprightly, mercifully, like God. Wherever there is faith, the same results will appear. He who believes that God is pledged to provide for him cannot be greedy, anxious, covetous; can only be liberal, even magnanimous. Any one can thus test his own faith. If he does not find that what God promises weighs substantially when put in the scales with gold; if he does not find that the accomplishment of God's purpose with him in the world is to him the most valuable thing, and actually compels him to think lightly of worldly position and ordinary success; if he does not find that in point of fact the gains which content a man of the world shrivel and lose interest, he may feel tolerably certain he has no faith and is not counting as certain what God has promised.

It is commonly observed that wealth pursues the men who part with it most freely. Abram had this experience. No sooner had he allowed Lot to choose his portion than God gave him assurance that the whole would be his. It is "the meek" who "inherit the earth." Not only have they, in their very losses and while suffering wrong at the hands of their fellows, a purer joy than those who wrong them; but they know themselves heirs of God with the certainty of enjoying all His possessions that can avail for their advantage. Declining to devote themselves as living sacrifices to business they hold their soul at leisure for what brings truest happiness, for friendship, for knowledge, for charity. Even in this life they may be said to inherit the earth, for all its richest fruits are theirs—the ground may belong to other men, but the beauty of the landscape is theirs without burden—and ever and anon they hear such words as were now uttered to Abram. They alone are inclined or able to receive renewed assurances that God is mindful of His promise and will abundantly bless them. It is they who are in no haste to be rich, and are content to abide in the retired hill-country where they can freely assemble round God's altar, it is they who seek first the kingdom of God and make sure of that, whatever else they put in hazard, to whom God's encouragements come. You wonder at the certainty with which others speak of hearing God's voice and that so seldom you have the joy of knowing that God is directing and encouraging you. Why should you wonder, if you very well know that your attention is directed mainly to the world, that your heart trembles and thrills with all the fluctuations of your earthly hopes, that you wait for news and listen to every hint that can affect your position in life? Can you wonder that an ear trained to be so sensitive to the near earthly sounds, should quite have lost the range of heavenly voices?

Of the assurance here given him Abram was probably much in need when Lot had withdrawn with his flocks and servants. When the warmth of feeling cooled and allowed the somewhat unpleasant facts of the case to press upon his mind; and when he heard his shepherds murmuring that after all the strife they had maintained for their master's rights, he should have weakly yielded these to Lot; and when he reflected, as now he inevitably would reflect, how selfish and ungrateful Lot had shown himself to be, he must have been tempted to think he had possibly made a mistake in dealing so generously with such a man. This reflection on himself might naturally grow into a reflection upon God, Who might have been expected so to order matters as to give the best country to the best man. All such reflections are precluded by the renewed grant he now receives of the whole land.

It is always as difficult to govern our heart wisely after as before making a sacrifice. It is as difficult to keep the will decided as to make the original decision; and it is more difficult to think affectionately of those for whom the sacrifice has been made, when the change in their condition and our own is actually accomplished. There is a natural reaction after a generous action which is not always sufficiently resisted. And when we see that those who refuse to make any sacrifices are more prosperous and less ruffled in spirit than ourselves we are tempted to take matters into our own hand, and, without waiting upon God, to use the world's quick ways. At such times we find how difficult it is to hold an advanced position, and how much unbelief mingles with the sincerest faith, and what vile dregs of selfishness sully the clearest generosity; we find our need of God and of those encouragements and assistances He can impart to the soul. Happy are we if we receive them and are enabled thereby to be constant in the good we have begun; for all sacrifice is good begun. And as Abram saw, when the cities of the plain were destroyed, how kindly God had guided him; so when our history is complete, we shall have no inclination to grumble at any passage of our life which we entered by generosity and faith in God, but shall see how tenderly God has held us back from much that our soul has been ardently desiring, and which we thought would be the making of us.

X
ABRAM'S RESCUE OF LOT

Genesis xiv.

This chapter evidently incorporates a contemporary account of the events recorded. So antique a document was it even when it found its place in this book, that the editor had to modernize some of its expressions that it might be intelligible. The places mentioned were no longer known by the names here preserved—Bela, the vale of Siddim, En-mishpat, the valley of Shaveh, all these names were unknown even to the persons who dwelt in the places once so designated. It can scarcely have been Abram who wrote down the narrative, for he himself is spoken of as Abram the Hebrew, the man born beyond the Euphrates, which is a way of speaking of himself no one would naturally adopt. From the clear outline given of the route followed by the expedition of Chedorlaomer, it might be supposed that some old staff-secretary had reported on the campaign. However that may be, the discoveries of the last two or three years have shed light on the outlandish names that have stood for four thousand years in this document, and on the relations subsisting between Elam and Palestine.

On the bricks now preserved in our own British Museum the very names we read in this chapter can be traced, in the slightly altered form which is always given to a name when pronounced by different races. Chedorlaomer is the Hebrew transliteration of Kudur Lagamar; Lagamar was the name of one of the Chaldean deities, and the whole name means Lagamar's son, evidently a name of dignity adopted by the king of Elam. Elam comprehended the broad and rich plains to the east of the lower course of the Tigris, together with the mountain range (8,000 to 10,000 feet high) that bounds them. Elam was always able to maintain its own against Assyria and Babylonia, and at this time it evidently exercised some kind of supremacy not only over these neighbouring powers, but as far west as the valley of the Jordan. The importance of keeping open the valley of the Jordan is obvious to every one who has interest enough in the subject to look at a map. That valley was the main route for trading caravans and for military expeditions between the Euphrates and Egypt. Whoever held that valley might prove a most formidable annoyance and indeed an absolute interruption to commercial or political relations between Egypt and Elam, or the Eastern powers. Sometimes it might serve the purpose of East and West to have a neutral power between them, as became afterwards clear in the history of Israel, but oftener it was the ambition of either Egypt or of the East to hold Canaan in subjection. A rebellion therefore of these chiefs occupying the vale of Siddim was sufficiently important to bring the king of Elam from his distant capital, attaching to his army as he came, his tributaries Amraphel king of Shinar or northern Chaldea, Arioch king of a district on the east of the Euphrates, and finally Tidal, or rather Tur-gal *i.e.* the great chief, who ruled over the nations or tribes to the north of Babylonia.

Susa, the capital of Elam, lies almost on the same parallel as the vale of Siddim, but between them lie many hundred miles of impracticable desert. Chedorlaomer and his army followed therefore much the same route as Terah in his emigration, first going north-west up the Euphrates and then crossing it probably at Carchemish, or above it, and coming southward towards Canaan. But the country to the east of the Jordan and the Dead Sea was occupied by warlike and marauding tribes who would have liked nothing better than to swoop down on a rich booty-laden Eastern army. With the sagacity of an old soldier therefore, Chedorlaomer makes it his first business to sweep this rough ground, and so cripple the tribes in his passage southwards, that when he swept round the lower end of the Dead Sea and up the Jordan valley he should have nothing to fear at least on his right flank. The tribe that first felt his sword was that of the Rephaim, or giants. Their stronghold was Ashteroth Karnaim, or Ashteroth of the two horns, a town dedicated to the goddess Astarte whose symbol was the crescent or two-horned moon. The Zuzims and the Emims, "a people great and many and tall," as we read in Deuteronomy, next fell before the invading host. The Horites, *i.e.* cave-dwellers or troglodytes, would scarcely hold Chedorlaomer long, though from their hilly fastnesses they might do him some damage. Passing through their mountains he came upon the great road between the Dead Sea and the Elanitic gulf—but he crossed this road and still held westward till he reached the edge of what is roughly known as the Desert of Sinai. Here, says the narrative (ver. 7), they returned, that is, this was their furthest point south and west, and here they turned and made for the vale of Siddim, smiting the Amalekites and the Amorites on their route.

This is the only part of the army's route that is at all obscure. The last place they are spoken of as touching before reaching the vale of Siddim is Hazezon-Tamar, or as it was afterwards and is still called Engedi. Now Engedi lies on the western shore of the Dead Sea about half way up from south to north. It lies on a very steep, indeed artificially made, pass and is a place of much greater importance on that account than its size would make it. The road between Moab and Palestine runs by the western margin of the Dead Sea up to this point, but beyond this point the shore is impracticable, and the only road is through the Engedi pass on to the higher ground above. If the army chose this route then they were compelled to force this pass; if on the other hand they preferred during their whole march from Kadesh to keep away west of the Dead Sea on the higher ground, then they would only detail a company to pounce upon Engedi, as the main army passed behind and above. In either case the main body must have been if not actually within sight of, yet only a few miles from, the encampment of Abram.

At length as they dropped down through the practicable passes into the vale of Siddim their grand object became apparent, and the kings of the five allied towns, probably warned by the hill-tribes weeks before, drew out to meet them. But it is not easy to check an army in full career, and the wells of bitumen, which those who knew the ground might have turned to good purpose against the foreigners, actually hindered the home troops and became a trap to them. The rout was complete. No second stand or rally was attempted. The towns were sacked, the fields swept, and so swift were the movements of the invaders that although Abram was barely twenty miles off, and no doubt started for the rescue of Lot the hour he got the news, he did not overtake the army, laden as it was with spoil and retarded by prisoners and wounded, until they had reached the sources of Jordan.

But well-conceived and brilliantly executed as this campaign had been, the experienced warrior had failed to take account of the most formidable opponent he would have to reckon with. Those that escaped from the slaughter at Sodom took to the hills, and either knowing they would find shelter with Abram or more probably blindly running on, found themselves at nightfall within sight of the encampment at Hebron. There is no delay on Abram's part; he hastily calls out his men, each snatching his bow, his sword, and his spear, and slinging over his shoulders a few days' provision. The neighbouring Amorite chiefs Aner, Mamre and Eshcol join them, probably with a troop each, and before many hours are lost they are down the passes and in hot pursuit. Not however till they had traversed a hundred and twenty miles or more do they overtake the Eastern army. But at Dan, at the very springs of the Jordan, they find them, and making a night attack throw them into utter confusion and pursue them as far as Hobah, a village near Damascus, that retains to this day the same name.

One is naturally curious to see how Abram will conduct himself in circumstances so unaccustomed. From leading a quiet pastoral life he suddenly becomes the most important man in the country, a man who can make himself felt from the Nile to the Tigris. From a herd he becomes a hero. But, notoriously, power tries a man, and, as one has often seen persons make very glaring mistakes in such altered circumstances and alter their characters and beliefs to suit and take advantage of the new material and opportunities presented to them, we are interested in seeing how a man whose one rule of action has hitherto been faith in a promise given him by God, will pass through such a trial. Can a spiritual quality like faith be of much service in rough campaigning and when the man of faith is mixed up with persons of doubtful character and unscrupulous conduct, and brought into contact with considerable political powers? Can we trace to Abram's faith any part of his action at this time? No sooner is the question put than we see that his faith in God's promise was precisely that which gave him balance and dignity, courage and generosity in dealing with the three prominent persons in the narrative. He could afford to be forgiving and generous to his grand competitor Lot, precisely because he felt sure God would deal generously with himself. He could afford to acknowledge Melchizedek and any other authority that might appear, as his superior, and he would not take advantage, even when at the head of his men eager for more fighting, of the peaceful king who came out to propitiate him, because he knew that God would give him his land without wronging other people. And he scorned the wages of the king of Sodom, holding himself to be no mercenary captain, nor indebted to any one but God. In a word, you see faith producing all that is of importance in his conduct at this time.

Lot is the person who of all others might have been expected to be forward in his expressions of gratitude to Abram—not a word of his is recorded. Ashamed he cannot but have been, for if Abram said not a word of reproach, there would be plenty of Lot's old friends among Abram's men who could not lose so good an opportunity of twitting him about the good choice he had made. And considering how humiliating it would have been for him to go back with Abram and abandon the district of his adoption, we can scarcely wonder that he should have gone quietly back to Sodom, well as he must by this time have known the nature of the risks he ran there. For, after all, this warning was not very loud. The same thing, or a similar thing, might have happened had he remained with Abram. The warning was unobtrusive as the warnings in life mostly are; audible to the ear that has been accustomed to listen to the still small voice of conscience, inaudible to the ear that is trained to hear quite other voices. God does not set angels and flaming swords in every man's path. The little whisper that no one hears but ourselves only and that says quite quietly that we are continuing in a wrong course, is as certain an indication that we are in danger, as if God were to proclaim our case from heaven with thunder or the voice of an archangel. And when a man has persistently refused to listen to conscience it ceases to speak, and he loses the power to discern between good and evil and is left wholly without a guide. He may be running straight to destruction and he does not know it. You cannot live under two principles of action, regard to worldly interest and regard to conscience. You can train yourself to great acuteness in perceiving and following out what is for your worldly advantage, or you can train yourself to great acuteness of conscience; but you must make your choice, for in proportion as you gain sensitiveness in the one direction you lose it in the other. If your eye is *single* your whole body is full of light; but if the light that is in thee be darkness, how great is that darkness!

Melchizedek is generally recognised as the most mysterious and unaccountable of historical personages; appearing here in the King's Vale no one knows whence, and disappearing no one knows whither, but coming with his hands full of substantial gifts for the wearied household of Abram, and the captive women that were with him. Of each of the patriarchs we can tell the paternity; the date of his birth, and the date of his death; but this man stands with none to claim him, he forms no part of any series of links by which the oldest and the present times are connected. Though possessed of the knowledge of the Most High God, his name is not found in any of those genealogies which show us how that knowledge passed from father to son. Of all the other great men whose history is recorded a careful genealogy is given; but here the writer breaks his rule, and breaks it where, had there not been substantial reason, he would most certainly have adhered to it. For here is the greatest man of the time, a man before whom Abram the father of the faithful, the honoured of all nations, bowed and paid tithes; and yet he appears and passes away likest to a vision of the night. Perhaps even in his own time there was none that could point to the chamber where first he was cradled, nor show the tent round which first he played in his boyhood, nor hoard up a single relic of the early years of the man that had risen to be the first man upon earth in those days. So that the Apostle speaks of him as a very type of all that is mysterious and abrupt in appearance and disappearance, "without father, without mother, without descent, having neither beginning of days, nor end of life," and as he significantly adds, "made like unto the Son of God." For as Melchizedek stands thus on the page of history, so our Lord in reality—as the one has no recorded pedigree, and holds an office beginning and ending in his own person, so our Lord, though born of a woman, stands separate from sinners and quite out of the ordinary line of generations, and exercises an office which he received hereditarily from none, and which he could commit to no successor. As the one stands apparently disconnected from all before and after him, so the Other in point of fact did thus suddenly emerge from eternity, a problem to all who saw Him; owning the authority of earthly parents, yet claiming an antiquity greater than Abram's; appearing suddenly to the captivity led captive, with His hands full of gifts, and His lips dropping words of blessing.

Melchizedek is the one personage on earth whom Abram recognises as his spiritual superior. Abram accepts his blessing and pays him tithes; apparently as priest of the Most High God; so that in paying to him, Abram is giving the tenth of his spoils to God. This is not any mere courtesy of private persons. It was done in presence of various parties of jealously watchful retainers. Men of rank and office and position *consider* how they should act to one another and who should take precedence. And Abram did deliberately and with a perfect perception of what he was doing, whatever he now did. Manifestly therefore God's revelation of Himself was not as yet confined to the one line running from Abram to Christ. Here was a man of whom we really do not know whether he was a Canaanite, a son of Ham or a son of Shem; yet Abram recognises him as having knowledge of the true God, and even bows to him as his spiritual superior in office if not in experience. This shows us how little jealousy Abram had of others being favoured by God, how little he thought *his* connection with God would be less secure if other men enjoyed a similar connection, and how heartily he welcomed those who with different rites and different prospects yet worshipped the living God. It shows us also how apt we are to limit God's ways of working; and how little we understand of the connections He has with those who are not situated as we ourselves are. Here while all our attention is concentrated on Abram as carrying the whole spiritual hope of the world, there emerges from an obscure Canaanite valley a man nearer to God than Abram is. From how many unthought-of places such men may at any time come out upon us, we really can never tell.

Again Melchizedek is evidently a title, not a name—the word means King of Righteousness, or Righteous King. It may have been a title adopted by a line of kings, or it may have been peculiar to this one man. But these old Canaanites, if Canaanites they were, had got hold of a great principle when they gave this title to the king of their city of Salem or Peace. They perceived that it was the righteousness, the justice, of their king that could best uphold their peaceful city. They saw that the right king for them was a man not grinding his neighbours by war and taxes, not overriding the rights of others and seeking always enlargement of his own dominion; nor a merely merciful man, inclined to treat sin lightly and leaning always to laxity; but the man they would choose to give them peace was the righteous man who might sometimes seem overscrupulous, sometimes over-stern, who would sometimes be called romantic and sometimes fanatical, but through all whose dealings it would be obvious that justice to all parties was the aim in view. Some of them might not be good enough to love a ruler who made no more of their special interest than he did of others, but all would possibly have wit enough to see that only by justice could they have peace. It is the reflex of God's government in which righteousness is the foundation of peace, a righteousness unflinching and invariable, promulgating holy laws and exacting punishment from all who break them. It is this that gives us hope of eternal peace, that we know God has not left out of account facts that must yet be reckoned with, nor merely lulled the unquiet forebodings of conscience, but has let every righteous law and principle find full scope, has done righteously in offering us pardon so that nothing can ever turn up to deprive us of our peace. And it is quite in vain that any individual holds before his mind the prospect of peace, *i.e.* of permanent satisfaction, so long as he is not seeking it by righteousness. In so far as he is keeping his conscience from interfering, in so far is he making it impossible to himself to enter into the condition for the sake of which he is keeping conscience from regulating his conduct.

Lastly, Abram's refusal of the king of Sodom's offers is significant. Naturally enough, and probably in accordance with well-established usage, the king proposes that Abram should receive the rescued goods and the spoil of the invading army. But Abram knew men, and knew that although now Sodom was eager to show that he felt himself indebted to Abram, the time would come when he would point to this occasion as laying the foundation of Abram's fortune. When a man rises in the world every one will tell you of the share he had in raising him, and will convey the impression that but for assistance rendered by the speaker he would not have been what he now is. Abram knows that he is destined to rise, and knows also by Whose help he is to rise. He intends to receive all from God; and therefore not a thread from Sodom. He puts his refusal in the form adopted by the man whose mind is made up beyond revisal. He has "vowed" it. He had anticipated such offers and had considered their bearing on his relations to God and man; and taking advantage of the unembarrassed season in which the offer was as yet only a possibility, he had resolved that when it was actually made he would refuse it, no matter what advantages it seemed to offer. So should we in our better seasons and when we know we are viewing things healthily, conscientiously, and righteously, determine what our conduct is to be, and if possible so commit ourselves to it that when the right frame is passed we cannot draw back from the right conduct. Abram had done so, and however tempting the spoils of the Eastern kings were, they did not move him. His vow had been made to the Possessor of heaven and earth, in Whose hand were riches beyond the gifts of Sodom.

Here again it is the man of faith that appears. He shows a noble jealousy of God's prerogative to bless him. He will not give men occasion to say that any earthly monarch has enriched him. It shall be made plain that it is on God he is depending. In all men of faith there will be something of this spirit. They cannot fail so to frame their life as to let it come clearly out that for happiness, for success, for comfort, for joy, they are in the main depending on God. That this cannot be done in the complex life of modern society, no one will venture to say in presence of this incident. Could we more easily have shown our reliance upon God in the hurry of a sudden foray, in the turmoil and intense action of a midnight attack and hand to hand conflict, in the excitement and elation of a triumphal progress, the kings of the country vying with one another to do us honour and the rescued captives lauding our valour and generosity? No one fails to see what it was that balanced Abram in this intoxicating march. No one asks what enabled him, while leading his armed followers flushed with success through a land weakened by recent dismay and disaster, to restrain them and himself from claiming the whole land as his. No one asks what gave him moral perception to see that the opportunity given him of winning the land by the sword was a temptation not a guiding providence. To every reader it is obvious that his dependence on God was his safeguard and his light. God would bring him by fair and honourable means to his own. There was no need of violence, no need of receiving help from doubtful allies. This is true nobility; and this, faith always produces. But it must be a faith like Abram's; not a quick and superficial growth, but a deeply-rooted principle. For against all temptations this only is our sure defence, that already our hearts are so filled with God's promise that other offers find no craving in us, no empty dissatisfied spot on which they can settle. To such faith God responds by the elevating and strengthening assurance, "I am thy shield, and thy exceeding great reward."

XI
COVENANT WITH ABRAM

Genesis xv.

Of the nine Divine manifestations made during Abram's life this is the fifth. At Ur, at Kharran, at the oak of Moreh, at the encampment between Bethel and Ai, and now at Mamre, he received guidance and encouragement from God. Different terms are used regarding these manifestations. Sometimes it is said "The Lord appeared unto him;" here for the first time in the course of God's revelation occurs that expression which afterwards became normal, "The word of the Lord came unto Abram." Throughout the subsequent history this word of the Lord continues to come, often at long intervals, but always meeting the occasion and needs of His people and joining itself on to what had already been declared, until at last the Word became flesh and dwelt among us, giving thus to all men assurance of the nearness and profound sympathy of their God. To repeat this revelation is impossible. A repetition of it would be a denial of its reality. For a second life on earth is allowed to no man; and were our Lord to live a second human life it were proof He was no true man, but an anomalous, unaccountable, uninstructive, appearance or simulacrum of a man.

But though these revelations of God are finished, though complete knowledge of God is given in Christ, God comes to the individual still through the Spirit Whose office it is to take of the things of Christ and show them to us. And in doing so the law is observed which we see illustrated here. God comes to a man with further encouragement and light for a new step when he has conscientiously used the light he already has. The temper that "seeks for a sign" and expects that some astounding Providence should be sent to make us religious is by no means obsolete. Many seem to expect that before they act on the knowledge they have, they will receive more. They put off giving themselves to the service of God under some kind of impression that some striking event or much more distinct knowledge is required to give them a decided turn to a religious life. In so doing they invert God's order. It is when we have conscientiously followed such light as we have, and faithfully done all that we know to be right, that God gives us further light. It was immediately on the back of faithful action that Abram received new help to his faith.

The time was seasonable for other reasons. Never did Abram feel more in need of such assurance. He had been successful in his midnight attack and had scattered the force from beyond Euphrates, but he knew the temper of these Eastern monarchs well enough to be aware that there was nothing they hailed with greater pleasure than a pretext for extending their conquests and adding to their territory. To Abram it must have appeared certain that the next campaigning season would see his country invaded and his little encampment swept away by the Eastern host. Most appropriate, therefore, are the words: "Fear not, Abram: I am thy shield."

But another train of thoughts occupied Abram's mind perhaps even more unceasingly at this time. After busy engagement comes dulness; after triumph, flatness and sadness. I have pursued kings, got myself a great name, led captivity captive. Men are speaking of me in Sodom, and finding that in me they have a useful and important ally. But what is all this to my purpose? Am I any nearer my inheritance? I have got all that men might think I needed; they may be unable to understand why now, of all times, I should seem heartless; but, O Lord, Thou knowest how empty these things seem to me, and what wilt Thou give me? Abram could not understand why he was kept so long waiting. The child given when he was a hundred years old might equally have been given twenty-five years before, when he first came to the land of Canaan. All Abram's servants had their children, there was no lack of young men born in his encampment. He could not leave his tent without hearing the shouts of other men's children, and having them cling to his garments—but "to me Thou hast given no seed; and lo! one born in mine house, a slave, is mine heir."

Thus it often is that while a man is receiving much of what is generally valued in the world, the one thing he himself most prizes is beyond his reach. He has his hope irremovably fixed on something which he feels would complete his life and make him a thoroughly happy man; there is one thing which, above all else, would be a right and helpful blessing to him. He speaks of it to God. For years it has framed a petition for itself when no other desire could make itself heard. Back and back to this his heart comes, unable to find rest in anything so long as this is withheld. He cannot help feeling that it is God who is keeping it from him. He is tempted to say, "What is the use of all else to me, why give me things Thou knowest I care little for, and reserve the one thing on which my happiness depends?" As Abram might have said; "Why make me a great name in the land, when there is no one to keep it alive in men's memories; why increase my possessions when there is none to inherit but a stranger?"

Is there then any resulting benefit to character in this so common experience of delayed expectations? In Abram's case there certainly was. It was in these years he was drawn close enough to God to hear Him say, "*I am thy exceeding great reward.*" He learned in the multitude of his debatings about God's promise and the delay of its fulfilment, that God was more than all His gifts. He had started as a mere hopeful colonist and founder of a family; these twenty-five years of disappointment made him the friend of God and the Father of the Faithful. Slowly do we also pass from delight in God's gifts to delight in Himself, and often by a similar experience. From what have you received truest and deepest pleasure in life? Is it not from your friendships? Not from what your friends have given you or done for you; rather from what you have done for them; but chiefly from your affectionate intercourse. You, being persons, must find your truest joy in persons, in personal love, personal goodness and wisdom. But friendship has its crown in the friendship of God. The man who knows God as his friend and is more certain of God's goodness and wisdom and steadfastness than he can be of the worth of the man he has loved and trusted and delighted in from his boyhood, the man who is always accompanied by a latent sense of God's observation and love, is truly living in the peace of God that passeth understanding. This raises him above the touch of worldly losses and restores him in all distresses, even to the surprise of observers; his language is, "There may be many that will say, Who will show us any good? Lord, lift Thou up the light of Thy countenance upon us. *Thou* hast put gladness in my heart more than in the time that their corn and their wine increased."

But evidently there was still another feeling in Abram's heart at this particular point in his career. He could not bear to think he was to miss that very thing which God had promised him. The keen yearning for an heir which God's promise had stirred in him was not lost sight of in the great saying, "*I* am thy exceeding great reward." When he was journeying back to his encampment not a shoestring richer than he left, and while he heard his men, disappointed of booty, murmuring that he should be so scrupulous, he cannot but have felt some soreness that he should be set before his little world as a man who had the enjoyment neither of this world's rewards nor of God. And here must have come the strong temptation that comes to every man: Might it not be as well to take what he could get, to enjoy what was put fairly within his reach, instead of waiting for what seemed so uncertain as God's gift? It is painful to be exposed to the observation of others or to our own observation, as persons who, on the one hand, refuse to seek happiness in the world's way, and yet are not finding it in God. You have possibly with some magnanimity rejected a tempting offer because there were conditions attached to which conscience could not reconcile itself; but you find that you are in consequence suffering greater privations than you expected and that no providential intervention seems to be made to reward your conscientiousness. Or you suddenly become aware that though you have for years refused to be mirthful or influential or successful or comfortable in the world's way and on the world's terms, you are yet getting no substitute for what you refuse. You will not join the world's mirth, but then you are morose and have no joy of any kind. You will not use means you disapprove of for influencing men, but neither have you the influence of a strong Christian character. In fact by giving up the world you seem to have contracted and weakened instead of enlarging and deepening your life.

In such a condition we can but imitate Abram and cast ourselves more resolutely on God. If you find it most weary and painful to deny yourself in these special ways which have fallen to be your experience, you can but utter your complaint to God, assured that in Him you will find consideration. He knows why He has called you, why He has given you strength to abandon worldly hopes; He appreciates your adherence to Him and He will renew your faith and hope. If day by day you are saying, "Lead Thou me on," if you say, "What wilt Thou give me?" not in complaint but in lively expectation, encouragement enough will be yours.

The means by which Abram's faith was renewed were appropriate. He has been seeing in the tumult and violence and disappointment of the world much to suggest the thought that God's promise could never work itself out in the face of the rude realities around him. So God leads him out and points him to the stars, each one called by his name, and thus reminds the Chaldæan who had so often gazed at and studied them in their silent steady courses, that his God has designs of infinite sweep and comprehension; that throughout all space His worlds obey His will and all harmoniously play their part in the execution of His vast design; that we and all our affairs are in a strong hand, but moving in orbits so immense that small portions of them do not show us their direction and may seem to be out of course. Abram is led out alone with the mighty God, and to every saved soul there comes such a crisis when before God's majesty we stand awed and humbled, all complaints hushed, and indeed our personal interests disappear or become so merged in God's purposes that we think only of Him; our mistakes and wrong-doing are seen now not so much as bringing misery upon ourselves as interrupting and perverting His purposes, and His word comes home to our hearts as stable and satisfying.

It was in this condition that Abram believed God, and He counted it to him for righteousness. Probably if we read this without Paul's commentary on it in the fourth of Romans, we should suppose it meant no more than that Abram's faith, exercised as it was in trying circumstances, met with God's cordial approval. The faith or belief here spoken of was a resolute renewal of the feeling which had brought him out of Chaldæa. He put himself fairly and finally into God's hand to be blessed in God's way and in God's time, and this act of resignation, this resolve that he would not force his own way in the world but would wait upon God, was looked upon by God as deserving the name of righteousness, just as much as honesty and integrity in his conduct with Lot or with his servants. Paul begs us to notice that an act of faith accepting God's favour is a very different thing from a work done for the sake of winning God's favour. God's favour is always a matter of grace, it is favour conferred on the undeserving; it is never a matter of debt, it is never favour conferred because it has been won. To put this beyond doubt he appeals to this righteousness of Abram's. How, he asks, did Abram achieve righteousness? Not by observing ordinances and commandments; for there were none to observe; but by trusting God, by believing that already without any working or winning of his, God loved him and designed blessedness for him, in short by referring his prospect of happiness and usefulness wholly to God and not at all to himself. This is the essential quality of the godly; and having this, Abram had that root which produced all actual righteousness and likeness to God.

It is sufficiently obvious in such a life as Abram's why faith is the one thing needful. Faith is required because it is only when a man believes God's promise and rests in His love that he can co-operate with God in severing himself from iniquitous prospects and in so living for spiritual ends as to enter the life and the blessedness God calls him to. The boy who does not believe his father, when he comes to him in the midst of his play and tells him he has something for him which will please him still better, suffers the penalty of unbelief by losing what his father would have given him. All missing of true enjoyment and blessedness results from unbelief in God's promise. Men do not walk in God's ways because they do not believe in God's ends. They do not believe that spiritual ends are as substantial and desirable as those that are physical.

Abram's faith is easily recognised, because not only had he not wrought for the blessing God promised him, but it was impossible for him even to see how it could be achieved. That which God promised was apparently quite beyond the reach of human power. It serves then as an admirable illustration of the essence of faith; and Paul uses it as such. It is not because faith is the root of all actual righteousness that Paul describes it as "imputed for righteousness." It is because faith at once gives a man possession of what no amount of working could ever achieve. God now offers in Christ righteousness, that is to say, justification, the forgiveness of sins and acceptance with God with all the fruits of this acceptance, the indwelling Divine Spirit and life everlasting. He offers this freely as he offered to Abram what Abram could never have won for himself. And all that we are asked to do is to accept it. This is all we are asked to do in order to our becoming the forgiven and accepted children of God. After becoming so, there of course remains an infinite amount of service to be rendered, of work to be done, of self-discipline to be undergone. But in answer to the awakened sinner's enquiry, "What must I do to be saved," Paul replies, "You are to *do* nothing; nothing you can do can win God's favour, because that favour is already yours; nothing you can do can achieve the rectification of your present condition, but Christ has achieved it. Believe that God is with you and that Christ can deliver you and commit yourself cordially to the life you are called to, hopeful that what is promised will be fulfilled."

Abram's faith cordial as it was, yet was not independent of some sensible sign to maintain it. The sign given was twofold: the smoking furnace and a prediction of the sojourn of Abram's posterity in Egypt. The symbols were similar to those by which on other occasions the presence of God was represented. Fire, cleansing, consuming, and unapproachable, seemed to be the natural emblem of God's holiness. In the present instance it was especially suitable, because the manifestation was made after sundown and when no other could have been seen. The cutting up of the carcases and passing between the pieces was one of the customary forms of contract. It was one of the many devices men have fallen upon to make sure of one another's word. That God should condescend to adopt these modes of pledging Himself to men is significant testimony to His love; a love so resolved on accomplishing the good of men that it resents no slowness of faith and accommodates itself to unworthy suspicions. It makes itself as obvious and pledges itself with as strong guarantees to men as if it were the love of a mortal whose feelings might change and who had not clearly foreseen all consequences and issues.

The prediction of the long sojourn of Abram's posterity in Egypt was not only helpful to those who had to endure the Egyptian bondage, but also to Abram himself. He no doubt felt the temptation, from which at no time the Church has been free, to consider himself the favourite of heaven before whose interests all other interests must bow. He is here taught that other men's rights must be respected as well as his, and that not one hour before absolute justice requires it, shall the land of the Amorites be given to his posterity. And that man is considerably past the rudimentary knowledge of God who understands that every act of God springs from justice and not from caprice, and that no creature upon earth is sooner or later unjustly dealt with, by the Supreme Ruler. In the life of Abram it becomes visible, how, by living with God and watching for every expression of His will, a man's knowledge of the Divine nature enlarges; and it is also interesting to observe that shortly after this he grounds all his pleading for Sodom on the truth he had learned here: "Shall not the Judge of *all the earth* do right?"

The announcement that a long interval must elapse before the promise was fulfilled must no doubt have been a shock to Abram; and yet it was sobering and educative. It is a great step we take when we come clearly to understand that God has a great deal to do with us before we can fully inherit the promise. For God's promise, so far from making everything in the future easy and bright, is that which above all else discloses how stern a reality life is; how severe and thorough that discipline must be which makes us capable of achieving God's purposes with us. A horror of great darkness may well fall upon the man who enters into covenant with God, who binds himself to that Being whom no pain nor sacrifice can turn aside from the pursuance of aims once approved. When we look forward and consider the losses, the privations, the self-denials, the delays, the pains, the keen and real discipline, the lowliness of the life to which fellowship with God leads men, darkness and gloom and smoke darken our prospect and discourage us; but the smoke is that which arises from a purifying fire that purges away all that prevents us from living spiritually, a darkness very different from that which settles over the life which amidst much present brightness carries in it the consciousness that its course is downwards, that the blows it suffers are deadening, that its sun is steadily nearing its setting and that everlasting night awaits it.

But over all other feelings this solemn transacting with God must have produced in Abram a humble ecstasy of confidence. The wonderful mercy and kindness of God in thus binding Himself to a weak and sinful man cannot but have given him new thoughts of God and new thoughts of himself. With fresh elevation of mind and superiority to ordinary difficulties and temptations would he return to his tent that night. In how different a perspective would all things stand to him now that the Infinite God had come so near to him. Things which yesterday fretted or terrified him seemed now remote: matters which had occupied his thought he did not now notice or remember. He was now the Friend of God, taken up into a new world of thoughts and hopes; hiding in his heart the treasure of God's covenant, brooding over the infinite significance and hopefulness of his position as God's ally.

For indeed this was a most extraordinary and a most encouraging event. The Infinite God drew near to Abram and made a contract with him.

God as it were said to him, I wish you to count upon Me, to make sure of Me: I therefore pledge Myself by these accustomed forms to be your Friend.

But it was not as an isolated person, nor for his own private interests alone that Abram was thus dealt with by God. It was as a medium of universal blessing that he was taken into covenant with God. The kindness of God which he experienced was merely an intimation of the kindness all men would experience. The laying aside of unapproachable dignity and entrance into covenant with a man was the proclamation of His readiness to be helpful to all and to bring Himself within reach of all. That you may have a God at hand He thus brought Himself down to men and human ways, that your life may not be vain and useless, dark and misguided, and that you may find that you have a part in a well-ordered universe in which a holy God cares for all and makes His strength and wisdom available for all. Do not allow these intimations of His mercy to go for nothing but use them as intended for your guidance and encouragement.

XII
BIRTH OF ISHMAEL

Genesis xvi.

In this unpretending chapter we have laid bare to us the origin of one of the most striking facts in the history of religion: namely, that from the one person of Abram have sprung Christianity and that religion which has been and still is its most formidable rival and enemy, Mohammedanism. To Ishmael, the son of Abram, the Arab tribes are proud to trace their pedigree. Through him they claim Abram as their father, and affirm that they are his truest representatives, the sons of his first-born. In Mohammed, the Arabian, they see the fulfilment of the blessing of Abram, and they have succeeded in persuading a large part of the world to believe along with them. Little did Sarah think when she persuaded Abram to take Hagar that she was originating a rivalry which has run with keenest animosity through all ages and which oceans of blood have not quenched. The domestic rivalry and petty womanish spites and resentments so candidly depicted in this chapter, have actually thrown on the world from that day to this one of its darkest and least hopeful shadows. The blood of our own countrymen, it may be of our own kindred, will yet flow in this unappeasable quarrel. So great a matter does a little fire kindle. So lasting and disastrous are the issues of even slight divergences from pure simplicity.

It is instructive to observe how long this matter of obtaining an heir for Abram occupies the stage of sacred history and in how many aspects it is shown. The stage is rapidly cleared of whatever else might naturally have invited attention, and interest is concentrated on the heir that is to be. The risks run by the appointed mother, the doubts of the father, the surrender now of the mother's rights,—all this is trivial if it concerned only one household, important only when you view it as significant for the race. It was thus men were taught thoughtfully to brood upon the future and to believe that, though Divine, blessing and salvation would spring from earth: man was to co-operate with God, to recognise himself as capable of uniting with God in the highest of all purposes. At the same time, this long and continually deferred expectation of Abram was the simple means adopted by God to convince men once for all that the promised seed is not of nature but of grace, that it is God who sends all effectual and determining blessing, and that we must learn to adapt ourselves to His ways and wait upon Him.

The first man, then, whose religious experience and growth are recorded for us at any length, has this one thing to learn, to trust God's word and wait for it. In this everything is included. But gradually it appears to us all that this is the great difficulty, to wait; to let God take His own time to bless us. It is hard to believe in God's perfect love and care when we are receiving no present comfort or peace; hard to believe we shall indeed be sanctified when we seem to be abandoned to sinful habit; hard to pass all through life with some pain, or some crushing trouble, or some harassing anxiety, or some unsatisfied craving. It is easy to start with faith, most trying to endure patiently to the end. It is thus God educates His children. Compelled to wait for some crowning gift, we cannot but study God's ways. It is thus we are forced to look below the surface of life to its hidden meanings and to construe God's dealings with ourselves apart from the experience of other men. It is thus we are taught actually to loosen our hold of things temporal and to lay hold on what is spiritual and real. He who leaves himself in God's hand will one day declare that the pains and sorrows he suffered were trifling in comparison with what he has won from them.

But Sarah could not wait. She seems to have fixed ten years as the period during which she would wait; but at the expiry of this term she considered herself justified in helping forward God's tardy providence by steps of her own. One cannot severely blame her. When our hearts are set upon some definite blessing, things seem to move too slowly and we can scarcely refrain from urging them on without too scrupulously enquiring into the character of our methods. We are willing to wait for a certain time, but beyond that we must take the matter into our own hand. This incident shows, what all life shows, that whatever be the boon you seek, you do yourself an injury if you cease to seek it in the best possible form and manner, and decline upon some lower thing which you can secure by some easy stratagem of your own.

The device suggested by Sarah was so common that the wonder is that it had not long before been tried. Jealousy or instinctive reluctance may have prevented her from putting it in force. She might no doubt have understood that God, always working out His purposes in consistency with all that is most honourable and pure in human conduct, requires of no one to swerve a hair's breadth from the highest ideal of what a human life should be, and that just in proportion as we seek the best gifts and the most upright and pure path to them does God find it easy to bless us. But in her case it was difficult to continue in this belief; and at length she resolved to adopt the easy and obvious means of obtaining an heir. It was unbelieving and foolish, but not more so than our adoption of practices common in our day and in our business which we know are not the best, but which we nevertheless make use of to obtain our ends because the most righteous means possible do not seem workable in our circumstances. Are you not conscious that you have sometimes used a means of effecting your purpose, which you would shrink from using habitually, but which you do not scruple to use to tide you over a difficulty, an extraordinary device for an extraordinary emergency, a Hagar brought in for a season to serve a purpose, not a Sarah accepted from God and cherished as an eternal helpmeet. It is against this we are here warned. From a Hagar can at the best spring only an Ishmael, while in order to obtain the blessing God intends we must betake ourselves to God's barren-looking means.

The evil consequences of Sarah's scheme were apparent first of all in the tool she made use of. Agur the son of Jakeh says: "For three things the earth is disquieted, and for four which it cannot bear. For a servant when he reigneth, and a fool when he is filled with meat; for an odious woman when she is married, and an handmaid that is heir to her mistress." Naturally this half-heathen girl, when she found that her son would probably inherit all Abram's possessions, forgot herself, and looked down on her present, nominal mistress. A flood of new fancies possessed her vacant mind and her whole demeanour becomes insulting to Sarah. The slave-girl could not be expected to sympathize with the purpose which Abram and Sarah had in view when they made use of her. They had calculated on finding only the unquestioning, mechanical obedience of the slave, even while raising her practically to the dignity of a wife. They had fancied that even to the deepest feelings of her woman's heart, even in maternal hopes, she would be plastic in their hands, their mere passive instrument. But they have entirely miscalculated. The slave has feelings as quick and tender as their own, a life and a destiny as tenaciously clung to as their God-appointed destiny. Instead of simplifying their life they have merely added to it another source of complexity and annoyance. It is the common fate of all who use others to satisfy their own desires and purposes. The instruments they use are never so soulless and passive as it is wished. If persons cannot serve you without deteriorating in their own character, you have no right to ask them to serve you. To use human beings as if they were soulless machines is to neglect radical laws and to inflict the most serious injury on our fellow-men.

Mistresses who do not treat their servants with consideration, recognising that they are as truly women as themselves, with all a woman's hopes and feelings, and with a life of their own to live, are committing a grievous wrong, and evil will come of it.

In such an emergency as now arose in Abram's household, character shows itself clearly. Sarah's vexation at the success of her own scheme, her recrimination and appeal for strange justice, her unjustifiable treatment of Hagar, Abram's Bedouin disregard of the jealousies of the women's tent, his Gallio-like repudiation of judgment in such quarrels, his regretful vexation and shame that through such follies, mistakes, and wranglings, God had to find a channel for His promise to flow—all this discloses the painful ferment into which Abram's household was thrown. Sarah's attempt to rid herself with a high hand of the consequences of her scheme was signally unsuccessful. In the same inconsiderate spirit in which she had put Hagar in her place, she now forces her to flee, and fancies that she has now rid herself and her household of all the disagreeable consequences of her experiment. She is grievously mistaken. The slave comes back upon her hands, and comes back with the promise of a son who should be a continual trouble to all about him. All through Ishmael's boyhood Abram and Sarah had painfully to reap the fruits of what they had sown. We only make matters worse when we endeavour by injustice and harshness to crush out the consequences of wrong-doing. The difficulties into which sin has brought us can only be effectually overcome by sincere contrition and humiliation. It is not all in a moment nor by one happy stroke you can rectify the sin or mistake of a moment. If by your wise devices you have begotten young Ishmaels, if something is every day grieving you and saying to you, "This comes of your careless inconsiderate conduct in the past," then see that in your vexation there is real penitence and not a mere indignant resentment against circumstances or against other people, and see that you are not actually continuing the fault which first gave birth to your present sorrow and entanglement.

When Hagar fled from her mistress she naturally took the way to her old country. Instinctively her feet carried her to the land of her birth. And as she crossed the desert country where Palestine, Egypt and Arabia meet, she halted by a fountain, spent with her flight and awed by the solitude and stillness of the desert. Her proud spirit is broken and tamed, the fond memories of her adopted home and all its customs and ways and familiar faces and occupations, overtake her when she pauses and her heart reacts from the first excitement of hasty purpose and reckless execution. To whom could she go in Egypt? Was there one there who would remember the little slave girl or who would care to show her a kindness? Has she not acted madly in fleeing from her only protectors? The desolation around her depicts her own condition. No motion stirs as far as her eye can reach, no bird flies, no leaf trembles, no cloud floats over the scorching sun, no sound breaks the death-like quiet; she feels as if in a tomb, severed from all life, forgotten of all. Her spirit is breaking under this sense of desolation, when suddenly her heart stands still as she hears a voice utter her own name "Hagar, Sarai's maid." As readily as every other person when God speaks to them, does Hagar recognise Who it is who has followed her into this blank solitude. In her circumstances to hear the voice of God left no room for disobedience. The voice of God made audible through the actual circumstances of our daily life acquires a force and an authority we never attached to it otherwise.

Probably, too, Hagar would have gone back to Abram's tents at the bidding of a less authoritative voice than this. Already she was softening and repenting. She but needed some one to say, "Go back." You may often make it easier for a proud man to do a right thing by giving him a timely word. Frequently men stand in the position of Hagar, knowing the course they ought to adopt and yet hesitating to adopt it until it is made easy to them by a wise and friendly word.

In the promise of a son which was here given to Hagar and the prediction concerning his destiny, while there was enough to teach both her and Abram that he was not to be the heir of the promise, there was also much to gratify a mother's pride and be to Hagar a source of continual satisfaction. The son was to bear a name which should commemorate God's remembrance of her in her desolation. As often as she murmured it over the babe or called it to the child or uttered it in sharp remonstrance to the refractory boy, she was still reminded that she had a helper in God who had heard and would hear her. The prediction regarding the child has been strikingly fulfilled in his descendants; the three characteristics by which they are distinguished being precisely those here mentioned. "He will be a wild man," literally, "a wild ass among men," reminding us of the description of this animal in Job: "Whose house I have made the wilderness, and the barren land his dwelling. He scorneth the multitude of the city, neither regardeth he the crying of the driver. The range of the mountains is his pasture, and he searcheth after every green thing." Like the zebra that cannot be domesticated, the Arab scorns the comforts of civilized life, and adheres to the primitive dress, food, and mode of life, delighting in the sensation of freedom, scouring the deserts, sufficient with his horse and spear for every emergency. His hand also is against every man, looking on all as his natural enemies or as his natural prey; in continual feud of tribe against tribe and of the whole race against all of different blood and different customs. And yet he "dwells in the presence of his brethren;" though so warlike a temper would bode his destruction and has certainly destroyed other races, this Ishmaelite stock continues in its own lands with an uninterrupted history. In the words of an authoritative writer: "They have roved like the moving sands of their deserts; but their race has been rooted while the individual wandered. That race has neither been dissipated by conquest, nor lost by migration, nor confounded with the blood of other countries. They have continued to dwell in the presence of all their brethren, a distinct nation, wearing upon the whole the same features and aspects which prophecy first impressed upon them."

What struck Hagar most about this interview was God's presence with her in this remote solitude. She awakened to the consciousness that duty, hope, God, are ubiquitous, universal, carried in the human breast, not confined to any place. Her hopes, her haughtiness, her sorrows, her flight, were all known. The feeling possessed her which was afterwards expressed by the Psalmist: "Thou knowest my down-sitting, and mine uprising, Thou understandest my thoughts afar off. Thou compassest my path and my lying down, and art acquainted with all my ways. Thou tellest my wanderings; put Thou my tears in Thy bottle; are they not in Thy book?" Even here where I thought to have escaped every eye, have I been following and at length found Him that seeth me. As truly and even more perceptibly than in Abram's tents, God is with her here in the desert. To evade duty, to leave responsibility behind us, is impossible. In all places we are God's children, bound to accept the responsibilities of our nature. In all places God is with us, not only to point out our duty but to give us the feeling that in adhering to duty we adhere to Him, and that it is because He values us that He presses duty upon us. With Him is no respect of persons; the servant is in his sight as vivid a personality as the mistress, and God appears not to the overbearing mistress but to the overborne servant.

Happy they who when God has thus met them and sent them back on their own footsteps, a long and weary return, have still been so filled with a sense of God's love in caring for them through all their errors, that they obey and return. All round about His people does God encamp, all round about His flock does the faithful Shepherd watch and drive back upon the fold each wanderer. Not only to those who are consciously seeking Him does God reveal Himself, but often to us at the very farthest point of our wandering, at our extremity, when another day's journey would land us in a region from which there is no return. When our regrets for the past become intolerably poignant and bitter; when we see a waste of years behind us barren as the sand of the desert, with nothing done but what should but cannot be undone; when the heart is stupefied with the sense of its madness and of the irretrievable loss it has sustained, or when we look to the future and are persuaded little can grow up in it out of such a past, when we see that all that would have prepared us for it has been lightly thrown aside or spent recklessly for nought, when our hearts fail us, this is God besetting us behind and before. And may He grant us strength to pray, "Show me Thy ways, O Lord, teach me Thy paths. Lead me in Thy truth and teach me: for Thou art the God of my salvation; on Thee do I wait all the day."

The quiet glow of hopefulness with which Hagar returned to Abram's encampment should possess the spirit of every one of us. Hagar's prospects were not in all respects inviting. She knew the kind of treatment she was likely to receive at the hands of Sarah. She was to be a bondwoman still. But God had persuaded her of His care and had given her a hope large enough to fill her heart. That hope was to be fulfilled by a return to the home she had fled from, by a humbling and painful experience. There is no person for whom God has not similar encouragement. Frequently persons forget that God is in their life, fulfilling His purposes. They flee from what is painful; they lose their bearings in life and know not which way to turn; they do not fancy there is help for them in God. Yet God is with them; by these very circumstances that reduce them to desolateness and despair He leads them to hope in Him. Each one of us has a place in His purpose; and that place we shall find not by fleeing from what is distressing but by submitting ourselves cheerfully to what He appoints. God's purpose is real, and life is real, meant to accomplish not our present passing pleasure, but lasting good in conformity with God's purpose. Be sure that when you are bidden back to duties that seem those of a slave, you are bidden to them by God, Whose purposes are worthy of Himself and Whose purposes include you and all that concerns you.

There are, I think, few truths more animating than this which is here taught us, that God has a purpose with each of us; that however insignificant we seem, however friendless, however hardly used, however ousted even from our natural place in this world's households, God has a place for us; that however we lose our way in life we are not lost from His eye; that even when we do not think of choosing Him He in His Divine, all-embracing love chooses us, and throws about us bonds from which we cannot escape. Of Hagar many were complacently thinking it was no great matter if she were lost, and some might consider themselves righteous because they said she deserved whatever mishap might befall her. But not so God. Of some of us, it may be, others may think no great blank would be made by our loss; but God's compassion and care and purpose comprehend the least worthy. The very hairs of your head are all numbered by Him. Nothing is so trivial and insignificant as to escape His attention, nothing so intractable that He cannot use it for good. Trust in Him, obey Him, and your life will yet be useful and happy.

XIII
THE COVENANT SEALED

Genesis xvii.

According to the dates here given fourteen years had passed since Abram had received any intimation of God's will regarding him. Since the covenant had been made some twenty years before, no direct communication had been received; and no message of any kind since Ishmael's birth. It need not, therefore, surprise us that we are often allowed to remain for years in a state of suspense, uncertain about the future, feeling that we need more light and yet unable to find it. All truth is not discovered in a day, and if that on which we are to found for eternity take us twenty years or a life's experience to settle it in its place, why should we on this account be overborne with discouragement? They who love the truth and can as little abstain from seeking it as the artist can abstain from admiring what is lovely, will assuredly have their reward. To be expectant yet not impatient, unsatisfied yet not unbelieving, to hold mind and heart open, assured that light is sown for the upright and that all that is has lessons for the teachable, this is our proper attitude.

> Think you, 'mid all this mighty sum
> Of things for ever speaking,
> That nothing of itself will come,
> But we must still be seeking?

We appreciate the significance of a revelation in proportion as we understand the state of mind to which it is made. Abram's state of mind is disclosed in the exclamation: "Oh, that Ishmael might live before Thee!" He had learned to love the bold, brilliant, domineering boy. He saw how the men liked to serve him and how proud they were of the young chief. No doubt his wild intractable ways often made his father anxious. Sarah was there to point out and exaggerate all his faults and to prognosticate mischief. But there he was, in actual flesh and blood, full of life and interest in everything, daily getting deeper into the affections of Abram, who allowed and could not but allow his own life to revolve very much around the dashing, attractive lad. So that the reminder that he was not the promised heir was not entirely welcome. When he was told that the heir of promise was to be Sarah's child, he could not repress the somewhat peevish exclamation: "Oh, that Ishmael might serve Thy turn!" Why call me off again from this actual attainment to the vague, shadowy, non-existent heir of promise, who surely can never have the brightness of eye and force of limb and lordly ways of this Ishmael? Would that what already exists in actual substance before the eye might satisfy Thee and fulfil Thine intention and supersede the necessity of further waiting! Must I again loosen my hold, and part with my chief attainment? Must I cut my moorings and launch again upon this ocean of faith with a horizon always receding and that seems absolutely boundless?

We are familiar with this state of mind. We wish God would leave us alone. We have found a very attractive substitute for what He promises, and we resent being reminded that our substitute is not, after all, the veritable, eternal, best possession. It satisfies our taste, our intellect, our ambition; it sets us on a level with other men and gives us a place in the world; but now and again we feel a void it does not fill. We have attained comfortable circumstances, success in our profession, our life has in it that which attracts applause and sheds a brilliance over it; and we do not like being told that this is not all. Our feeling is Oh, that this might do! that this might be accepted as perfect attainment! it satisfies me (all but a little bit); might it not satisfy God? Why summon me again away from domestic happiness, intellectual enjoyment, agreeable occupations, to what really seems so unattainable as perfect fellowship with God in the fulfilment of His promise? Why spend all my life in waiting and seeking for high spiritual things when I have so much with which I can be moderately satisfied? For our complaint often is not that God gives so little but that He offers too much, more than we care to have: that He never will let us be content with anything short of what perfectly fulfils His perfect love and purpose.

This being Abram's state of mind, he is aroused from it by the words: "I am the Almighty God; walk before Me and be thou perfect." I am the Almighty God, able to fulfil your highest hopes and accomplish for you the brightest ideal that ever My words set before you. There is no need of paring down the promise till it square with human probabilities, no need of relinquishing one hope it has begotten, no need of adopting some interpretation of it which may make it seem easier to fulfil, and no need of striving to fulfil it in any second-rate way. All possibility lies in this: I am the Almighty God. Walk before Me and be thou perfect, therefore. Do not train your eye to earthly distances and earthly magnitudes and limit your hope accordingly, but live in the presence of the Almighty God. Do not defer the advices of conscience and of your purest aspirations to some other possible world; do not settle down at the low level of godless nature and of the men around you; do not give way to what you yourself know to be weakness and evidence of defeat; do not let self-indulgence take the place of My commandments, indolence supplant resolution and the likelihoods of human calculation obliterate the hopes stirred by the Divine call: Be thou perfect. Is not this a summons that comes appropriately to every man? Whatever be our contentment, our attainments, our possessions, a new light is shed upon our condition when we measure it by God's idea and God's resources. Is my life God's ideal? Does that which satisfies me satisfy Him?

The purpose of God's present appearance to Abram was to renew the covenant, and this He does in terms so explicit, so pregnant, so magnificent that Abram must have seen more distinctly than ever that he was called to play a very special part in God's providence. That kings should spring from him, a mere pastoral nomad in an alien country, could not suggest itself to Abram as a likely thing to happen. Indeed, though a line of kings or two lines of kings did spring from him through Isaac, the terms of the prediction seem scarcely exhausted by that fulfilment. And accordingly Paul without hesitation or reserve transfers this prediction to a spiritual region, and is at pains to show that the many nations of whom Abram was to be the father, were not those who inherited his blood, his natural appearance, his language and earthly inheritance, but those who inherited his spiritual qualities and the heritage in God to which his faith gave him entrance. And he argues that no difference of race or disadvantages of worldly position can prevent any man from serving himself heir to Abram, because the seed, to whom as well as to Abram the promise was made, was Christ, and in Christ there is neither Jew nor Gentile, bond nor free, but all are one.

In connection then with this covenant in which God promised that He would be a God to Abram and to his seed, two points of interest to us emerge. First that Christ is Abram's heir. In His use of God's promise we see its full significance. In His life-long appropriation of God we see what God meant when He said, "I will be a God to thee and to thy seed." We find our Lord from the first living as one who felt His life encompassed by God, embraced and comprehended in that higher life which God lives through all and in all. His life was all and whole a life in God. He recognised what it is to have a God, one Whose will is supreme and unerringly good, Whose love is constant and eternal, Who is the first and the last, beyond Whom and from under Whom we can never pass. He moved about in the world in so perfectly harmonious a correspondence with God, so merging Himself in God and His purpose and with so unhesitating a reliance upon Him, that He seemed and was but a manifestation of God, God's will embodied, God's child, God expressing Himself in human nature. He showed us once for all the blessedness of true dependence, fidelity and faith. He showed us how that simple promise 'I will be a God to thee,' received in faith, lifts the human life into fellowship with all that is hopeful and inspiring, with all that is purifying, with all that is real and abiding.

But a second point is, that Jesus was the heir of Abram not merely because He was his descendant, a Jew with all the advantages of the Jew, but because, like Abram, He was full of faith. God was the atmosphere of His life. But He claimed God not because He was Jewish, but because He was human. Through the Jews God had made Himself known, but it was to what was human not to what was Jewish He appealed. And it was as Son of man not as son of Israel or of Adam that Jesus responded to God and lived with Him as His God. Not by specially Jewish rites did Jesus approach and rest in God, but by what is universal and human, by prayer to the Father, by loving obedience, by faith and submission. And thus we too may be joint-heirs with Christ and possess God. And if we think of ourselves as left to struggle with natural defects amidst irreversible natural laws; if we begin to pray very heartlessly, as if He who once listened were now asleep or could do nothing; if our life seems profitless, purposeless, and all unhinged; then let us look back to this sure promise of God, that He will be our God: our God, for, if Christ's God, then ours, for if we be Christ's then are we Abram's seed and heirs according to the promise. How few in any given day are living on this promise: how few attach reality to God's continuous revelation of Himself, the reality in this world's transitory history: how few can believe in the nearness and observance and love of God, how few can strenuously seek to be holy or understand where abiding happiness is to be found; for all these things are here. Yet who knocks at this door? Who makes, as Christ made, his life a unity with God, undismayed, unmurmuring, unreluctant, neither fearful of God nor disobedient, but diligent, earnest, jubilant, because God has said, "I will be thy God." Do you believe these things and can you forbear to use them? Do you believe that it is open to you, whosoever you are, to have the Eternal and Supreme God for your God, that He may use all His Divine nature in your behalf; have you conceived what it is that God means when He extends to you this offer, and can you decline to accept it, can you do otherwise than cherish it and seek to find more and more in it every day you live?

Two seals were at this time affixed to the covenant: the one for Abram himself, the other for every one who shared with him in his blessings of the covenant. The first consisted in the change of his own name to Abraham, "the father of a multitude," and of his wife's to Sarah, "princess" or "queen," because she was now announced as the destined mother of kings. And however Abraham would be annoyed to see the hardly suppressed smile on the ironical faces of his men as he boldly commanded them to call him by a name whose verification seemed so grievously to lag; and however indignant and pained he may have been to hear the young Ishmael jeering Sarah with her new name, and lending to it every tone of mockery and using it with insolent frequency, yet Abraham knew that these names were not given to deceive; and probably as the name of Abraham has become one of the best known names on earth, so to himself did it quickly acquire a preciousness as God's voice abiding with him, God's promise renewed to him through every man that addressed him, until at length the child of promise lying on his knees took up its first syllable and called him "Abba."

This seal was special to Abraham and Sarah, the other was public. All who desired to partake with Abraham in the security, hope, and happiness of having God as their God, were to submit to circumcision. This sign was to determine who were included in the covenant. By this outward mark encouragement and assurance of faith were to be quickened in the heart of all Abraham's descendants.

The mark chosen was significant. It was indeed not distinctive in its outward form; so little so that at this day no fewer than one hundred and fifty millions of the race make use of the same rite for one purpose or other. All the descendants of Ishmael of course continue it, but also all who have their religion, that is, all Mohammedans; but besides these, some tribes in South America, some in Australia, some in the South Sea Islands, and a large number of Kaffir tribes. The ancient Egyptians certainly practised it, and it has been suggested that Abraham may have become acquainted with the practice during his sojourn in Egypt. It is however uncertain whether the practice in Egypt runs back to so early a time. If it were an established Egyptian usage, then of course Hagar would demand for her boy at the usual age the rite which she had always associated with entrance on a new stage of life. But even supposing this was the case, the rite was none the less available for the new use to which it was now put. The rainbow existed before the Flood; bread and wine existed before the night of the Lord's Supper; baptisms of various kinds were practised before the days of the Apostles. And for this very reason, when God desired a natural emblem of the stability of the seasons He chose a striking feature of nature on which men were already accustomed to look with pleasure and hope; when He desired symbols of the body and blood of the Redeemer He took those articles which already had a meaning as the most efficacious human nutriment; when He desired to represent to the eye the renunciation of the old life and the birth to a new life which we have by union with Christ, He took that rite which was already known as the badge of discipleship; and when He desired to impress men by symbol with the impurity of nature and with our dependence on God for the production of all acceptable life, He chose that rite which, whether used before or not, did most strikingly represent this.

With the significance of circumcision to other men who practise it, we have here nothing to do. It is as the chief sacrament of the old covenant, by which God meant to aid all succeeding generations of Hebrews in believing that God was their God. And this particular mark was given, rather than any other, that they might recognise and ever remember that human nature was unable to generate its own Saviour, that in man there is a native impurity which must be laid aside when he comes into fellowship with the Holy God. And these circumcised races, although in many respects as unspiritual as others, have yet in general perceived that God is different from nature, a Holy Being to Whom we cannot attain by any mere adherence to nature, but only by the aid He Himself extends to us in ways for which nature makes no provision. The lesson of circumcision is an old one and rudely expressed, but it is vital; and no abhorrence of the circumcised for the uncircumcised too strongly, however unjustly, emphasizes the distinction that actually subsists between those who believe in nature and those who believe in God.

The lesson is old, but the circumcision of the heart to which the outward mark pointed, is ever required. That is the true seal of our fellowship with God; the earnest of the Spirit which gives promise of eternal union with the Holy One; the relentings, the shame, the softening of heart, the adoration and reverence for the holiness of God, the thirst for Him, the joy in His goodness, these are the first fruits of the Spirit, which lead on to our calling God Father, and feeling that to be alone with Him is our happiness. It is this putting aside of our natural confidence in nature and absorption in nature, and this turning to God as our confidence and our life, which constitutes the true circumcision of the heart.

Believing as Abraham was, he could not forbear smiling when God said that Sarah would be the mother of the promised seed. This incredulity of Abraham was so significant that it was commemorated in the name of Isaac, the laugher. This heir was typical of all God's best gifts, at first reckoned impossible, at last filling the heart with gladness. The smile of incredulity became the laughter of joy when the child was born and Sarah said, "God hath made me to laugh, so that all that hear will laugh with me." It is they who expect things so incongruous and so impossible to nature unaided that they smile even while they believe, who will one day find their hopes fulfilled and their hearts running over with joyful laughter. If your heart is fixed only on what you can accomplish for yourself, no great joy can ever be yours. But frame your actual hopes in accordance with the promise of God, expect holiness, fulness of joy, animating partnership with God in the highest matters, the resurrection of the dead, the life everlasting, and one day you will say, "God hath made me to laugh." But Abraham prostrating himself to hide a smile is the symbol of our common attitude. We profess to believe in a God of unspeakable power and goodness, but even while we do so we find it impossible to attach a sense of reality to His promises. They are kindly, well-intentioned words, but are apparently spoken in neglect of solid, obstinate facts. How hard is it for us to learn that God is the great reality, and that the reality of all else may be measured by its relation to Him.

Sarah's laughter had a different meaning. Indeed Sarah does not appear to have been by any means a blameless character. Her conduct towards Hagar showed us that she was a woman capable of generous impulses but not of the strain of continued magnanimous conduct. She was capable of yielding her wifely rights on the impulse of the brilliant scheme that had struck her, but like many other persons who can begin a magnanimous or generous course of conduct, she could not follow it up to the end, but failed disgracefully in her conduct towards her rival. So now again she betrays characteristic weakness. When the strangers came to Abraham's tent, and announced that she was to become a mother, she smiled in superior, self-assured, woman's wisdom. When the promise threatened no longer to hover over her household as a mere sublime and exalting idea which serves its purpose if it keep them in mind that God has spoken to them, but to take place now among the actualities of daily occurrence, she hails this announcement with a laugh of total incredulity. Whatever she had made of God's word, she had not thought it was really and veritably to come to pass; she smiled at the simplicity which could speak of such an unheard-of thing.

This is true to human nature. It reminds you how you have dealt with God's promises,—nay, with God's commandments—when they offered to make room for themselves in the everyday life of which you are masters, every detail of which you have arranged, seeming to know absolutely the laws and principles on which your particular line of life must be carried on. Have you never smiled at the simplicity which could set about making actual, about carrying out in practical life, in society, in work, in business, those thoughts, feelings and purposes, which God's promises beget? Sarah did not laugh outright, but smiled behind the Lord; she did not mock Him to His face, but let the compassionate expression pass over her face with which we listen to the glowing hopes of the young enthusiast who does not know the world. Have we not often put aside God's voice precisely thus; saying within us, We know what kind of things can be done by us and others and what need not be attempted; we know what kind of frailties in social intercourse we must put up with, and not seek to amend; what kind of practices it is vain to think of abolishing; we know what use to make of God's promise and what use not to make of it; how far to trust it, and how far to give greater weight to our knowledge of the world and our natural prudence and sense? Does not our faith, like Sarah's, vary in proportion as the promise to be believed is unpractical? If the promise seems wholly to concern future things, we cordially and devoutly assent; but if we are asked to believe that God intends within the year to do so-and-so, if we are asked to believe that the result of God's promise will be found taking a substantial place among the results of our own efforts—then the derisive smile of Sarah forms on our face.

To look at the crowds of persons professing religion, one would suppose nothing was commoner than faith. There is nothing rarer. Devoutness is common; righteousness of life is common; a contempt for every kind of fraud and underhand practice is common; a highminded disregard for this world's gains and glories is common; an abhorrence of sensuality and an earnest thirst for perfection are common—but faith? Will the Son of man when He comes find it on earth? May not the messengers of God yet say, Who hath believed our report? Why, the great majority of Christian people have never been near enough to spiritual things to know whether they are or are not, they have never narrowly weighed spiritual issues and trembled as they watched the uncertain balance, they say they believe God and a future of happiness because they really do not know what they are talking about—they have not measured the magnitude of these things. Faith is not a blind and careless assent to matters of indifference, faith is not a state of mental suspense with a hope that things may turn out to be as the Bible says. Faith is the firm persuasion that these things are so. And he who at once knows the magnitude of these things and believes that they are so, must be filled with a joy that makes him independent of the world, with an enthusiasm which must seem to the world like insanity. It is quite a different world in which the man of faith lives.

XIV
ABRAHAM'S INTERCESSION FOR SODOM

Genesis xviii.

The scene with which this chapter opens is one familiar to the observer of nomad life in the East. During the scorching heat and glaring light of noon, while the birds seek the densest foliage and the wild animals lie panting in the thicket and everything is still and silent as midnight, Abraham sits in his tent door under the spreading oak of Mamre. Listless, languid, and dreamy as he is, he is at once aroused into brightest wakefulness by the sudden apparition of three strangers. Remarkable as their appearance no doubt must have been, it would seem that Abraham did not recognise the rank of his visitors; it was, as the writer to the Hebrews says, "unawares" that he entertained angels. But when he saw them stand as if inviting invitation to rest, he treated them as hospitality required him to treat any wayfarers. He sprang to his feet, ran and bowed himself to the ground, and begged them to rest and eat with him. With the extraordinary, and as it seems to our colder nature extravagant courtesy of an Oriental, he rates at the very lowest the comforts he can supply; it is only a little water he can give to wash their feet, a morsel of bread to help them on their way, but they will do him a kindness if they accept these small attentions at his hands. He gives, however, much more than he offered, seeks out the fatted calf and serves while his guests sit and eat. The whole scene is primitive and Oriental, and "presents a perfect picture of the manner in which a modern Bedawee Sheykh receives travellers arriving at his encampment;" the hasty baking of bread, the celebration of a guest's arrival by the killing of animal food not on other occasions used even by large flock-masters; the meal spread in the open air, the black tents of the encampment stretching back among the oaks of Mamre, every available space filled with sheep, asses, camels,—the whole is one of those clear pictures which only the simplicity of primitive life can produce.

Not only, however, as a suitable and pretty introduction which may ensure our reading the subsequent narrative is it recorded how hospitably Abraham received these three. Later writers saw in it a picture of the beauty and reward of hospitality. It is very true, indeed, that the circumstances of a wandering pastoral life are peculiarly favourable to the cultivation of this grace. Travellers being the only bringers of tidings are greeted from a selfish desire to hear news as well as from better motives. Life in tents, too, of necessity makes men freer in their manners. They have no door to lock, no inner rooms to retire to, their life is spent outside, and their character naturally inclines to frankness and freedom from the suspicions, fears, and restraints of city life. Especially is hospitality accounted the indispensable virtue, and a breach of it as culpable as a breach of the sixth commandment, because to refuse hospitality is in many regions equivalent to subjecting a wayfarer to dangers and hardships under which he is almost certain to succumb.

> "This tent is mine," said Yussouf, "but no more
> Than it is God's; come in, and be at peace;
> Freely shalt thou partake of all my store,
> As I of His Who buildeth over these
> Our tents His glorious roof of night and day,
> And at Whose door none ever yet heard Nay."

Still we are of course bound to import into our life all the suggestions of kindly conduct which any other style of living gives us. And the writer to the Hebrews pointedly refers to this scene and says, "Let us not be forgetful to entertain strangers, for thereby some have entertained angels unawares." And often in quite a prosaic and unquestionable manner does it become apparent to a host, that the guest he has been entertaining has been sent by God, an angel indeed ministering to his salvation, renewing in him thoughts that had been dying out, filling his home with brightness and life like the smile of God's own face, calling out kindly feelings, provoking to love and to good works, effectually helping him onwards and making one more stage of his life endurable and even blessed. And it is not to be wondered at that our Lord Himself should have continually inculcated this same grace; for in His whole life and by His most painful experience were men being tested as to who among them would take the stranger in. He who became man for a little that He might for ever consecrate the dwelling of Abraham and leave a blessing in his household, has now become man for evermore, that we may learn to walk carefully and reverentially through a life whose circumstances and conditions, whose little socialities and duties, and whose great trials and strains He found fit for Himself for service to the Father. This tabernacle of our human body has by His presence been transformed from a tent to a temple, and this world and all its ways that He approved, admired, and walked in, is holy ground. But as He came to Abraham trusting to his hospitality, not sending before him a legion of angels to awe the patriarch but coming in the guise of an ordinary wayfarer; so did He come to His own and make His entrance among us, claiming only the consideration which He claims for the least of His people, and granting to whoever gave Him *that* the discovery of His Divine nature. Had there been ordinary hospitality in Bethlehem that night before the taxing, then a woman in Mary's condition had been cared for and not superciliously thrust among the cattle, and our race had been delivered from the everlasting reproach of refusing its God a cradle to be born and sleep His first sleep in, as it refused Him a bed to die in, and left chance to provide Him a grave in which to sleep His latest sleep. And still He is coming to us all requiring of us this grace of hospitality, not only in the case of every one who asks of us a cup of cold water and whom our Lord Himself will personate at the last day and say, "*I* was a stranger and ye took Me in;" but also in regard to those claims upon our heart's reception which He only in His own person makes.

But while we are no doubt justified in gathering such lessons from this scene, it can scarcely have been for the sake of inculcating hospitality that these angels visited Abraham. And if we ask, Why did God on this occasion use this exceptional form of manifesting Himself; why, instead of approaching Abraham in a vision or in word as had been found sufficient on former occasions, did He now adopt this method of becoming Abraham's guest and eating with him?—the only apparent reason is that He meant this also to be the test applied to Sodom. There too His angels were to appear as wayfarers, dependent on the hospitality of the town, and by the people's treatment of these unknown visitors their moral state was to be detected and judged. The peaceful meal under the oaks of Mamre, the quiet and confidential walk over the hills in the afternoon when Abraham in the humble simplicity of a godly soul was found to be fit company for these three—this scene where the Lord and His messengers receive a becoming welcome and where they leave only blessing behind them, is set in telling contrast to their reception in Sodom, where their coming was the signal for the outburst of a brutality one blushes to think of, and elicited all the elements of a mere hell upon earth.

Lot would fain have been as hospitable as Abraham. Deeper in his nature than any other consideration was the traditional habit of hospitality. To this he would have sacrificed everything—the rights of strangers were to him truly inviolable. Lot was a man who could as little see strangers without inviting them to his house as Abraham could. He would have treated them handsomely as his uncle; and what he could do he did. But Lot had by his choice of a dwelling made it impossible he should afford safe and agreeable lodging to any visitor. He did his best, and it was not his reception of the angels that sealed Sodom's doom, and yet what shame he must have felt that he had put himself in circumstances in which his chief virtue could not be practised. So do men tie their own hands and cripple themselves so that even the good they would take pleasure in doing is either wholly impossible or turns to evil.

In divulging to Abraham His purpose in visiting Sodom, it is enounced here that God acted on a principle which seems afterwards to have become almost proverbial. Surely the Lord will do nothing but He revealeth His secret unto His servants the prophets. There are indeed two grounds stated for making known to Abraham this catastrophe. The reason that we should naturally expect, viz. that he might go on and warn Lot is not one of them. Why then make any announcement to Abraham if the catastrophe cannot be averted, and if Abraham is to turn back to his own encampment? The first reason is: "Shall I hide from Abraham that thing which I do? *Seeing that Abraham* shall surely become a great and mighty nation, and all the nations of the earth shall be blessed in him." In other words, Abraham has been made the depository of a blessing for all nations, and account must therefore be given to him when any people is summarily removed beyond the possibility of receiving this blessing. If a man has got a grant for the emancipation of the slaves in a certain district, and is informed on landing to put this grant in force that fifty slaves are to be executed that day, he has certainly a right to know and he will inevitably desire to know that this execution is to be, and why it is to be. When an officer goes to negotiate an exchange of prisoners, if two of the number cannot be exchanged, but are to be shot, he must be informed of this and account of the matter must be given him. Abraham often brooding on God's promise, living indeed upon it, must have felt a vague sympathy with all men, and a sympathy not at all vague, but most powerful and practical with the men in the Jordan valley whom he had rescued from Chedorlaomer. If he was to be a blessing to any nation it must surely be to those who were within an afternoon's walk of his encampment and among whom his nephew had taken up his abode. Suppose he had not been told, but had risen next morning and seen the dense cloud of smoke overhanging the doomed cities, might he not with some justice have complained that although God had spoken to him the previous day, not one word of this great catastrophe had been breathed to him.

The second reason is expressed in the nineteenth verse; God had chosen Abraham that he might command his children and his household after him to keep the way of the Lord, to do justice and judgment that the Lord might fulfil His promise to Abraham. That is to say, as it was only by obedience and righteousness that Abraham and his seed were to continue in God's favour, it was fair that they should be encouraged to do so by seeing the fruits of unrighteousness. So that as the Dead Sea lay throughout their whole history on their borders reminding them of the wages of sin, they might never fail rightly to interpret its meaning, and in every great catastrophe read the lesson "except ye repent ye shall all likewise perish." They could never attribute to chance this predicted judgment. And in point of fact frequent and solemn reference was made to this standing monument of the fruit of sin.

As yet there was no moral law proclaimed by any external authority. Abraham had to discover what justice and goodness were from the dictates of his own conscience and from his observation upon men and things. But he was at all events persuaded that only so long as he and his sought honestly to live in what they considered to be righteousness would they enjoy God's favour. And they read in the destruction of Sodom a clear intimation that certain forms of wickedness were detestable to God.

The earnestness with which Abraham intercedes for the cities of the plain reveals a new side of his character. One could understand a strong desire on his part that Lot should be rescued, and no doubt the preservation of Lot formed one of his strongest motives to intercede, yet Lot is never named, and it is, I think, plain that he had more than the safety of Lot in view. He prayed that the city might be spared, not that the righteous might be delivered out of its ruin. Probably he had a lively interest in the people he had rescued from captivity, and felt a kind of protectorate over them as he sometimes looked down on them from the hills near his own tents. He pleads for them as he had fought for them, with generosity, boldness and perseverance; and it was his boldness and unselfishness in fighting for them that gave him boldness in praying for them.

There has come into vogue in this country a kind of intercession which is the exact reverse of this of Abraham—an obtuse, mechanical intercession about whose efficacy one may cherish a reasonable suspicion. The Bible and common sense bid us pray with the Spirit and with the *understanding*; but at some meetings for prayer you are asked to pray for people you do not know and have no real interest in. You are not told even their names, so that if an answer is sent you could not identify the answer, nor is any clue given you by which if God should propose to use you for their help you could know where the help was to be applied. For all you know the slip of paper handed in among a score of others may misrepresent the circumstances; and even supposing it does not, what likeness to the effectual fervent prayer of an anxious man has the petition that is once read in your hearing and at once and for ever blotted from your mind by a dozen others of the same kind. Not so did Abraham pray: he prayed for those he knew and had fought for; and I see no warrant for expecting that our prayers will be heard for persons whose good we seek in no other way than prayer, in none of those ways which in all other matters our conduct proves we judge more effectual than prayer. When Lot was carried captive Abraham did not think it enough to put a petition for him in his evening prayer. He went and *did* the needful thing, so that now when there is nothing else he can do but pray, he intercedes, as few of us can without self-reproach or feeling that had we only done our part there might now be no need of prayer. What confidence can a parent have in praying for a son who is going to a country where vice abounds, if he has done little or nothing to infix in his boy's mind a love of virtue? In some cases the very persons who pray for others are themselves the obstacles preventing the answer. Were we to ask ourselves how much we are prepared to do for those for whom we pray, we should come to a more adequate estimate of the fervency and sincerity of our prayers.

The element in Abraham's intercession that jars on the reader is the trading temper that strives always to get the best possible terms. Abraham seems to think God can be beaten down and induced to make smaller and smaller demands. No doubt this style of prayer was suggested to Abraham by the statement on God's part that He was going to Sodom to see if its iniquity was so great as it was reported; that is, to number, as it were, the righteous men in it. Abraham seizes upon this and asks if He would not spare it if fifty were found in it. But Abraham knowing Sodom as he did could not have supposed this number would be found. Finding, then, that God meets him so far, he goes on step by step getting larger in his demands, until when he comes to ten he feels that to go farther would be intolerably presumptuous. Along with this audacious beating down of God, there is a genuine and profound reverence and humility which at each renewal of the petition dictate some such expression as: "I who am but dust and ashes," "Let not my Lord be angry."

It is remarkable too that, throughout, it is for justice Abraham pleads, and for justice of a limited and imperfect kind. He proceeds on the assumption that the town will be judged as a town, and either wholly saved or wholly destroyed. He has no idea of individual discrimination being made, those only suffering who had sinned. And yet it is this principle of discrimination on which God ultimately proceeds, rescuing Lot. Yet is not this intercession the history of what every one who prays passes through, beginning with the idea that God is to be won over to more liberal views and a more munificent intention, and ending with the discovery that God gives what we should count it shameless audacity to ask? We begin to pray,

> "As if ourselves were better certainly
> Than what we come to—Maker and High Priest"

and we leave off praying assured that the whole is to be managed by a righteousness and love and wisdom, which we cannot plan for, which any love or desire of ours would only limit the action of, and which must be left to work out its own purposes in its own marvellous ways. We begin, feeling that we have to beat down a reluctant God and that we can guide the mind of God to some better thing than He intends: when the answer comes we recognise that what we set as the limit of our expectation God has far overstepped, and that our prayer has done little more than show our inadequate conception of God's mercy.

Not only in this respect but throughout this chapter there is betrayed an inadequate conception of God. The language is adapted to the use of men who are as yet unable to conceive of one Infinite, Eternal Spirit. They think of Him as one who needs to come down and institute an inquiry into the state of Sodom, if He is to know with accuracy the moral condition of its inhabitants. We can freely use the same language, but we put into it a meaning that the words do not literally bear: Abraham and his contemporaries used and accepted the words in their literal sense. And yet the man who had ideas of God in some respects so rudimentary was God's Friend, received singular tokens of His favour, found His whole life illuminated with His presence, and was used as the point of contact between heaven and earth, so that if you desire the first lessons in the knowledge of God which will in time grow into full information, it is to the tent of Abraham, you must go. This surely is encouraging; for who is not conscious of much difficulty in thinking rightly of God? Who does not feel that precisely here, where the light should be brightest, clouds and darkness seem to gather? It may indeed be said that what was excusable in Abraham is inexcusable in us; that we have that day, that full noon of Christ to which he could only, out of the dusky dawn, look forward. But after all may not a man with some justice say: Give me an afternoon with God, such as Abraham had; give me the opportunity of converse with a God submitting Himself to question and answer, to those means and instruments of ascertaining truth which I daily employ in other matters, and I will ask no more? Christ has given us entrance into the final stage of our knowledge of God, teaching us that God is a Spirit and that we cannot see the Father; that Christ Himself left earth and withdrew from the bodily eye that we might rely more upon spiritual modes of apprehension and think of God as a Spirit. But we are not at all times able to receive this teaching, we are children still and fall back with longing for the times when God walked and spoke with man. And this being so, we are encouraged by the experience of Abraham. We shall not be disowned by God though we do not know Him perfectly. We can but begin where we are, not pretending that that is clear and certain to us which in fact is not so, but freely dealing with God according to the light we have, hoping that we too, like Abraham, shall see the day of Christ and be glad; shall one day stand in the full light of ascertained and eternal truth, knowing as we are known.

In conclusion, we shall find when we read the following chapter, and especially the prayer of Lot that he might not be driven to the wild mountain district, but might occupy the little town of Zoar which was saved for his sake—we shall find, that much light is reflected on this prayer of Abraham. Without trenching on what may be more fitly spoken of afterwards, it may now be observed that the difference between Lot and Abraham, as between man and man generally, comes out nowhere more strikingly than in their prayers. Abraham had never prayed for himself with a tithe of the persistent earnestness with which he prays for Sodom—a town which was much indebted to him, but towards which for more reasons than one a smaller man would have borne a grudge. Lot, on the other hand, much indebted to Sodom, identified indeed with it, one of its leading citizens, connected by marriage with its inhabitants, is in no agony about its destruction, and has indeed but one prayer to offer, and that is, that when all his fellow-townsmen are destroyed, he may be comfortably provided for. While the men he has bargained and feasted with, the men he has made money out of and married his daughters to, are in the agonies of an appalling catastrophe and so near that the smoke of their torment sweeps across his retreat, he is so disengaged from regrets and compassion that he can nicely weigh the comparative comfort and advantage of city and rural life. One would have thought better of the man if he had declined the angelic rescue and resolved to stand by those in death whose society he had so coveted in life. And it is significant that while the generous, large-hearted, devout pleading of Abraham is in vain, the miserable, timorous, selfish petition of Lot is heard and answered. It would seem as if sometimes God were hopeless of men, and threw to them in contempt the gifts they crave, giving them the poor stations in this life their ambition is set upon, because He sees they have made themselves incapable of enduring hardness, and so quelling their lower nature. An answered prayer is not always a blessing, sometimes it is a doom: "He sent them meat to the full: but while their meat was yet in their mouths, the wrath of God came upon them and slew the fattest of them."

Probably had Lot felt any inclination to pray for his townsmen he would have seen that for him to do so would be unseemly. His circumstances, his long association with the Sodomites, and his accommodation of himself to their ways had both eaten the soul out of him and set him on quite a different footing towards God from that occupied by Abraham. A man cannot on a sudden emergency lift himself out of the circumstances in which he has been rooted, nor peel off his character as if it were only skin deep. Abraham had been living an unworldly life in which intercourse with God was a familiar employment. His prayer was but the seasonable flower of his life, nourished to all its beauty by the habitual nutriment of past years. Lot in his need could only utter a peevish, pitiful, childish cry. He had aimed all his life at being comfortable, he could not now wish anything more than to be comfortable. "Stand out of my sunshine," was all he could say, when he held by the hand the plenipotentiary of heaven, and when the roar of the conflict of moral good and evil was filling his ears—a decent man, a righteous man, but the world had eaten out his heart till he had nothing to keep him in sympathy with heaven.

Such is the state to which men in our society, as in Sodom, are brought by risking their spiritual life to make the most of this world.

XV
DESTRUCTION OF THE CITIES OF THE PLAIN

Genesis xix.

While Abraham was pleading with the Lord the angels were pursuing their way to Sodom. And in doing so they apparently observed the laws of those human forms which they had assumed. They did not spread swift wings and alight early in the afternoon at the gates of the city; but taking the usual route, they descended from the hills which separated Abraham's encampment from the plain of the Jordan, and as the sun was setting reached their destination. In the deep recess which is found at either side of the gateway of an Eastern city, Lot had taken his accustomed seat. Wearied and vexed with the din of the revellers in the street, and oppressed with the sultry doom-laden atmosphere, he was looking out towards the cool and peaceful hills, purple with the sinking sun behind them, and letting his thoughts first follow and then outrun his eye; he was now picturing and longing for the unseen tents of Abraham, and almost hearing the cattle lowing round at evening and all the old sounds his youth had made familiar.

He is recalled to the actual present by the footfall of the two men, and little knowing the significance of his act, invites them to spend the night under his roof. It has been observed that the historian seems to intend to bring out the quietness and the ordinary appearance of the entire circumstances. All goes on as usual. There is nothing in the setting sun to say that for the last time it has shone on these rich meadows, or that in twelve hours its rising will be dimmed by the smoke of the burning cities. The ministers of so appalling a justice as was here displayed enter the city as ordinary travellers. When a crisis comes, men do not suddenly acquire an intelligence and insight they have not habitually cultivated. They cannot suddenly put forth an energy nor exhibit an apt helpfulness which only character can give. When the test comes, we stand or fall not according to what we would wish to be and now see the necessity of being, but according to what former self-discipline or self-indulgence has made us.

How then shall this angelic commission of enquiry proceed? Shall it call together the elders of Sodom—or shall it take Lot outside the city and cross-examine him, setting down names and dates and seeking to come to a fair judgment. Not at all—there is a much surer way of detecting character than by any process of examination by question and answer. To each of us God says:

> "Since by its *fruit* a tree is judged,
> Show me thy fruit, the *latest act* of thine!
> For in the *last* is summed the first, and all,—
> What thy life last put heart and soul into,
> There shall I taste thy product."

It is thus these angels proceed. They do not startle the inhabitants of Sodom into any abnormal virtue nor present opportunity for any unwonted iniquity. They give them opportunity to act in their usual way. Nothing could well be more ordinary than the entrance to the city of two strangers at sunset. There is nothing in this to excite, to throw men off their guard, to overbalance the daily habit, or give exaggerated expression to some special feature of character. It is thus we are all judged—by the insignificant circumstances in which we act without reflection, without conscious remembrance of an impending judgment, with heart and soul and full enjoyment.

First Lot is judged. Lot's character is a singularly mixed one. With all his selfishness, he was hospitable and public-spirited. Lover of good living, as undoubtedly he was, his courage and strength of character are yet unmistakable. His sitting at the gate in the evening to offer hospitality may fairly be taken as an indication of his desire to screen the wickedness of his townsmen, and also to shield the stranger from their brutality. From the style in which the mob addressed him, it is obvious that he had made himself offensive by interfering to prevent wrong-doing. He was nicknamed "the Censor," and his eye was felt to carry condemnation. It is true there is no evidence that his opposition had been of the slightest avail. How could it avail with men who knew perfectly well that with all his denunciation of their wicked ways, he preferred their money-making company to the desolation of the hills, where he would be vexed with no filthy conversation, but would also find no markets? Still it is to Lot's credit that in such a city, with none to observe, none to applaud, and none to second him, he should have been able to preserve his own purity of life and steadily to resist wrong-doing. It would be cynical to say that he cultivated austerity and renounced popular vices as a salve to a conscience wounded by his own greed.

That he had the courage which lies at the root of strength of character became apparent as the last dark night of Sodom wore on. To go out among a profligate, lawless mob, wild with passion and infuriated by opposition—to go out and shut the door behind him—was an act of true courage. His confidence in the influence he had gained in the town cannot have blinded him to the temper of the raging crowd at his door. To defend his unknown guests he put himself in a position in which men have frequently lost life.

In the first few hours of his last night in Sodom, there is much that is admirable and pathetic in Lot's conduct. But when we have said that he was bold and that he hated other men's sins, we have exhausted the more attractive side of his character. The inhuman collectedness of mind with which, in the midst of a tremendous public calamity, he could scheme for his own private well-being is the key to his whole character. He had no feeling. He was cold-blooded, calculating, keenly alive to his own interest, with all his wits about him to reap some gain to himself out of every disaster; the kind of man out of whom wreckers are made, who can with gusto strip gold rings off the fingers of doomed corpses; out of whom are made the villains who can rifle the pockets of their dead comrades on a battlefield, or the politicians who can still ride on the top of the wave that hurls their country on the rocks. When Abraham gave him his choice of a grazing ground, no rush of feeling, no sense of gratitude, prevented him from making the most of the opportunity. When his house was assailed, he had coolness, when he went out to the mob, to shut the door behind him that those within might not hear his bargain. When the angel, one might almost say, was flurried by the impending and terrible destruction, and was hurrying him away, he was calm enough to take in at a glance the whole situation and on the spot make provision for himself. There was no need to tell him not to look back as his wife did: no deep emotion would overmaster him, no unconquerable longing to see the last of his dear friends in Sodom would make him lose one second of his time. Even the loss of his wife was not a matter of such importance as to make him forget himself and stand to mourn. In every recorded act of his life appears this same unpleasant characteristic.

Between Lot and Judas there is an instructive similarity. Both had sufficient discernment and decision of character to commit themselves to the life of faith, abandoning their original residence and ways of life. Both came to a shameful end, because the motive even of the sacrifices they made was self-interest. Neither would have had so dark a career had he more justly estimated his own character and capabilities, and not attempted a life for which he was unfit. They both put themselves into a false position; than which nothing tends more rapidly to deteriorate character. Lot was in a doubly false position, because in Sodom as well as in Abraham's shifting camp he was out of place. He voluntarily bound himself to men he could not love. One side of his nature was paralysed; and that the side which in him especially required development. It is the influence of home life, of kindly surroundings, of friendships, of congenial employment, of everything which evokes the free expression of what is best in us; it is this which is a chief factor in the development of every man. But instead of the genial and fertilising influence of worthy friendships, and ennobling love, Lot had to pretend good-will where he felt none, and deceit and coldness grew upon him in place of charity. Besides, a man in a false position in life, out of which he can by any sacrifice deliver himself, is never at peace with God until he does deliver himself. And any attempt to live a righteous life with an evil conscience is foredoomed to failure.

And if it still be felt that Lot was punished with extreme severity, and that if every man who chose a good grazing ground or a position in life which was likely to advance his fortune were thereby doomed to end his days in a cave and under the darkest moral brand, society would be quite disintegrated, it must be remembered, that in order to advance his interests in life, Lot sacrificed much that a man is bound by all means to cherish; and further, it must be said that our destinies are thus determined. The whole iniquity and final consequences of our disposition are not laid before us in the mass; but to give the rein to any evil disposition is to yield control of our own life and commit ourselves to guidance which cannot result in good, and is of a nature to result in utter shame and wretchedness.

Turning from the rescued to the destroyed, we recognise how sufficient a test of their moral condition the presence of the angels was. The inhabitants of Sodom quickly afford evidence that they are ripe for judgment. They do nothing worse than their habitual conduct led them to do. It is not for this one crime they are punished; its enormity is only the legible instance which of itself convicts them. They are not aware of the frightful nature of the crime they seek to commit. They fancy it is but a renewal of their constant practice. They rush headlong on destruction and do not know it. How can it be otherwise? If a man *will not* take warning, if he will persist in sin, then the day comes when he is betrayed into iniquity the frightful nature of which he did not perceive, but which is the natural result of the life he has led. He goes on and will not give up his sin till at last the final damning act is committed which seals his doom. Character tends to express itself in one perfectly representative act. The habitual passion, whatever it is, is always alive and seeking expression. Sometimes one consideration represses it, sometimes another; but these considerations are not constant, while the passion is, and must therefore one day find its opportunity—its opportunity not for that moderate, guarded, disguised expression which passes without notice, but for the full utterance of its very essence. So it was here, the whole city, small and great, young and old, from every quarter came together unanimous and eager in prosecuting the vilest wickedness. No further investigation or proof was needed: it has indeed passed into a proverb: "they *declare* their sin as Sodom."

To punish by a special commission of enquiry is quite unusual in God's government. Nations are punished for immorality or for vicious administration of law or for neglect of sanitary principles by the operation of natural laws. That is to say, there is a distinctly traceable connection between the crime and its punishment; the one being the natural cause of the other. That nations should be weakened, depopulated, and ultimately sink into insignificance, is the natural result of a development of the military spirit of a country and the love of glory. That a population should be decimated by cholera or small-pox is the inevitable result of neglecting intelligible laws of health. It seems to me absurd to put this destruction of Sodom in the same category. The descent of meteoric stones from the sky is not the natural result of immorality. The vices of these cities have disastrous national results which are quite legibly written in some races existing in the present day. We have here to do not with what is natural but with what is miraculous. Of course it is open to any one to say, "It was merely accidental—it was a mere coincidence that a storm of lightning so violent as to set fire to the bituminous soil should rage in the valley, while on the hills a mile or two off all was serene; it was a mere coincidence that meteoric stones or some instrument of conflagration should set on fire just these cities, not only one of them but four of them, and no more." And certainly were there nothing more to go upon than the fact of their destruction, this coincidence, however extraordinary, must still be admitted as wholly natural, and having no relation to the character of the people destroyed. It might be set down as pure accident, and be classed with storms at sea, or volcanic eruptions, which are due to physical causes and have no relation to the moral character of those involved, but indiscriminately destroy all who happen to be present.

But we have to account not only for the fact of the destruction but for its prediction both to Abraham and to Lot. Surely it is only reasonable to allow that such prediction was supernatural; and the prediction being so, it is also reasonable to accept the account of the event given by the predicters of it, and understand it not as an ordinary physical catastrophe, but as an event contrived with a view to the moral character of those concerned, and intended as an infliction of punishment for moral offences. And before we object to a style of dealing with nations so different from anything we now detect, we must be sure that a quite different style of dealing was not at that time required. If there is an intelligent training of the world, it must follow the same law which requires that a parent deal in one way with his boy of ten and in another with his adult son.

Of Lot's wife the end is recorded in a curt and summary fashion. "His wife looked back from behind him, and she became a pillar of salt." The angel, knowing how closely on the heels of the fugitives the storm would press, had urgently enjoined haste, saying, "Look not behind thee, neither stay thou in all the plain." Rapid in its pursuit as a prairie fire, it was only the swift who could escape it. To pause was to be lost. The command, "Look not behind thee" was not given because the scene was too awful to behold for what men can endure, men may behold, and Abraham looked upon it from the hill above. It was given simply from the necessity of the case and from no less practical and more arbitrary reason. Accordingly when the command was neglected, the consequence was felt. Why the infatuated woman looked back one can only conjecture. The woful sounds behind her, the roar of the flame and of Jordan driven back, the crash of falling houses and the last forlorn cry of the doomed cities, all the confused and terrific din that filled her ear, may well have paralysed her and almost compelled her to turn. But the use our Lord makes of her example shows us that He ascribed her turning to a different motive. He uses her as a warning to those who seek to save out of the destruction more than they have time to save, and so lose all. "He which shall be on the housetop, and his stuff in the house, let him not come down to take it away; and he that is in the field, let him likewise not return back. Remember Lot's wife." It would seem, then, as if our Lord ascribed her tragic fate to her reluctance to abandon her household stuff. She was a wife after Lot's own heart, who in the midst of danger and disaster had an eye to her possessions. The smell of fire, the hot blast in her hair, the choking smoke of blazing bitumen, suggested to her only the thought of her own house decorations, her hangings, and ornaments, and stores. She felt keenly the hardship of leaving so much wealth to be the mere food of fire. The thought of such intolerable waste made her more breathless with indignation than her rapid flight. Involuntarily as she looks at the bleak, stony mountains before her, she thinks of the rich plain behind; she turns for one last look, to see if it is impossible to return, impossible to save anything from the wreck. The one look transfixes her, rivets her with dismay and horror. Nothing she looked for can be seen; all is changed in wildest confusion. Unable to move, she is overtaken and involved in the sulphurous smoke, the bitter salts rise out of the earth and stifle her and encrust around her and build her tomb where she stands.

Lot's wife by her death proclaims that if we crave to make the best of both worlds, we shall probably lose both. Her disposition is not rare and exceptional as the pillar of salt which was its monument. She is not the only woman whose heart is so fixedly set upon her household possessions that she cannot listen to the angel-voices that would guide her. Are there none but Lot's wife who show that to them there is nothing so important, nothing else indeed to live for at all, but the management of a house and the accumulation of possessions? If all who are of the same mind as Lot's wife shared her fate the world would present as strange a spectacle as the Dead Sea presents at this day. For radically it was her divided mind which was her ruin. She had good impulses, she saw what she ought to do, but she did not do it with a mind made up. Other things divided her thoughts and diverted her efforts. What else is it ruins half the people who suppose themselves well on the way of life? The world is in their heart; they cannot pursue with undivided mind the promptings of a better wisdom. Their heart is with their treasure, and their treasure is really not in spiritual excellence, not in purity of character, not in the keen bracing air of the silent mountains where God is known, but in the comforts and gains of the luxurious plain behind.

We are to remember Lot's wife that we may bear in mind how possible it is that persons who promise well and make great efforts and bid fair to reach a place of safety may be overtaken by destruction. We can perhaps tell of exhausting effort, we may have outstripped many in practical repentance, but all this may only be petrified by present carelessness into a monument recording how nearly a man may be saved and yet be destroyed. "Have ye suffered all these things in vain, if it be yet in vain?" "Ye have run well, what now hinders you?" The question always is, not, what have you done, but what are you now doing? Up to the site of the pillar, Lot's wife had done as well as Lot, had kept pace with the angels; but her failure at that point destroyed her.

The same urgency may not be felt by all; but it should be felt by all to whose conscience it has been distinctly intimated that they have become involved in a state of matters which is ruinous. If you are conscious that in your life there are practices which may very well issue in moral disaster, an angel has taken you by the hand and bid you flee. For you to delay is madness. Yet this is what people will do. Sagacious men of the world, even when they see the probability of disaster, cannot bear to come out with loss. They will always wait a little longer to see if they cannot rescue something more, and so start on a fresh course with less inconvenience. They will not understand that it is better to live bare and stripped with a good conscience and high moral achievement, than in abundance with self-contempt. What they have, always seems more to them than what they are.

XVI
SACRIFICE OF ISAAC

Genesis xxii.

The sacrifice of Isaac was the supreme act of Abraham's life. The faith which had been schooled by so singular an experience and by so many minor trials was here perfected and exhibited as perfect. The strength which he had been slowly gathering during a long and trying life was here required and used. This is the act which shines like a star out of those dark ages, and has served for many storm-tossed souls over whom God's billows have gone, as a mark by which they could still shape their course when all else was dark. The devotedness which made the sacrifice, the trust in God that endured when even such a sacrifice was demanded, the justification of this trust by the event, and the affectionate fatherly acknowledgment with which God gloried in the man's loyalty and strength of character— all so legibly written here—come home to every heart in the time of its need. Abraham has here shown the way to the highest reach of human devotedness and to the heartiest submission to the Divine will in the most heart-rending circumstances. Men and women living our modern life are brought into situations which seem as torturing and overwhelming as those of Abraham, and all who are in such conditions find, in his loyal trust in God, sympathetic and effectual aid.

In order to understand God's part in this incident and to remove the suspicion that God imposed upon Abraham as a duty what was really a crime, or that He was playing with the most sacred feelings of His servant, there are one or two facts which must not be left out of consideration. In the first place, Abraham did not think it wrong to sacrifice his son. His own conscience did not clash with God's command. On the contrary, it was through his own conscience God's will impressed itself upon him. No man of Abraham's character and intelligence could suppose that any word of God could make that right which was in itself wrong, or would allow the voice of conscience to be drowned by some mysterious voice from without. If Abraham had supposed that in all circumstances it was a crime to take his son's life, he could not have listened to any voice that bade him commit this crime. The man who in our day should put his child to death and plead that he had a Divine warrant for it would either be hanged or confined as insane. No miracle would be accepted as a guarantee for the Divine dictation of such an act. No voice from heaven would be listened to for a moment, if it contradicted the voice of the universal conscience of mankind. But in Abraham's day the universal conscience had only approbation to express for such a deed as this. Not only had the father absolute power over the son, so that he might do with him what he pleased; but this particular mode of disposing of a son would be considered singular only as being beyond the reach of ordinary virtue. Abraham was familiar with the idea that the most exalted form of religious worship was the sacrifice of the first-born. He felt, in common with godly men in every age, that to offer to God cheap sacrifices while we retain for ourselves what is truly precious, is a kind of worship that betrays our low estimate of God rather than expresses true devotion. He may have been conscious that in losing Ishmael he had felt resentment against God for depriving him of so loved a possession; he may have seen Canaanite fathers offering their children to gods he knew to be utterly unworthy of any sacrifice; and this may have rankled in his mind until he felt shut up to offer his all to God in the person of his son, his only son, Isaac. At all events, however it became his conviction that God desired him to offer his son, this was a sacrifice which was in no respect forbidden by his own conscience.

But although not wrong in Abraham's judgment, this sacrifice was wrong in the eye of God; how then can we justify God's command that He should make it? We justify it precisely on that ground which lies patent on the face of the narrative—God meant Abraham to make the sacrifice in spirit, not in the outward act; He meant to write deeply on the Jewish mind the fundamental lesson regarding sacrifice, that it is in the spirit and will all true sacrifice is made. God intended what actually happened, that Abraham's sacrifice should be complete and that human sacrifice should receive a fatal blow. So far from introducing into Abraham's mind erroneous ideas about sacrifice, this incident finally dispelled from his mind such ideas and permanently fixed in his mind the conviction that the sacrifice God seeks is the devotion of the living soul not the consumption of a dead body. God met him on the platform of knowledge and of morality to which he had attained, and by requiring him to sacrifice his son taught him and all his descendants in what sense alone such sacrifice can be acceptable. God meant Abraham to sacrifice his son, but not in the coarse material sense. God meant him to yield the lad truly to Him; to arrive at the consciousness that Isaac more truly belonged to God than to him, his father. It was needful that Abraham and Isaac should be in perfect harmony with the Divine will. Only by being really and absolutely in God's hand could they, or can any one, reach the whole and full good designed for them by God.

How old Isaac was at the time of this sacrifice there is no means of accurately ascertaining. He was probably in the vigour of early manhood. He was able to take his share in the work of cutting wood for the burnt offering and carrying the faggots a considerable distance. It was necessary too that this sacrifice should be made on Isaac's part not with the timorous shrinking or ignorant boldness of a boy, but with the full comprehension and deliberate consent of maturer years. It is probable that Abraham was already preparing, if not to yield to Isaac the family headship, yet to introduce him to a share in the responsibilities he had so long borne alone. From the touching confidence in one another which this incident exhibits, a light is reflected on the fond intercourse of former years. Isaac was at that time of life when a son is closest to a father, mature but not independent; when all that a father can do has been done, but while as yet the son has not passed away into a life of his own.

And Isaac was no ordinary son. The man of business who has encouraged and solaced himself in his toil by the hope that his son will reap the fruit of it and make his old age easy and honoured, but who outlives his son and sees the effort of his life go for nothing; the proprietor who bears an ancient name and sees his heir die—these are familiar objects of pathetic interest, and no heart is so hard as to refuse a tear of sympathy when brought into view of such heart-withering bereavements. But in Abraham all fatherly feelings had been evoked and strengthened and deepened by a quite peculiar experience. By a special and most effectual discipline he had been separated from the objects which ordinarily divide men's attention and eke out their contentment in life, and his whole hopes had been compelled to centre in his son. It was not the perpetuation of a name nor the transmission of a well-known and valuable property; it was not even the gratification of the most justifiable and tender of human affections, that was crushed and thwarted in Abraham by this command; but it was also and especially that hope which had been aroused and fostered in him by extraordinary providences and which concerned, as he believed, not himself alone but all men.

Manifestly no harder task could have been set to Abraham, than that which was imposed on him by the command, "Take now thy son, thine only son, Isaac, whom thou lovest," this son of thine in whom all the promises are yea and amen to thee, this son for whose sake thou gavest up home and kindred, and banished thy firstborn Ishmael, this son whom thou lovest, and offer him for a burnt-offering. This son, Abraham might have said, whom I have been taught to cherish, putting aside all other affections that I might love him above all, I am now with my own hand to slay, to slay with all the terrible niceties and formalities of sacrifice *and with all the love and adoration of sacrifice*. I am with my own hand to destroy all that makes life valuable to me, and as I do so I am to love and worship Him who commands this sacrifice. I am to go to Isaac, whom I have taught to look forward to the fairest happiest life, and I am to contradict all I ever told him and tell him now that he has only grown to maturity that he might be cut down in the flush and hope of opening manhood. What can Abraham have thought? Possibly the thought would occur that God was now recalling the great gift He had made. There is always enough conscience of sin in the purest human heart to engender self-reproach and fear on the faintest occasion; and when so signal a token of God's displeasure as this was sent, Abraham may well have believed himself to have been unwittingly guilty of some great crime against God, or have now thought with bitterness of the languid devotion he had been offering Him. I have in sacrificing a lamb been as if I had been cutting off a dog's neck, profane and thoughtless in my worship, and now God is solemnising me indeed. I have in thought or desire kept back the prime of my flock, and God is now teaching me that a man may not rob God. Who could have been surprised if in this horror of great darkness the mind of Abraham had become unhinged? Who could wonder if he had slain *himself* to make the loss of Isaac impossible? Who could wonder if he had sullenly ignored the command, waited for further light, or rejected an alliance with God which involved such lamentable conditions? Nothing that could befall him in consequence of disobedience, he might have supposed, could exceed in pain the agony of obedience. And it is always easier to endure the pain inflicted upon us by circumstances than to do with our own hand and free will what we know will involve us in suffering. It is not mere resignation but active obedience that was required of Abraham. His was not the passive resignation of the man out of whose reach death or disaster has swept his dearest treasures, and who is helped to resignation by the consciousness that no murmuring can bring them back—his was the far more difficult active resignation, which has still in possession all that it prizes, and may withhold these treasures if it pleases, but is called by a higher voice than that of self-pleasing to sacrifice them all.

But though Abraham was the chief, he was not the sole actor in this trying scene. To Isaac this was the memorable day of his life, and quiescent and passive as his character seems to have been, it cannot but have been stirred and strained now in every fibre of it. Abraham could not find it in his heart to disclose to his son the object of the journey; even to the last he kept him unconscious of the part he was himself to play. Two long days' journey, days of intense inward commotion to Abraham, they went northward. On the third day the servants were left, and father and son went on alone, unaccompanied and unwitnessed. "So they went," as the narrative twice over says, "both of them together," but with minds how differently filled; the father's heart torn with anguish, and distracted by a thousand thoughts, the son's mind disengaged, occupied only with the new scenes and with passing fancies. Nowhere in the narrative does the completeness of the mastery Abraham had gained over his natural feelings appear more strikingly than in the calmness with which he answers Isaac's question. As they approach the place of sacrifice Isaac observes the silent and awe-struck demeanour of his father, and fears that it may have been through absence of mind he has neglected to bring the lamb. With a gentle reverence he ventures to attract Abraham's attention: "My father;" and he said, "Here am I, my son." And he said, "Behold the fire and the wood, but where is the lamb for a burnt offering?" It is one of those moments when only the strongest heart can bear up calmly and when only the humblest faith has the right word to say. "My son, the Lord will provide Himself a lamb for a burnt offering."

Not much longer could the terrible truth be hidden from Isaac. With what feelings must he have seen the agonised face of his father as he turned to bind him and as he learned that he must prepare not to sacrifice but to be sacrificed. Here then was the end of those great hopes on which his youth had been fed. What could such contradiction mean? Was he to submit even to his father in such a matter? Why should he not expostulate, resist, flee? Such ideas seem to have found short entertainment in the mind of Isaac. Trained by long experience to trust his father, he obeys without complaint or murmur. Still it cannot cease to be matter of admiration and astonishment that a young man should have been able on so brief a notice, through so shocking a way, and with so startling a reversal of his expectations, to forego all right to choose for himself, and yield himself implicitly to what he believed to be God's will. By a faith so absolute Isaac became indeed the heir of Abraham. When he laid himself on the altar, trusting his father and his God, he came of age as the true seed of Abraham and entered on the inheritance, making God his God. At that supreme moment he made himself over to God, he put himself at God's disposal; if his death was to be helpful in fulfilling God's purpose he was willing to die. It was God's will that must be done, not his. He knew that God could not err, could not harm His people; he was ignorant of the design which his death could fulfil, but he felt sure that his sacrifice was not asked in vain. He had familiarised himself with the thought that he belonged to God; that he was on earth for God's purposes not for his own; so that now when he was suddenly summoned to lay himself formally and finally on God's altar, he did not hesitate to do so. He had learned that there are possessions more worth preserving than life itself, that

> "Manhood is the one immortal thing
> Beneath Time's changeful sky" —

he had learned that "length of days is knowing when to die."

No one who has measured the strain that such sacrifice puts upon human nature can withhold his tribute of cordial admiration for so rare a devotedness, and no one can fail to see that by this sacrifice Isaac became truly the heir of Abraham. And not only Isaac, but every man attains his majority by sacrifice. Only by losing our life do we begin to live. Only by yielding ourselves truly and unreservedly to God's purpose do we enter the true life of men. The giving up of self, the abandonment of an isolated life, the bringing of ourselves into connection with God, with the Supreme and with the whole, this is the second birth. To reach that full stream of life which is moved by God's will and which is the true life of men, we must so give ourselves up to God, that each of His commandments, each of His providences, all by which He comes into connection with us, has its due effect upon us. If we only seek from God help to carry out our own conception of life, if we only desire His power to aid us in making of this life what we have resolved it shall be, we are far indeed from Isaac's conception of God and of life. But if we desire that God fulfil in us, and through us His own conception of what our life should be, the only means of attaining this desire is to put ourselves fairly into God's hand, unflinchingly to do what we believe to be His will irrespective of present darkness and pain and privation. He who thus bids an honest farewell to earth and lets himself be bound and laid upon God's altar, is conscious that in renouncing himself he has won God and become His heir.

Have you thus given yourselves to God? I do not ask if your sacrifice has been perfect, nor whether you do not ever seek great things still for yourselves; but do you know what it is thus to yield yourself to God, to put God first, yourself second or nowhere? Are you even occasionally quite willing to sink your own interests, your own prospects, your own native tastes, to have your own worldly hopes delayed or blighted, your future darkened? Have you even brought your intellect to bear upon this first law of human life, and determined for yourself whether it is the case or not that man's life, in order to be profitable, joyful, and abiding, must be lived in God? Do you recognise that human life is not for the individual's good, but for the common good, and that only in God can each man find his place and his work? All that we give up to Him we have in an ampler form. The very affections which we are called to sacrifice are purified and deepened rather than lost. When Abraham resigned his son to God and received him back, their love took on a new delicacy and tenderness. They were more than ever to one another after this interference of God. And He meant it to be so. Where our affections are thwarted or where our hopes are blasted, it is not our injury, but our good, that is meant, a fineness and purity, an eternal significance and depth, are imparted to affections that are annealed by passing through the fire of trial.

Not till the last moment did God interpose with the gladdening words, "Lay not thine hand upon the lad, neither do thou anything unto him; for now I know that thou fearest God, seeing thou hast not withheld thy son, thine only son, from Me." The significance of this was so obvious that it passed into a proverb: "In the mount of the Lord it shall be provided." It was there, and not at any earlier point, Abraham saw the provision that had been made for an offering. Up to the moment when he lifted the knife over all he lived for, it was not seen that other provision was made. Up to the moment when it was indubitable that both he and Isaac were obedient unto death, and when in will and feeling they had sacrificed themselves, no substitute was visible, but no sooner was the sacrifice complete in spirit than God's provision was disclosed. It was the spirit of sacrifice, not the blood of Isaac, that God desired. It was the noble generosity of Abraham that God delighted in, not the fatherly grief that would have followed the actual death of Isaac. It was the heroic submission of father and son that God saw with delight, rejoicing that men were found capable of the utmost of heroism, of patient and unflinching adherence to duty. At any point short of the consummation, interposition would have come too soon, and would have prevented this educative and elevating display of the capacity of men for the utmost that life can require of them. Had the provision of God been made known one minute before the hand of Abraham was raised to strike, it would have remained doubtful whether in the critical moment one or other of the parties might not have failed. But when the sacrifice was complete, when already the bitterness of death was past, when all the agonizing conflict was over, the anguish of the father mastered, and the dismay of the son subdued to perfect conformity with the supreme will, then the full reward of victorious conflict was given, and God's meaning flashed through the darkness, and His provision was seen.

This is the universal law. We find God's provision only on the mount of sacrifice, not at any stage short of this, but only there. We must go the whole way in faith; what lies before us as duty, we must do; often in darkness and utter misery, seeing no possibility of escape or relief, we must climb the hill where we are to abandon all that has given joy and hope to our life; and not before the sacrifice has been actually made can we enter into the heaven of victory God provides. You may be called to sacrifice your youth, your hopes of a career, your affections, that you may uphold and soothe the lingering days of one to whom you are naturally bound. Or your whole life may have centred in an affection which circumstances demand you shall abandon; you may have to sacrifice your natural tastes and give up almost everything you once set your heart on; and while to others the years bring brightness and variety and scope, to you they may be bringing only monotonous fulfilment of insipid and uncongenial tasks. You may be in circumstances which tempt you to say, Does God see the inextricable difficulty I am in? Does He estimate the pain I must suffer if immediate relief do not come? Is obedience to Him only to involve me in misery from which other men are exempt? You may even say that although a substitute was found for Isaac, no substitute has been found for the sacrifice you have had to make, but you have been compelled actually to lose what was dear to you as life itself. But when the character has been fully tried, when the utmost good to character has been accomplished, and when delay of relief would only increase misery, then relief comes. Still the law holds good, that as soon as you in spirit yield to God's will, and with a quiet submissiveness consent to the loss or pain inflicted upon you, in that hour your whole attitude to your circumstances is transformed, you find rest and assured hope. Two things are certain: that, however painful your condition is, God's intention is not to injure, but to advance you, and that hopeful submission is wiser, nobler, and every way better than murmuring and resentment.

Finally, these words, "The Lord will provide," which Abraham uttered in that exalted frame of mind which is near to the prophetic ecstasy, have been the burden sung by every sincere and thoughtful worshipper as he ascended the hill of God to seek forgiveness of his sin, the burden which the Lord's worshipping congregation kept on its tongue through all the ages, till at length, as the angel of the Lord had opened the eyes of Abraham to see the ram provided, the voice of the Baptist "crying in the wilderness" to a fainting and well-nigh despairing few turned their eye to God's great provision with the final announcement, "Behold the Lamb of God." Let us accept this as a motto which we may apply, not only in all temporal straits, when we can see no escape from loss and misery, but also in all spiritual emergency, when sin seems a burden too great for us to bear, and when we seem to lie under the uplifted knife of God's judgment. Let us remember that God's desire is not that we suffer pain, but that we learn obedience, that we be brought to that true and thorough confidence in Him which may fit us to fulfil His loving purposes. Let us, above all, remember that we cannot know the grace of God, cannot experience the abundant provision He has made for weak and sinful men, until we have climbed the mount of sacrifice and are able to commit ourselves wholly to Him. Not by attacking our manifold enemies one by one, nor by attempting the great work of sanctification piecemeal, shall we ever make much growth or progress, but by giving ourselves up wholly to God and by becoming willing to live in Him and as His.

XVII
ISHMAEL AND ISAAC

Gen. xxi., xxii.

"Abraham had two sons, the one by a bondmaid, the other by a freewoman. * * * Which things are an allegory."—Galatians iv. 22.

"Abraham stretched forth his hand, and took the knife to slay his son."—Genesis xxii. 10.

In the birth of Isaac, Abraham at length sees the long-delayed fulfilment of the promise. But his trials are by no means over. He has himself introduced into his family the seeds of discord and disturbance, and speedily the fruit is borne. Ishmael, at the birth of Isaac, was a lad of fourteen years, and, reckoning from Eastern customs, he must have been over sixteen when the feast was made in honour of the weaned child. Certainly he was quite old enough to understand the important and not very welcome alteration in his prospects which the birth of this new son effected. He had been brought up to count himself the heir of all the wealth and influence of Abraham. There was no alienation of feeling between father and son: no shadow had flitted over the bright prospect of the boy as he grew up; when suddenly and unexpectedly there was interposed between him and his expectation the effectual barrier of this child of Sarah's. The importance of this child to the family was in due course indicated in many ways offensive to Ishmael; and when the feast was made, his spleen could no longer be repressed. This weaning was the first step in the direction of an independent existence, and this would be the point of the feast in celebration. The child was no longer a mere part of the mother, but an individual, a member of the family. The hopes of the parents were carried forward to the time when he should be quite independent of them.

But in all this there was great food for the ridicule of a thoughtless lad. It was precisely the kind of thing which could easily be mocked without any great expenditure of wit by a boy of Ishmael's age. The too visible pride of the aged mother, the incongruity of maternal duties with ninety years, the concentration of attention and honours on so small an object,—all this was, doubtless, a temptation to a boy who had probably at no time too much reverence. But the words and gestures which others might have disregarded as childish frolic, or, at worst, as the unseemly and ill-natured impertinence of a boy who knew no better, stung Sarah, and left a poison in her blood that infuriated her. "Cast out that bondwoman and her son," she demanded of Abraham. Evidently she feared the rivalry of this second household of Abraham, and was resolved it should come to an end. The mocking of Ishmael is but the violent concussion that at last produces the explosion, for which material has long been laid in train. She had seen on Abraham's part a clinging to Ishmael, which she was unable to appreciate. And though her harsh decision was nothing more than the dictate of maternal jealousy, it did prevent things from running on as they were until even a more painful family quarrel must have been the issue.

The act of expulsion was itself unaccountably harsh. There was nothing to prevent Abraham sending the boy and his mother under an escort to some safe place; nothing to prevent him from giving the lad some share of his possessions sufficient to provide for him. Nothing of this kind was done. The woman and the boy were simply put to the door; and this, although Ishmael had for years been counted Abraham's heir, and though he was a member of the covenant made with Abraham. There may have been some law giving Sarah absolute power over her maid; but if any law gave her power to do what was now done, it was a thoroughly barbarous one, and she was a barbarous woman who used it.

It is one of those painful cases in which one poor creature, clothed with a little brief authority, stretches it to the utmost in vindictive maltreatment of another. Sarah happened to be mistress, and, instead of using her position to make those under her happy, she used it for her own convenience, for the gratification of her own spite, and to make those beneath her conscious of her power by their suffering. She happened to be a mother, and instead of bringing her into sympathy with all women and their children, this concentrated her affection with a fierce jealousy on her own child. She breathed freely when Hagar and Ishmael were fairly out of sight. A smile of satisfied malice betrayed her bitter spirit. No thought of the sufferings to which she had committed a woman who had served her well for years, who had yielded everything to her will, and who had no other natural protector but her, no glimpses of Abraham's saddened face, visited her with any relentings. It mattered not to her what came of the woman and the boy to whom she really owed a more loving and careful regard than to any except Abraham and Isaac. It is a story often repeated. One who has been a member of the household for many years is at last dismissed at the dictate of some petty pique or spite as remorselessly and inhumanly as a piece of old furniture might be parted with. Some thoroughly good servant, who has made sacrifices to forward his employer's interest, is at last, through no offence of his own, found to be in his employer's way, and at once all old services are forgotten, all old ties broken, and the authority of the employer, legal but inhuman, is exercised. It is often those who can least defend themselves who are thus treated; no resistance is possible, and also, alas! the party is too weak to face the wilderness on which she is thrown out, and if any cares to follow her history, we may find her at the last gasp under a bush.

Still, both for Abraham and for Ishmael it was better this severance should take place. It was grievous to Abraham; and Sarah saw that for this very reason it was necessary. Ishmael was his first-born, and for many years had received the whole of his parental affection: and, looking on the little Isaac, he might feel the desirableness of keeping another son in reserve, lest this strangely-given child might as strangely pass away. Coming to him in a way so unusual, and having perhaps in his appearance some indication of his peculiar birth, he might seem scarcely fit for the rough life Abraham himself had led. On the other hand, it was plain that in Ishmael were the very qualities which Isaac was already showing that he lacked. Already Abraham was observing that with all his insolence and turbulence there was a natural force and independence of character which might come to be most useful in the patriarchal household. The man who had pursued and routed the allied kings could not but be drawn to a youth who already gave promise of capacity for similar enterprises—and this youth his own son. But can Abraham have failed to let his fancy picture the deeds this lad might one day do at the head of his armed slaves? And may he not have dreamt of a glory in the land not altogether such as the promise of God encouraged him to look for, but such as the tribes around would acknowledge and fear? All the hopes Abraham had of Ishmael had gained firm hold of his mind before Isaac was born; and before Isaac grew up, Ishmael must have taken the most influential place in the house and plans of Abraham. His mind would thus have received a strong bias towards conquest and forcible modes of advance. He might have been led to neglect, and, perhaps, finally despise, the unostentatious blessings of heaven.

If, then, Abraham was to become the founder, not of one new warlike power in addition to the already too numerous warlike powers of the East, but of a religion which should finally develop into the most elevating and purifying influence among men, it is obvious that Ishmael was not at all a desirable heir. Whatever pain it gave to Abraham to part with him, separation in some form had become necessary. It was impossible that the father should continue to enjoy the filial affection of Ishmael, his lively talk, and warm enthusiasm, and adventurous exploits, and at the same time concentrate his hope and his care on Isaac. He had, therefore, to give up, with something of the sorrow and self-control he afterwards underwent in connection with the sacrifice of Isaac, the lad whose bright face had for so many years shone in all his paths. And in some such way are we often called to part with prospects which have wrought themselves very deep into our spirit, and which, indeed, just because they are very promising and seductive, have become dangerous to us, upsetting the balance of our life, and throwing into the shade objects and purposes which ought to be outstanding. And when we are thus required to give up what we were looking to for comfort, for applause, and for profit, the voice of God in its first admonition sometimes seems to us little better than the jealousy of a woman. Like Sarah's demand, that none should share with her son, does the requirement seem which indicates to us that we must set nothing on a level with God's direct gifts to us. We refuse to see why we may not have all the pleasures and enjoyments, all the display and brilliance that the world can give. We feel as if we were needlessly restricted. But this instance shows us that when circumstances compel us to give up something of this kind which we have been cherishing, room is given for a better thing than itself to grow.

For Ishmael himself, too, wronged as he was in the mode of his expulsion, it was yet far better that he should go. Isaac *was* the true heir. No jeering allusions to his late birth or to his appearance could alter that fact. And to a temper like Ishmael's it was impossible to occupy a subordinate, dependent position. All he required to call out his latent powers was to be thrown thus on his own resources. The daring and high spirit and quickness to take offence and use violence, which would have wrought untold mischief in a pastoral camp, were the very qualities which found fit exercise in the desert, and seemed there only in keeping with the life he had to lead. And his hard experience at first would at his age do him no harm, but good only. To be compelled to face life single-handed at the age of sixteen is by no means a fate to be pitied. It was the making of Ishmael, and is the making of many a lad in every generation.

But the two fugitives are soon reminded that, though expelled from Abraham's tents and protection, they are not expelled from his God. Ishmael finds it true that when father and mother forsake him, the Lord takes him up. At the very outset of his desert life he is made conscious that God is still his God, mindful of his wants, responsive to his cry of distress. It was not through Ishmael the promised seed was to come, but the descendants of Ishmael had every inducement to retain faith in the God of Abraham, who listened to their father's cry. The fact of being excluded from certain privileges did not involve that they were to be excluded from all privileges. God still "heard the voice of the lad, and the angel of God called to Hagar out of heaven."

It is this voice of God to Hagar that so speedily, and apparently once for all, lifts her out of despair to cheerful hope. It would appear as if her despair had been needless; at least from the words addressed to her, "What aileth thee, Hagar?" it would appear as if she might herself have found the water that was close at hand, if only she had been disposed to look for it. But she had lost heart, and perhaps with her despair was mingled some resentment, not only at Sarah, but at the whole Hebrew connection, including the God of the Hebrews, who had before encouraged her. Here was the end of the magnificent promise which that God had made her before her child was born—a helpless human form gasping its life away without a drop of water to moisten the parched tongue and bring light to the glazing eyes, and with no easier couch than the burning sand. Was it for this, the bitterest drop that, apart from sin, can be given to any parent to drink, she had been brought from Egypt and led through all her past? Had her hopes been nursed by means so extraordinary only that they might be so bitterly blighted? Thus she leapt to her conclusions, and judged that because her skin of water had failed God had failed her too. No one can blame her, with her boy dying before her, and herself helpless to relieve one pang of his suffering. Hitherto in the well-furnished tents of Abraham she had been able to respond to his slightest desire. Thirst he had never known, save as the relish to some boyish adventure. But now, when his eyes appeal to her in dying anguish, she can but turn away in helpless despair. She cannot relieve his simplest want. Not for her own fate has she any tears, but to see her pride, her life and joy, perishing thus miserably, is more than she can bear.

No one can blame, but every one may learn from her. When angry resentment and unbelieving despair fill the mind, we may perish of thirst in the midst of springs. When God's promises produce no faith, but seem to us so much waste paper, we are necessarily in danger of missing their fulfilment. When we ascribe to God the harshness and wickedness of those who represent Him in the world, we commit moral suicide. So far from the promises given to Hagar being now at the point of extinction, this was the first considerable step towards their fulfilment. When Ishmael turned his back on the familiar tents, and flung his last gibe at Sarah, he was really setting out to a far richer inheritance, so far as this world goes, than ever fell to Isaac and his sons.

But the chief use Paul makes of this entire episode in the history is to see in it an allegory, a kind of picture made up of real persons and events, representing the impossibility of law and gospel living harmoniously together, the incompatibility of a spirit of service with a spirit of sonship. Hagar, he says, is in this picture the likeness of the law given from Sinai, which gendereth to bondage. Hagar and her son, that is to say, stand for the law and the kind of righteousness produced by the law,—not superficially a bad kind; on the contrary, a righteousness with much dash and brilliance and strong manly force about it, but at the root defective, faulty in its origin, springing from the slavish spirit. And first Paul bids us notice how the freeborn is persecuted and mocked by the slave-born, that is, how the children of God who are trying to live by love and faith in Christ are put to shame and made uneasy by the law. They believe they are God's dear children, that they are loved by Him, and may go out and in freely in His house as their own home, using all that is His with the freedom of His heirs; but the law mocks them, frightens them, tells them *it* is God's first-born, law lying far back in the dimness of eternity, coeval with God Himself. It tells them they are puny and weak, scarcely out of their mother's arms, tottering, lisping creatures, doing much mischief, but none of the housework, at best only getting some little thing to pretend to work at. In contrast to their feeble, soft, unskilled weakness, it sets before them a finely-moulded, athletic form, becoming disciplined to all work, and able to take a place among the serviceable and able-bodied. But with all this there is in that puny babe a life begun which will grow and make it the true heir, dwelling in the house and possessing what it has not toiled for, while the vigorous, likely-looking lad must go into the wilderness and make a possession for himself with his own bow and spear.

Now, of course, righteousness of life and character, or perfect manhood, is the end at which all that we call salvation aims, and that which can give us the purest, ripest character is salvation for us; that which can make us, for all purposes, most serviceable and strong. And when we are confronted with persons who might speak of service we cannot render, of an upright, unfaltering carriage we cannot assume, of a general human worthiness we can make no pretension to, we are justly perturbed, and should regain our equanimity only under the influence of the most undoubted truth and fact. If we can honestly say in our hearts, "Although we can show no such work done, and no such masculine growth, yet we have a life in us which is of

God, and will grow;" if we are sure that we have the spirit of God's children, a spirit of love and dutifulness, we may take comfort from this incident. We may remind ourselves that it is not he who has at the present moment the best appearance who always abides in the father's home, but he who is by birth the heir. Have we or have we not the spirit of the Son? not feeling that we must every evening make good our claim to another night's lodging by showing the task we have accomplished, but being conscious that the interests in which we are called to work are our own interests, that we are heirs in the father's house, so that all we do for the house is really done for ourselves. Do we go out and in with God, feeling no need of His commands, our own eye seeing where help is required, and our own desires being wholly directed towards that which engages all His attention and work?

For Paul would have each of us apply, allegorically, the words, Cast out the bondwoman and her son, that is, cast out the legal mode of earning a standing in God's house, and with this legal mode cast out all the self-seeking, the servile fear of God, the self-righteousness, and the hard-heartedness it engenders. Cast out wholly from yourself the spirit of the slave, and cherish the spirit of the son and heir. The slave-born may seem for a while to have a firm footing in the father's house, but it cannot last. The temper and tastes of Ishmael are radically different from those of Abraham, and when the slave-born becomes mature, the wild Egyptian strain will appear in his character. Moreover, he looks upon the goods of Abraham as plunder; he cannot rid himself of the feeling of an alien, and this would, at length, show itself in a want of frankness with Abraham—slowly, but surely, the confidence between them would be worn out. Nothing but being a child of God, being born of the Spirit, can give the feeling of intimacy, confidence, unity of interest, which constitutes true religion. All we do as slaves goes for nothing; that is to say, all we do, not because we see the good of it, but because we are commanded; not because we have any liking for the thing done, but because we wish to be paid for it. The day is coming when we shall attain our majority, when it will be said to us by God, Now, do whatever you like, whatever you have a mind to; no surveillance, no commands are now needed; I put all into your own hand. What, in these circumstances, should we straightway do? Should we, for the love of the thing, carry on the same work to which God's commands had driven us; should we, if left absolutely in charge, find nothing more attractive than just to prosecute that idea of life and the world set before us by Christ? Or, should we see that we had merely been keeping ourselves in check for a while, biding our time, untamed as Ishmael, craving the rewards but not the life of the children of God? The most serious of all questions these—questions that determine the issues of our whole life, that determine whether our home is to be where all the best interests of men and the highest blessings of God have their seat, or in the pathless desert where life is an aimless wandering, dissociated from all the forward movements of men.

The distinction between the servile spirit and the spirit of sonship being thus radical, it could be by no mere formality, or exhibition of his legal title, that Isaac became the heir of God's heritage. His sacrifice on Moriah was the requisite condition of his succession to Abraham's place; it was the only suitable celebration of his majority. Abraham himself had been able to enter into covenant with God only by sacrifice; and sacrifice not of a dead and external kind, but vivified by an actual surrender of himself to God, and by so true a perception of God's holiness and requirements, that he was in a horror of great darkness. By no other process can any of his heirs succeed to the inheritance. A true resignation of self, in whatever outward form this resignation may appear, is required that we may become one with God in His holy purposes and in His eternal blessedness. There could be no doubt that Abraham had found a true heir, when Isaac laid himself on the altar and steadied his heart to receive the knife. Dearer to God, and of immeasurably greater value than any service, was this surrender of himself into the hand of his Father and his God. In this was promise of all service and all loving fellowship. "Precious in the sight of the Lord is the death of His saints. O Lord, truly I am Thy servant; I am Thy servant, the son of Thine handmaid: Thou hast loosed my bonds."

So incomparable with the most distinguished service did this sacrifice of Isaac's self appear, that the record of his active life seems to have had no interest to his contemporaries or successors. There was but this one thing to say of him. No more seemed needful. The sacrifice was indeed great, and worthy of commemoration. No act could so conclusively have shown that Isaac was thoroughly at one with God. He had much to live for; from his birth there hovered around him interests and hopes of the most exciting and flattering nature; a new kind of glory such as had not yet been attained on earth was to be attained, or, at any rate, approached in him. This glory was certain to be realised, being guaranteed by God's promise, so that his hopes might launch out in the boldest confidence and give him the aspect and bearing of a king; while it was uncertain in the time and manner of its realisation, so that the most attractive mystery hung around his future. Plainly his was a life worth entering on and living through; a life fit to engage and absorb a man's whole desire, interest, and effort; a life such as might well make a man gird himself and resolve to play the man throughout, that so each part of it might reveal its secret to him, and that none of its wonder might be lost. It was a life which, above all others, seemed worth protecting from all injury and risk, and for which, no doubt, not a few of the home-born servants in the patriarchal encampment would have gladly ventured their own. There have, indeed, been few, if any, lives of which it could so truly be said, The world cannot do without this—at all hazards and costs this must be cherished. And all this must have been even more obvious to its owner than to any one else, and must have begotten in him an unquestioning assurance, that he at least had a charmed life, and would live and see good days. Yet with whatever shock the command of God came upon him, there is no word of doubt or remonstrance or rebellion. He gave his life to Him who had first given it to him. And thus yielding himself to God, he entered into the inheritance, and became worthy to stand to all time the representative heir of God, as Abraham by his faith had become the father of the faithful.

XVIII
PURCHASE OF MACHPELAH

Genesis xxiii.

It may be supposed to be a needless observation that our life is greatly influenced by the fact that it speedily and certainly ends in death. But it might be interesting, and it would certainly be surprising, to trace out the various ways in which this fact influences life. Plainly every human affair would be altered if we lived on here for ever, supposing that were possible. What the world would be had we no predecessors, no wisdom but what our own past experience and the genius of one generation of men could produce, we can scarcely imagine. We can scarcely imagine what life would be or what the world would be did not one generation succeed and oust another and were we contemporary with the whole process of history. It is the grand irreversible and universal law that we give place and make room for others. The individual passes away, but the history of the race proceeds. Here on earth in the meantime, and not elsewhere, the history of the race is being played out, and each having done his part, however small or however great, passes away. Whether an individual, even the most gifted and powerful, could continue to be helpful to the race for thousands of years, supposing his life were continued, it is needless to inquire. Perhaps as steam has force only at a certain pressure, so human force requires the condensation of a brief life to give it elastic energy. But these are idle speculations. They show us, however, that our life beyond death will be not so much a prolongation of life as we now know it as an entire change in the form of our existence; and they show us also that our little piece of the world's work must be quickly done if it is to be done at all, and that it will not be done at all unless we take our life seriously and own the responsibilities we have to ourselves, to our fellows, to our God.

Death comes sadly to the survivor, even when there is as little untimeliness as in the case of Sarah; and as Abraham moved towards the familiar tent the most intimate of his household would stand aloof and respect his grief. The stillness that struck upon him, instead of the usual greeting, as he lifted the tent-door; the dead order of all inside; the one object that lay stark before him and drew him again and again to look on what grieved him most to see; the chill which ran through him as his lips touched the cold, stony forehead and gave him sensible evidence how gone was the spirit from the clay—these are shocks to the human heart not peculiar to Abraham. But few have been so strangely bound together as these two were, or have been so manifestly given to one another by God, or have been forced to so close a mutual dependence. Not only had they grown up in the same family, and been together separated from their kindred, and passed through unusual and difficult circumstances together, but they were made co-heirs of God's promise in such a manner that neither could enjoy it without the other. They were knit together, not merely by natural liking and familiarity of intercourse, but by God's choosing them as the instrument of His work and the fountain of His salvation. So that in Sarah's death Abraham doubtless read an intimation that his own work was done, and that his generation is now out of date and ready to be supplanted.

Abraham's grief is interrupted by the sad but wholesome necessity which forces us from the blank desolation of watching by the dead to the active duties that follow. She whose beauty had captivated two princes must now be buried out of sight. So Abraham stands up from before his dead. Such a moment requires the resolute fortitude and manly self-control which that expression seems intended to suggest. There is something within us which rebels against the ordinary ongoing of the world side by side with our great woe; we feel as if either the whole world must mourn with us, or we must go aside from the world and have our grief out in private. The bustle of life seems so meaningless and incongruous to one whom grief has emptied of all relish for it. We seem to wrong the dead by every return of interest we show in the things of life which no longer interest *him*. Yet he speaks truly who says:—

> "When sorrow all our heart would ask,
> We need not shun our daily task,
> And hide ourselves for calm;
> The herbs we seek to heal our woe,
> Familiar by our pathway grow,
> Our common air is balm."

We must resume our duties, not as if nothing had happened, not proudly forgetting death and putting grief aside as if this life did not need the chastening influence of such realities as we have been engaged with, or as if its business could not be pursued in an affectionate and softened spirit, but acknowledging death as real and as humbling and sobering.

Abraham then goes forth to seek a grave for Sarah, having already with a common predilection fixed on the spot where he himself would prefer to be laid. He goes accordingly to the usual meeting-place or exchange of these times, the city-gate, where bargains were made, and where witnesses for their ratification could always be had. Men who are familiar with Eastern customs rather spoil for us the scene described in this chapter by assuring us that all these courtesies and large offers are merely the ordinary forms preliminary to a bargain, and were as little meant to be literally understood as we mean to be literally understood when we sign ourselves "your most obedient servant." Abraham asks the Hittite chiefs to approach Ephron on the subject, because all bargains of the kind are negotiated through mediators. Ephron's offer of the cave and field is merely a form. Abraham quite understood that Ephron only indicated his willingness to deal, and so he urges him to state his price, which Ephron is not slow to do; and apparently his price was a handsome one such as he could not have asked from a poorer man, for he adds, "What are four hundred shekels between wealthy men like you and me? Without more words let the bargain be closed—bury thy dead."

The first landed property, then, of the patriarchs is a grave. In this tomb were laid Abraham and Sarah, Isaac and Rebecca; here, too, Jacob buried Leah, and here Jacob himself desired to be laid after his death, his last words being, "Bury me with my fathers in the cave that is in the field of Ephron the Hittite." This grave, therefore, becomes the centre of the land. Where the dust of our fathers is, there is our country; and as you may often hear aged persons, who are content to die and have little else to pray for, still express a wish that they may rest in the old well-remembered churchyard where their kindred lie, and may thus in the weakness of death find some comfort, and in its solitariness some companionship from the presence of those who tenderly sheltered the helplessness of their childhood; so does this place of the dead become henceforth the centre of attraction for all Abraham's seed to which still from Egypt their longings and hopes turn, as to the one magnetic point which, having once been fixed there, binds them ever to the land. It is this grave which binds them to the land. This laying of Sarah in the tomb is the real occupation of the land.

During the lapse of ages, all around this spot has been changed again and again; but at some remote period, possibly as early as the time of David, the reverence of the Jews built these tombs round with masonry so substantial that it still endures. Within the space thus enclosed there stood for long a Christian church, but since the Mohammedan domination was established, a mosque has covered the spot. This mosque has been guarded against Christian intrusion with a jealousy almost as rigid as that which excludes all unbelievers from approaching Mecca. And though the Prince of Wales was a few years ago allowed to enter the mosque, he was not permitted to make any examination of the vaults beneath, where the original tomb must be.

It is evident that this narrative of the purchase of Machpelah and the burial of Sarah was preserved, not so much on account of the personal interest which Abraham had in these matters, as on account of the manifest significance they had in connection with the history of his faith. He had recently heard from his own kindred in Mesopotamia, and it might very naturally have occurred to him that the proper place to bury Sarah was in his fatherland. The desire to lie among one's people is a very strong Eastern sentiment. Even tribes which have no dislike to emigration make provision that at death their bodies shall be restored to their own country. The Chinese notoriously do so. Abraham, therefore, could hardly have expressed his faith in a stronger form than by purchasing a burying-ground for himself in Canaan. It was equivalent to saying in the most emphatic form that he believed this country would remain in perpetuity the country of his children and people. He had as yet given no such pledge as this was, that he had irrevocably abandoned his fatherland. He had bought no other landed property; he had built no house. He shifted his encampment from place to place as convenience dictated, and there was nothing to hinder him from returning at any time to his old country. But now he fixed himself down; he said, as plainly as acts can say, that his mind was made up that this was to be in all time coming his land; this was no mere right of pasture rented for the season, no mere waste land he might occupy with his tents till its owner wished to reclaim it; it was no estate he could put into the market whenever trade should become dull and he might wish to realise or to leave the country; but it was a kind of property which he could not sell and could not abandon.

Again, his determination to hold it in perpetuity is evident not only from the nature of the property, but also from the formal purchase and conveyance of it—the complete and precise terms in which the transaction is completed. The narrative is careful to remind us again and again that the whole transaction was negotiated in the audience of the people of the land, of all those who went in at the gate, that the sale was thoroughly approved and witnessed by competent authorities. The precise subjects made over to Abraham are also detailed with all the accuracy of a legal document—"the field of Ephron, which was in Machpelah, which was before Mamre, the field and the cave which was therein, and all the trees that were in the field, that were in all the borders round about, were made sure unto Abraham for a possession in the presence of the children of Heth, before all that went in at the gate of his city." Abraham had no doubt of the friendliness of such men as Aner, Eshcol, and Mamre, his ancient allies, but he was also aware that the best way to maintain friendly relations was to leave no loophole by which difference of opinion or disagreement might enter. Let the thing be in black and white, so that there may be no misunderstanding as to terms, no expectations doomed to be unfulfilled, no encroachments which must cause resentment, if not retaliation. Law probably does more to prevent quarrels than to heal them. As statesmen and historians tell us that the best way to secure peace is to be prepared for war, so legal documents seem no doubt harsh and unfriendly, but really are more effective in maintaining peace and friendliness than vague promises and benevolent intentions. In arranging affairs and engagements one is always tempted to say, Never mind about the money, see how the thing turns out and we can settle that by-and-bye; or, in looking at a will, one is tempted to ask, of what strength is Christian feeling—not to say family affection—if all these hard-and-fast lines need to be drawn round the little bit of property which each is to have? But experience shows that this is false delicacy, and that kindliness and charity may be as fully and far more safely expressed in definite and legal terms than in loose promises or mere understandings.

Again, Abraham's idea in purchasing this sepulchre is brought out by the circumstance that he would not accept the offer of the children of Heth to use one of their sepulchres. This was not pride of blood or any feeling of that sort, but the right feeling that what God had promised as His own peculiar gift must not seem to be given by men. Possibly no great harm might have come of it if Abraham had accepted the gift of a mere cave, or a shelf in some other man's burying-ground; but Abraham could not bear to think that any captious person should ever be able to say that the inheritance promised by God was really the gift of a Hittite.

Similar captiousness appears not only in the experience of the individual Christian, but also in the treatment religion gets from the world. It is quite apparent, that is to say, that the world counts itself the real proprietor here, and Christianity a stranger fortunately or unfortunately thrown upon its shores and upon *its mercy*. One cannot miss noticing the patronising way of the world towards the Church and all that is connected with it, as if it alone could give it those things needful for its prosperity—and especially willing is it to come forward in the Hittite fashion and offer to the sojourner a sepulchre where it may be decently buried, and as a dead thing lie out of the way.

But thoughts of a still wider reach were no doubt suggested to Abraham by this purchase. Often must he have brooded on the sacrifice of Isaac, seeking to exhaust its meaning. Many a talk in the dusk must his son and he have had about that most strange experience. And no doubt the one thing that seemed always certain about it was, that it is through death a man truly becomes the heir of God; and here again in this purchase of a tomb for Sarah it is the same fact that stares him in the face. He becomes a proprietor when death enters his family; he himself, he feels, is likely to have no more than this burial-acre of possession of his land; it is only by dying he enters on actual possession. Till then he is but a tenant, not a proprietor; as he says to the children of Heth, he is but a stranger and a sojourner among them, but at death he will take up his permanent dwelling in their midst. Was this not to suggest to him that there might be a deeper meaning underlying this, and that possibly it was only by death he could enter fully into all that God intended he should receive? No doubt in the first instance it was a severe trial to his faith to find that even at his wife's death he had acquired no firmer foothold in the land. No doubt it was the very triumph of his faith that though he himself had never had a settled, permanent residence in the land, but had dwelt in tents, moving about from place to place, just as he had done the first year of his entrance upon it, yet he died in the unalterable persuasion that the land was his, and that it would one day be filled with his descendants. It was the triumph of his faith that he believed in the performance of the promise as he had originally understood it; that he believed in the gift of the actual visible land. But it is difficult to believe that he did not come to the persuasion that God's friendship was more than any single thing He promised; difficult to suppose he did not feel something of what our Lord expressed in the words that God is the God of the living, not of the dead; that those who are His enter by death into some deeper and richer experience of His love.

Such is the interpretation put upon Abraham's attitude of mind by the writer, who of all others saw most deeply into the moving principles of the Old Testament dispensation and the connection between old things and new—I mean the writer of the Epistle to the Hebrews. He says that persons who act as Abraham did declare plainly that they seek a country; and if on finding they did not get the country in which they sojourned they thought the promise had failed, they might, he says, have found opportunity to return to the country whence they came at first. And why did they not do so? Because they sought a better, that is, an heavenly country. Wherefore God is not ashamed to be called their God, for He hath prepared for them a city; as if He said, God would have been ashamed of Abraham if he had been content with less, and had not aspired to something more than he received in the land of Canaan.

Now how else could Abraham's mind have been so effectually lifted to this exalted hope as by the disappointment of his original and much tamer hope? Had he gained possession of the land in the ordinary way of purchase or conquest, and had he been able to make full use of it for the purposes of life; had he acquired meadows where his cattle might graze, towns where his followers might establish themselves, would he not almost certainly have fallen into the belief that in these pastures and by his worldly wealth and quiet and prosperity he was already exhausting God's promise regarding the land? But buying the land for his dead he is forced to enter upon it from the right side, with the idea that not by present enjoyment of its fertility is God's promise to him exhausted. Both in the getting of his heir and in the acquisition of his land his mind is led to contemplate things beyond the range of earthly vision and earthly success. He is led to the thought that God having become his God, this means blessing eternal as God Himself. In short Abraham came to believe in a life beyond the grave on very much the same grounds as many people still rely on. They feel that this life has an unaccountable poverty and meagreness in it. They feel that they themselves are much larger than the life here allotted to them. They are out of proportion. It may be said that this is their own fault; they should make life a larger, richer thing. But that is only apparently true; the very brevity of life, which no skill of theirs can alter, is itself a limiting and disappointing condition. Moreover, it seems unworthy of God as well as of man. As soon as a worthy conception of God possesses the soul, the idea of immortality forthwith follows it. We instinctively feel that God can do far more for us than is done in this life. Our knowledge of Him here is most rudimentary; our connection with Him obscure and perplexed, and wanting in fulness of result; we seem scarcely to know whose we are, and scarcely to be reconciled to the essential conditions of life, or even to God;—we are, in short, in a very different kind of life from that which we can conceive and desire. Besides, a serious belief in God, in a personal Spirit, removes at a touch all difficulties arising from materialism. If God lives and yet has no senses or bodily appearance, we also may so live; and if His is the higher state and the more enjoyable state, we need not dread to experience life as disembodied spirits.

It is certainly a most acceptable lesson that is read to us here—viz., that God's promises do not shrivel, but grow solid and expand as we grasp them. Abraham went out to enter on possession of a few fields a little richer than his own, and he found an eternal inheritance. Naturally we think quite the opposite of God's promises; we fancy they are grandiloquent and magnify things, and that the actual fulfilment will prove unworthy of the language describing it. But as the woman who came to touch the hem of Christ's garment with some dubious hope that thus her body might be healed, found herself thereby linked to Christ for evermore, so always, if we meet God at any one point and honestly trust Him for even the smallest gift, He makes that the means of introducing Himself to us and getting us to understand the value of His better gifts. And indeed, if this life were all, might not God well be ashamed to call Himself our God? When He calls Himself our God He bids us expect to find in Him inexhaustible resources to protect and satisfy and enrich us. He bids us cherish boldly all innocent and natural desires, believing that we have in Him one who can gratify every such desire. But if this life be all, who can say existence has been perfectly satisfactory—if there be no reversal of what has here gone wrong, no restoration of what has here been lost, if there be no life in which conscience and ideas and hopes find their fulfilment and satisfaction, who can say he is content and could ask no more of God? Who can say he does not see what more God could do for him than has here been done? Doubtless there are many happy lives, doubtless there are lives which carry in them a worthiness and a sacredness which manifest God's presence, but even such lives only more powerfully suggest a state in which all lives shall be holy and happy, and in which, freed from inward uneasiness and shame and sorrow, we shall live unimpeded the highest life, life as we feel it ought to be. The very joys men have here experienced suggest to them the desirableness of continued life; the love they have known can only intensify their yearning for this perpetual enjoyment; their whole experience of this life has served to reveal to them the endless possibilities of growth and of activity that are bound up in human nature; and if death is to end all this, what more has life been to any of us than a seed-time without a harvest, an education without any sphere of employment, a vision of good that can never be ours, a striving after the unattainable? If this is all that God can give us we must indeed be disappointed in Him.

But He is disappointed in us if we do not aspire to more than this. In this sense also He is ashamed to be called our God. He is ashamed to be known as the God of men who never aspire to higher blessings than earthly comfort and present prosperity. He is ashamed to be known as connected with those who think so lightly of His power that they look for nothing beyond what every man calculates on getting in this world. God means all present blessings and all blessings of a lower kind to lure us on to trust Him and seek more and more from Him. In these early promises of His He says nothing expressly and distinctly of things eternal. He appeals to the immediate wants and present longings of men—just as our Lord while on earth drew men to Himself by healing their diseases. Take, then, any one promise of God, and, however small it seems at first, it will grow in your hand; you will find always that you get more than you bargained for, that you cannot take even a little without going further and receiving all.

XIX
ISAAC'S MARRIAGE

Genesis xxiv.

"Favour is deceitful, and beauty is vain: but a woman that feareth the Lord, she shall be praised."—Prov. xxxi. 30.

"When a son has attained the age of twenty years, his father, if able, should marry him, and then take his hand and say, I have disciplined thee, and taught thee, and married thee; I now seek refuge with God from thy mischief in the present world and the next." This Mohammedan tradition expresses with tolerable accuracy the idea of the Eastern world, that a father has not discharged his responsibilities towards his son until he finds a wife for him. Abraham no doubt fully recognised his duty in this respect, but he had allowed Isaac to pass the usual age. He was thirty-seven at his mother's death, forty when the events of this chapter occurred. This delay was occasioned by two causes. The bond between Isaac and his mother was an unusually strong one; and alongside of that imperious woman a young wife would have found it even more difficult than usual to take a becoming place. Besides, where was a wife to be found? No doubt some of Abraham's Hittite friends would have considered any daughter of theirs exceptionally fortunate who should secure so good an alliance. The heir of Abraham was no inconsiderable person even when measured by Hittite expectations. And it may have taxed Abraham's sagacity to find excuses for not forming an alliance which seemed so natural, and which would have secured to him and his heirs a settled place in the country. This was so obvious, common, easily accomplished a means of gaining a footing for Isaac among somewhat dangerous neighbours, that it stands to reason Abraham must often have weighed its advantages.

But as often as he weighed the advantages of this solution of his difficulty, so often did he reject them. He was resolved that the race should be of pure Hebrew blood. His own experience in connection with Hagar had given this idea a settled prominence in his mind. And, accordingly, in his instructions to the servant whom he sent to find a wife for Isaac, two things were insisted on—1st, that she should not be a Canaanite; and, 2nd, that on no pretext should Isaac be allowed to leave the land of promise and visit Mesopotamia. The steward, knowing something of men and women, foresaw that it was most unlikely that a young woman would forsake her own land and preconceived hopes and go away with a stranger to a foreign country. Abraham believes she will be persuaded. But in any case, he says, one thing must be seen to; Isaac must on no account be induced to leave the promised land even to visit Mesopotamia. God will furnish Isaac with a wife without putting him into circumstances of great temptation, without requiring him to go into societies in the slightest degree injurious to his faith. In fact, Abraham refused to do what countless Christian mothers of marriageable sons and daughters do without compunction. He had an insight into the real influences that form action and determine careers which many of us sadly lack.

And his faith was rewarded. The tidings from his brother's family arrived in the nick of time. Light, he found, was sown for the upright. It happened with him as it has doubtless often happened with ourselves, that though we have been looking forward to a certain time with much anxiety, unable even to form a plan of action, yet when the time actually came, things seemed to arrange themselves, and the thing to do became quite obvious. Abraham was persuaded God would send His angel to bring the affair to a happy issue. And when we seem drifting towards some great upturning of our life, or when things seem to come all of a sudden and in crowds upon us, so that we cannot judge what we should do, it is an animating thought that another eye than ours is penetrating the darkness, finding for us a way through all entanglement and making crooked things straight for us.

But the patience of Isaac was quite as remarkable as the faith of Abraham. He was now forty years old, and if, as he had been told, the great aim of his life, the great service he was to render to the world, was bound up with the rearing of a family, he might with some reason be wondering why circumstances were so adverse to the fulfilment of this vocation. Must he not have been tempted, as his father had been, to take matters into his own hand? Fathers are perhaps too scrupulous about telling their sons instructive passages from their own experience; but when Abraham saw Isaac exercised and discomposed about this matter, he can scarcely have failed to strengthen his spirit by telling him something of his own mistakes in life. Abraham must have seen that everything depended on Isaac's conduct, and that he had a very difficult part to play. He himself had been supernaturally encouraged to leave his own land and sojourn in Canaan;

on the other hand, by the time Jacob grew up, the idea of the promised land had become traditional and fixed; though even Jacob, had he found Laban a better master, might have permanently renounced his expectations in Canaan. But Isaac enjoyed the advantages neither of the first nor of the third generation. The coming into Canaan was not his doing, and he saw how little of the land Abraham had gained. He was under strong temptation to disbelieve. And when he measured his condition with that of other young men, he certainly required unusual self-control. And to every one who would urge, Youth is passing, and I am not getting what I expected at God's hand; I have not received that providential leading I was led to expect, nor do I find that my life is made simpler; it is very well to tell me to wait, but life is slipping away, and we may wait too long—to every one whose heart urges such murmurs, Abraham through Isaac would say: But if you wait for God you get something, some positive good, and not some mere appearance of good; you at last do get begun, you get into life at the right door; whereas if you follow some other way than that which you believe God wishes to lead you in, you get nothing.

Isaac's continence had its reward. In the suitableness of Rebekah to a man of his nature, we see the suitableness of all such gifts of God as are really waited for at His hand. God may keep us longer waiting than the world does, but He gives us never the wrong thing. Isaac had no idea of Rebekah's character; he could only yield himself to God's knowledge of what he needed; and so there came to him, from a country he had never seen, a help-meet singularly adapted to his own character. One cannot read of her lively, bustling, almost forward, but obliging and generous conduct at the well, nor of her prompt, impulsive departure to an unknown land, without seeing, as no doubt Eliezer very quickly saw, that this was exactly the woman for Isaac. In this eager, ardent, active, enterprising spirit, his own retiring and contemplative, if not sombre disposition found its appropriate relief and stimulus. Hers was a spirit which might indeed, with so mild a lord, take more of the management of affairs than was befitting; and when the wear and tear of life had tamed down the girlish vivacity with which she spoke to Eliezer at the well, and leapt from the camel to meet her lord, her active-mindedness does appear in the disagreeable shape of the clever scheming of the mother of a family. In her sons you see her qualities exaggerated: from her, Esau derived his activity and open-handedness; and in Jacob, you find that her self-reliant and unscrupulous management has become a self-asserting craft which leads him into much trouble, if it also sometimes gets him out of difficulties. But such as Rebekah was, she was quite the woman to attract Isaac and supplement his character.

So in other cases where you find you must leave yourself very much in God's hand, what He sends you will be found more precisely adapted to your character than if you chose it for yourself. You find your whole nature has been considered,—your aims, your hopes, your wants, your position, whatever in you waits for something unattained. And as in giving to Isaac the intended mother of the promised seed, God gave him a woman who fitted in to all the peculiarities of his nature, and was a comfort and a joy to him in his own life; so we shall always find that God, in satisfying His own requirements, satisfies at the same time our wants—that God carries forward His work in the world by the satisfaction of the best and happiest feelings of our nature, so that it is not only the result that is blessedness, but blessing is created along its whole course.

Abraham's servant, though not very sanguine of success, does all in his power to earn it. He sets out with an equipment fitted to inspire respect and confidence. But as he draws nearer and nearer to the city of Nahor, revolving the delicate nature of his errand, and feeling that definite action must now be taken, he sees so much room for making an irreparable mistake that he resolves to share his responsibility with the God of his master. And the manner in which he avails himself of God's guidance is remarkable. He does not ask God to guide him to the house of Bethuel; indeed, there was no occasion to do so, for any child could have pointed out the house to him. But he was a cautious person, and he wished to make his own observations on the appearance and conduct of the younger women of the household, before in any way committing himself to them. He was free to make these observations at the well; while he felt it must be very awkward to enter Laban's house with the possibility of leaving it dissatisfied. At the same time, he felt it was for God rather than for him to choose a wife for Isaac. So he made an arrangement by which the interposition of God was provided for. He meant to make his own selection, guided necessarily by the comparative attractiveness of the women who came for water, possibly also by some family likeness to Sarah or Isaac he might expect to see in any women of Bethuel's house; but knowing the deceitfulness of appearances, he asked God to confirm and determine his own choice by moving the girl he should address to give him a certain answer. Having arranged this, "Behold! Rebekah came out with her pitcher upon her shoulder, and the damsel was very fair to look upon." In the Bible the beauty of women is frankly spoken of without prudery or mawkishness as an influence in human affairs. The beauty of Rebekah at once disposed Eliezer to address her, and his first impression in her favour was confirmed by the obliging, cheerful alacrity with which she did very much more than she was asked, and, indeed, took upon herself, through her kindness of disposition, a task of some trouble and fatigue.

It is important to observe then in what sense and to what extent this capable servant asked a sign. He did not ask for a bare, intrinsically insignificant sign. He might have done so. He might have proposed as a test, Let her who stumbles on the first step of the well be the designed wife of Isaac; or, Let her who comes with a certain-coloured flower in her hand— or so forth. But the sign he chose was significant, because dependent on the character of the girl herself; a sign which must reveal her good-heartedness and readiness to oblige and courteous activity in the entertainment of strangers—in fact, the outstanding Eastern virtue. So that he really acted very much as Isaac himself must have done. He would make no approach to any one whose appearance repelled him; and when satisfied in this particular, he would test her disposition. And of course it was these qualities of Rebekah which afterwards caused Isaac to feel that this was the wife God had designed for him. It was not by any arbitrary sign that he or any man could come to know who was the suitable wife for him, but only by the love she aroused within him. God has given this feeling to direct choice in marriage; and where this is wanting, nothing else whatever, no matter how astoundingly providential it seems, ought to persuade a man that such and such a person is designed to be his wife.

There are turning points in life at once so momentous in their consequence, and affording so little material for choice, that one is much tempted to ask for more than providential leading. Not only among savages and heathen have omens been sought. Among Christians there has been manifest a constant disposition to appeal to the lot, or to accept some arbitrary way of determining which course we should follow. In very many predicaments we should be greatly relieved were there some one who could at once deliver us from all hesitation and mental conflict by one authoritative word. There are, perhaps, few things more frequently and determinedly wished for, nor regarding which we are so much tempted to feel that such a thing should be, as some infallible guide before whom we could lay every difficulty; who would tell us at once what ought to be done in each case, and whether we ought to continue as we are or make some change. But only consider for a moment what would be the consequence of having such a guide. At every important step of your progress you would, of course, instantly turn to him; as soon as doubt entered your mind regarding the moral quality of an action, or the propriety of a course you think of adopting, you would be at your counsellor. And what would be the consequence? The consequence would be, that instead of the various circumstances, experiences, and temptations of this life being a training to you, your conscience would every day become less able to guide you, and your will less able to decide, until, instead of being a mature son of God, who has learned to conform his conscience and will to the will of God, you would be quite imbecile as a moral creature. What God desires by our training here is, that we become like to Him; that there be nurtured in us a power to discern between good and evil; that by giving our own voluntary consent to His appointments, and that by discovering in various and perplexing circumstances what is the right thing to do, we may have our own moral natures as enlightened, strengthened, and fully developed every way as possible. The object of God in declaring His will to us is not to point out particular steps, but to bring our wills into conformity with His, so that whether we err in any particular step or no, we shall still be near to Him in intention. He does with us as we with children. We do not always at once relieve them from their little difficulties, but watch with interest the working of their own conscience regarding the matter, and will give them no sign till they themselves have decided.

Evidently, therefore, before we may dare to ask a sign from God, the case must be a very special one. If you are at present engaged in something that is to your own conscience doubtful, and if you are not hiding this from God, but would very willingly, so far as you know your own mind, do in the matter what He pleases—if no further light is coming to you, and you feel a growing inclination to put it to God in this way: "Grant, O Lord, that something may happen by which I may know Thy mind in this matter"—this is asking from God a kind of help which He is very ready to give, often leading men to clearer views of duty by events which happen within their knowledge, and which having no special significance to persons whose minds are differently occupied, are yet most instructive to those who are waiting for light on some particular point. The danger is not here, but in fixing God down to the special thing which shall happen as a sign between Him and you; which, when it happens, gives no fresh light on the subject, leaves your mind still *morally* undecided, but only binds you, by an arbitrary bargain of your own, to follow one course rather than another. This matter that you would so summarily dispose of may be the very thread of your life which God means to test you by; this state of indecision which you would evade, God may mean to continue until your moral character grows strong enough to rise above it to the right decision.

No one will suppose that Rebekah's readiness to leave her home was due to mere light-mindedness. Her motives were no doubt mixed. The worldly position offered to her was good, and there was an attractive spice of romance about the whole affair which would have its charm. She may also be credited with some apprehension of the great future of Isaac's family. In after life she certainly showed a very keen sense of the value of the blessings peculiar to that household. And, probably above all, she had an irresistible feeling that this was her destiny. She saw the hand of God in her selection, and with a more or less conscious faith in God she passed to her new life.

Her first meeting with her future husband is not the least picturesque passage in this most picturesque narrative. Isaac had gone out on that side of the encampment by which he knew his father's messenger was most likely to approach. He had gone out "to meditate at even-tide;" his meditation being necessarily directed and intensified by his attitude of critical expectancy.

The evening light, in our country hanging dubiously between the glare of noon and the darkness of midnight, invites to that condition of mind which lies between the intense alertness of day and the deep oblivion of sleep, and which seems the most favourable for the meditation of divine things. The dusk of evening seems interposed between day and night to invite us to that reflection which should intervene betwixt our labour and our rest from labour, that we may leave our work behind us satisfied that we have done what we could, or, seeing its faultiness, may still lay us down to sleep with God's forgiveness. It is when the bright sunlight has gone, and no more reproaches our inactivity, that friends can enjoy prolonged intercourse, and can best unbosom to one another, as if the darkness gave opportunity for a tenderness which would be ashamed to show itself during the twelve hours in which a man shall work. And all that makes this hour so beloved by the family circle, and so conducive to friendly intercourse, makes it suitable also for such intercourse with God as each human soul can attempt. Most of us suppose we have some little plot of time railed off for God morning and evening, but how often does it get trodden down by the profane multitude of this world's cares, and quite occupied by encroaching secular engagements. But evening is the time when many men are, and when all men ought to be least hurried; when the mind is placid, but not yet prostrate; when the body requires rest from its ordinary labour, but is not yet so oppressed with fatigue as to make devotion a mockery; when the din of this world's business is silenced, and as a sleeper wakes to consciousness when some accustomed noise is checked, so the soul now wakes up to the thought of itself and of God. I know not whether those of us who have the opportunity have also the resolution to sequester ourselves evening by evening, as Isaac did; but this I do know, that he who does so will not fail of his reward, but will very speedily find that his Father who seeth in secret is manifestly rewarding him. What we all need above all things is to let the mind *dwell* on divine things—to be able to sit down knowing we have so much clear time in which we shall not be disturbed, and during which we shall think directly under God's eye—to get quite rid of the feeling of getting through with something, so that without distraction the soul may take a deliberate survey of its own matters. And so shall often God's gifts appear on our horizon when we lift up our eyes, as Isaac "lifted up his eyes and saw the camels coming" with his bride.

Twilight, "nature's vesper-bell," or the light shaded at evening by the hills of Palestine, seems, then, to have called Isaac to a familiar occupation. This long-continued mourning for his mother, and his lonely meditation in the fields, are both in harmony with what we know of his character, and of his experience on Mount Moriah. Retiring and contemplative, willing to conciliate by concession rather than to assert and maintain his rights against opposition, glad to yield his own affairs to the strong guidance of some other hand, tender and deep in his affections, to him this lonely meditation seems singularly appropriate. His dwelling, too, was remote, on the edge of the wilderness, by the well which Hagar had named Lahai-roi. Here he dwelt as one consecrated to God, feeling little desire to enter deeper into the world, and preferring the place where the presence of God was least disturbed by the society of men. But at this time he had come from the south, and was awaiting at his father's encampment the result of Eliezer's mission. And one can conceive the thrill of keen expectancy that shot through him as he saw the female figure alighting from the camel, the first eager exchange of greetings, and the gladness with which he brought Rebekah into his mother Sarah's tent and was comforted after his mother's death. The readiness with which he loved her seems to be referred in the narrative to the grief he still felt for his mother; for as a candle is never so easily lit as just after it has been put out, so the affection of Isaac, still emitting the sad memorial of a past love, more quickly caught at the new object presented. And thus was consummated a marriage which shows us how thoroughly interwrought are the plans of God and the life of man, each fulfilling the other.

For as the salvation God introduces into the world is a practical, everyday salvation to deliver us from the sins which this life tempts us to, so God introduced this salvation by means of the natural affections and ordinary arrangements of human life. God would have us recognise in our lives what He shows us in this chapter, that He has made provision for our wants, and that if we wait upon Him He will bring us into the enjoyment of all we really need. So that if we are to make any advance in appropriating to ourselves God's salvation, it can only be by submitting ourselves implicitly to His providence, and taking care that in the commonest and most secular actions of our lives we are having respect to His will with us, and that in those actions in which our own feelings and desires seem sufficient to guide us, we are having regard to His controlling wisdom and goodness. We are to find room for God everywhere in our lives, not feeling embarrassed by the thought of His claims even in our least constrained hours, but subordinating to His highest and holiest ends everything that our life contains, and acknowledging as His gift what may seem to be our own most proper conquest or earning.

XX
ESAU AND JACOB

Genesis xxv.

"He goeth as an ox goeth to the slaughter, till a dart strike through his liver; as a bird hasteth to the snare, and knoweth not that it is for his life."—Prov. vii. 22, 23.

The character and career of Isaac would seem to tell us that it is possible to have too great a father. Isaac was dwarfed and weakened by growing up under the shadow of Abraham. Of his life there was little to record, and what was recorded was very much a reproduction of some of the least glorious passages of his father's career. The digging of wells for his flocks was among the most notable events in his commonplace life, and even in this he only re-opened the wells his father had dug.

In him we see the result of growing up under too strong and dominant an external influence. The free and healthy play of his own capacities and will was curbed. The sons of outstanding fathers are much tempted to follow in the wake of *their* success, and be too much controlled and limited by the example therein set to them. There is a great deal to induce a son to do so; this calling has been successful in his father's case, what better can he do than follow? Also he may get the use of his *wells*—those sources his father has opened for the easier or more abundant maintenance of those dependent on him, the business he has established, the practice he has made, the connections he has formed—these are useful if he follows in his father's line of life. But all this tends, as in Isaac's case, to the stunting of the man himself. Life is made too easy for him.

Isaac has been called "the Wordsworth of the Old Testament," but his meditative disposition seems to have degenerated into mere dreamy apathy, which, at last, made him the tool of the more active-minded members of his family, and was also attended by its common accompaniment of sensuality. It seems also to have brought him to a condition of almost entire bodily prostration, for a comparison of dates shows that he must have spent forty or fifty years in blindness and incapacity for all active duty. Neither can this greatly surprise us, for it is abundantly open to our own observation that men of the finest spiritual discernment, and of whose godliness in the main one cannot doubt, are also frequently the prey of the most childish tastes, and most useless even to the extent of doing harm in practical matters. They do not see the evil that is growing in their own family; or, if they see it, they cannot rouse themselves to check it.

Isaac's marriage, though so promising in the outset, brought new trial into his life. Rebekah had to repeat the experience of Sarah. The intended mother of the promised seed was left for twenty years childless—to contend with the doubts, surmises, evil proposals, proud challengings of God, and murmurings, which must undoubtedly have arisen even in so bright and spirited a heart as Rebekah's. It was thus she was taught the seriousness of the position she had chosen for herself, and gradually led to the implicit faith requisite for the discharge of its responsibilities. Many young persons have a similar experience. They seem to themselves to have chosen a wrong position, to have made a thorough mistake in life, and to have brought themselves into circumstances in which they only retard, or quite prevent, the prosperity of those with whom they are connected. In proportion as Rebekah loved Isaac, and entered into his prospects, must she have been tempted to think she had far better have remained in Padan-aram. It is a humbling thing to stand in some other person's way; but if it is by no fault of ours, but in obedience to affection or conscience we are in this position, we must, in humility and patience, wait upon Providence as Rebekah did, and resist all morbid despondency.

This second barrenness in the prospective mother of the promised seed was as needful to all concerned as the first was; for the people of God, no more than any others, can learn in one lesson. They must again be brought to a real dependence on God as the Giver of the heir. The prayer with which Isaac "entreated" the Lord for his wife "because she was barren" was a prayer of deeper intensity than he could have uttered had he merely remembered the story that had been told him of his own birth. God must be recognised again and again and throughout as the Giver of life to the promised line. We are all apt to suppose that when once we have got a thing in train and working we can get on without God. How often do we pray for the bestowal of a blessing, and forget to pray for its continuance? How often do we count it enough that God has conferred some gift, and, not inviting Him to continue His agency, but trusting to ourselves, we mar His gift in the use? Learn, therefore, that although God has given you means of working out His salvation, your Rebekah will be barren without His continued activity. On His own means you must re-invite His blessing, for without the continuance of His aid you will make nothing of the most beautiful and appropriate helps He has given you.

It was by pain, anxiety, and almost dismay, that Rebekah received intimation that her prayer was answered. In this she is the type of many whom God hears. Inward strife, miserable forebodings, deep dejection, are often the first intimations that God is listening to our prayer and is beginning to work within us. You have prayed that God would make you more a blessing to those about you, more useful in your place, more answerable to His ends: and when your prayer has risen to its highest point of confidence and expectation, you are thrown into what seems a worse state than ever, your heart is broken within you, you say, Is this the answer to my prayer, is this God's blessing; if it be so, why am I thus? For things that make a man serious, happen when God takes him in hand, and they that yield themselves to His service will not find that that service is all honour and enjoyment. Its first steps will often land us in a position we can make nothing of, and our attempts to aid others will get us into difficulties with them; and especially will our desire that Christ be formed in us bring into such lively action the evil nature that is in us, that we are torn by the conflict, and our heart lies like the ground of a fierce struggle, seamed and furrowed, tossed and confused. As soon as there is a movement within us in one direction, immediately there is an opposing movement: as soon as one of the natures says, Do this; the other says, Do it not. The better nature is gaining slightly the upper hand, and by a long, steady strain, seems to be wearying out the other, when suddenly there is one quick stroke and the evil nature conquers. And every movement of the parties is with pain to ourselves; either conscience is wronged, and gives out its cry of shame, or our natural desires are trodden down, and that also is pain. And so disconnected and connected are we, so entirely one with both parties, and yet so able to contemplate both that Rebekah's distress seems aptly enough to symbolize our own. And whether the symbol be apt or no, there can be no question that he who enquires of the Lord as she did, will receive a similar assurance that there are two natures within him, and that "the elder shall serve the younger," the nature last formed, and that seems to give least promise of life, shall master the original, eldest born child of the flesh.

The children whose birth and destinies were thus predicted, at once gave evidence of a difference even greater than that which will often strike one as existing between two brothers, though rarely between twins. The first was born, all over like a hairy garment, presenting the appearance of being rolled up in a fur cloak or the skin of an animal—an appearance which did not pass away in childhood, but so obstinately adhered to him through life, that an imitation of his hands could be produced with the hairy skin of a kid. This was by his parents considered ominous. The want of the hairy covering which the lower animals have, is one of the signs marking out man as destined for a higher and more refined life than they; and when their son appeared in this guise, they could not but fear it prognosticated his sensual, animal career. So they called him Esau. And so did the younger son from the first show his nature, catching the heel of his brother, as if he were striving to be firstborn; and so they called him Jacob, the heel-catcher or supplanter—as Esau afterwards bitterly observed, a name which precisely suited his crafty, plotting nature, shown in his twice over tripping up and overthrowing his elder brother. The name which Esau handed down to his people was, however, not his original name, but one derived from the colour of that for which he sold his birthright. It was in that exclamation of his, "Feed me with that same *red*," that he disclosed his character.

So different in appearance at birth, they grew up of very different character; and as was natural, he who had the quiet nature of his father was beloved by the mother, and he who had the bold, practical skill of the mother was clung to by the father. It seems unlikely that Rebekah was influenced in her affection by anything but natural motives, though the fact that Jacob was to be the heir must have been much on her mind, and may have produced the partiality which maternal pride sometimes begets. But before we condemn Isaac, or think the historian has not given a full account of his love for Esau, let us ask what we have noticed about the growth and decay of our own affections. We are ashamed of Isaac; but have we not also been sometimes ashamed of ourselves on seeing that our affections are powerfully influenced by the gratification of tastes almost or quite as low as this of Isaac's? He who cunningly panders to our taste for applause, he who purveys for us some sweet morsel of scandal, he who flatters or amuses us, straightway takes a place in our affections which we do not accord to men of much finer parts, but who do not so minister to our sordid appetites.

The character of Jacob is easily understood. It has frequently been remarked of him that he is thoroughly a Jew, that in him you find the good and bad features of the Jewish character very prominent and conspicuous. He has that mingling of craft and endurance which has enabled his descendants to use for their own ends those who have wronged and persecuted them. The Jew has, with some justice and some injustice, been credited with an obstinate and unscrupulous resolution to forward his own interests, and there can be no question that in this respect Jacob is the typical Jew—ruthlessly taking advantage of his brother, watching and waiting till he was sure of his victim; deceiving his blind father, and robbing him of what he had intended for his favourite son; outwitting the grasping Laban, and making at least his own out of all attempts to rob him; unable to meet his brother without stratagem; not forgetting prudence even when the honour of his family is stained; and not thrown off his guard even by his true and deep affection for Joseph. Yet, while one recoils from this craftiness and management, one cannot but admire the quiet force of character, the indomitable tenacity, and, above all, the capacity for warm affection and lasting attachments, that he showed throughout.

But the quality which chiefly distinguished Jacob from his hunting and marauding brother was his desire for the friendship of God and sensibility to spiritual influences. It may have been Jacob's consciousness of his own meanness that led him to crave connection with some Being or with some prospect that might ennoble his nature and lift him above his innate disposition. It is an old, old truth that not many noble are called; and, seeing quite as plainly as others see their feebleness and meanness, the ignoble conceive a self-loathing which is sometimes the beginning of an unquenchable thirst for the high and holy God. The consciousness of your bad, poor nature may revive within you day by day, as the remembrance of physical weakness returns to the invalid with every morning's light; but to what else can God so effectively appeal when he offers you present fellowship with Himself and eventual conformity to His own nature?

It has been pointed out that the weakness in Esau's character which makes him so striking a contrast to his brother is his inconstancy.

> "That one error
> Fills him with faults; makes him run through all the sins."

Constancy, persistence, dogged tenacity is certainly the striking feature of Jacob's character. He could wait and bide his time; he could retain one purpose year after year till it was accomplished. The very motto of his life was, "I will not let Thee go except Thou bless me." He watched for Esau's weak moment, and took advantage of it. He served fourteen years for the woman he loved, and no hardship quenched his love. Nay, when a whole lifetime intervened, and he lay dying in Egypt, his constant heart still turned to Rachel, as if he had parted with her but yesterday. In contrast with this tenacious, constant character stands Esau, led by impulse, betrayed by appetite, everything by turns and nothing long. To-day despising his birthright, to-morrow breaking his heart for its loss; to-day vowing he will murder his brother, to-morrow falling on his neck and kissing him; a man you cannot reckon upon, and of too shallow a nature for anything to root itself deeply in.

The event in which the contrasted characters of the twin brothers were most decisively shown, so decisively shown that their destinies were fixed by it, was an incident which, in its external circumstances, was of the most ordinary and trivial kind. Esau came in hungry from hunting: from dawn to dusk he had been taxing his strength to the utmost, too eagerly absorbed to notice either his distance from home or his hunger; it is only when he begins to return depressed by the ill-luck of the day, and with nothing now to stimulate him, that he feels faint; and when at last he reaches his father's tents, and the savoury smell of Jacob's lentiles greets him, his ravenous appetite becomes an intolerable craving, and he begs Jacob to give him some of his food. Had Jacob done so with brotherly feeling there would have been nothing to record. But Jacob had long been watching for an opportunity to win his brother's birthright, and though no one could have supposed that an heir to even a little property would sell it in order to get a meal five minutes sooner than he could otherwise get it, Jacob had taken his brother's measure to a nicety, and was confident that present appetite would in Esau completely extinguish every other thought.

It is perhaps worth noticing that the birthright in Ishmael's line, the guardianship of the temple at Mecca, passed from one branch of the family to another in a precisely similar way. We read that when the guardianship of the temple and the governorship of the town "fell into the hands of Abu Gabshan, a weak and silly man, Cosa, one of Mohammed's ancestors, circumvented him while in a drunken humour, and bought of him the keys of the temple, and with them the presidency of it, for a bottle of wine. But Abu Gabshan being gotten out of his drunken fit, sufficiently repented of his foolish bargain; from whence grew these proverbs among the Arabs: More vexed with late repentance than Abu Gabshan; and, More silly than Abu Gabshan—which are usually said of those who part with a thing of great moment for a small matter."

Which brother presents the more repulsive spectacle of the two in this selling of the birthright it is hard to say. Who does not feel contempt for the great, strong man, declaring he will die if he is required to wait five minutes till his own supper is prepared; forgetting, in the craving of his appetite, every consideration of a worthy kind; oblivious of everything but his hunger and his food; crying, like a great baby, Feed me with that *red*! So it is always with the man who has fallen under the power of sensual appetite. He is always going to die if it is not immediately gratified. He *must* have his appetite satisfied. No consideration of consequences can be listened to or thought of; the man is helpless in the hands of his appetite—it rules and drives him on, and he is utterly without self-control; nothing but physical compulsion can restrain him.

But the treacherous and self-seeking craft of the other brother is as repulsive; the cold-blooded, calculating spirit that can hold every appetite in check, that can cleave to one purpose for a life-time, and, without scruple, take advantage of a twin-brother's weakness. Jacob knows his brother thoroughly, and all his knowledge he uses to betray him. He knows he will speedily repent of his bargain, so he makes him swear he will abide by it. It is a relentless purpose he carries out—he deliberately and unhesitatingly sacrifices his brother to himself.

Still, in two respects, Jacob is the superior man. He can appreciate the birthright in his father's family, and he has constancy. Esau might be a pleasant companion, far brighter and more vivacious than Jacob on a day's hunting; free and open-handed, and not implacable; and yet such people are not satisfactory friends. Often the most attractive people have similar inconstancy; they have a superficial vivacity, and brilliance, and charm, and good-nature, which invite a friendship they do not deserve.

Parents frequently make the mistake of Isaac, and think more highly of the gay, sparkling, but shallow child, than of the child who cannot be always smiling, but broods over what he conceives to be his wrongs. Sulkiness is itself not a pleasing feature in a child's character, but it may only be the childish expression of constancy, and of a depth of character which is slow to let go any impression made upon it. On the other hand, frankness and a quick throwing aside of passion and resentment are pleasing features in a child, but often these are only the expressions of a fickle character, rapidly changing from sun to shower like an April day, and not to be trusted for retaining affection or good impressions any longer than it retains resentment.

But Esau's despising of his birthright is that which stamps the man and makes him interesting to each generation. No one can read the simple account of his reckless act without feeling how justly we are called upon to "look diligently lest there be among us any profane person as Esau, who, for one morsel of meat, sold his birthright." Had the birthright been something to eat, Esau would not have sold it. What an exhibition of human nature! What an exposure of our childish folly and the infatuation of appetite! For Esau has company in his fall. We are all stricken by his shame. We are conscious that if God had made provision for the flesh we should have listened to Him more readily. "But what will this birthright profit us?" We do not see the good it does: were it something to keep us from disease, to give us long unsated days of pleasure, to bring us the fruits of labour without the weariness of it, to make money for us, where is the man who would not value it—where is the man who would lightly give it up? But because it is only the favour of God that is offered, His endless love, His holiness made ours, this we will imperil or resign for every idle desire, for every lust that bids us serve it a little longer. Born the sons of God, made in His image, introduced to a birthright angels might covet, we yet prefer to rank with the beasts of the field, and let our souls starve if only our bodies be well tended and cared for.

There is in Esau's conduct and after-experience so much to stir serious thought, that one always feels reluctant to pass from it, and as if much more ought to be made of it. It reflects so many features of our own conduct, and so clearly shows us what we are from day to day liable to, that we would wish to take it with us through life as a perpetual admonition. Who does not know of those moments of weakness, when we are fagged with work, and with our physical energy our moral tone has become relaxed? Who does not know how, in hours of reaction from keen and exciting engagements, sensual appetite asserts itself, and with what petulance we inwardly cry, We shall die if we do not get this or that paltry gratification? We are, for the most part, inconstant as Esau, full of good resolves to-day, and to-morrow throwing them to the winds—to-day proud of the arduousness of our calling, and girding ourselves to self-control and self-denial, to-morrow sinking back to softness and self-indulgence. Not once as Esau, but again and again we barter peace of conscience and fellowship with God and the hope of holiness, for what is, in simple fact, no more than a bowl of pottage. Even after recognising our weakness and the lowness of our tastes, and after repenting with self-loathing and misery, some slight pleasure is enough to upset our steadfast mind, and make us as plastic as clay in the hand of circumstances. It is with positive dismay one considers the weakness and blindness of our hours of appetite and passion: how one goes then like an ox to the slaughter, all unconscious of the pitfalls that betray and destroy men, and how at any moment we ourselves may truly sell our birthright.

XXI
JACOB'S FRAUD

Genesis xxvii.

"The counsel of the Lord standeth for ever." —Psalm xxxiii. 11.

There are some families whose miserable existence is almost entirely made up of malicious plottings and counter-plottings, little mischievous designs, and spiteful triumphs of one member or party in the family over the other. It is not pleasant to have the veil withdrawn, and to see that where love and eager self-sacrifice might be expected their places are occupied by an eager assertion of rights, and a cold, proud, and always petty and stupid, nursing of some supposed injury. In the story told us so graphically in this page, we see the family whom God has blessed sunk to this low level, and betrayed by family jealousies into unseemly strife on the most sacred ground. Each member of the family plans his own wicked device, and God by the evil of one defeats the evil of another, and saves His own purpose to bless the race from being frittered away and lost. And it is told us in order that, amidst all this mess of human craft and selfishness, the righteousness and stability of God's word of promise may be more vividly seen. Let us look at the sin of each of the parties in order, and the punishment of each.

In the Epistle to the Hebrews Isaac is commended for his faith in blessing his sons. It was commendable in him that, in great bodily weakness, he still believed himself to be the guardian of God's blessing, and recognised that he had a great inheritance to bequeath to his sons. But, in unaccountable and inconsistent contempt of God's expressed purpose, he proposes to hand over this blessing to Esau. Many things had occurred to fix his attention upon the fact that Esau was not to be his heir. Esau had sold his birthright, and had married Hittite women, and his whole conduct was, no doubt, of a piece with this, and showed that, in his hands, any spiritual inheritance would be both unsafe and unappreciated. That Isaac had some notion he was doing wrong in giving to Esau what belonged to God, and what God meant to give to Jacob, is shown from his precipitation in bestowing the blessing. He has no feeling that he is authorized by God, and therefore he cannot wait calmly till God should intimate, by unmistakable signs, that he is near his end; but, seized with a panic lest his favourite should somehow be left unblessed, he feels, in his nervous alarm, as if he were at the point of death, and, though destined to live for forty-three years longer, he calls Esau that he may hand over to him his dying testament. How different is the nerve of a man when he knows he is doing God's will, and when he is but fulfilling his own device. For the same reason, he has to stimulate his spirit by artificial means. The prophetic ecstasy is not felt by him; he must be exhilarated by venison and wine, that, strengthened and revived in body, and having his gratitude aroused afresh towards Esau, he may bless him with all the greater vigour. The final stimulus is given when he smells the garments of Esau on Jacob, and when that fresh earthy smell which so revives us in spring, as if our life were renewed with the year, and which hangs about one who has been in the open air, entered into Isaac's blood, and lent him fresh vigour.

It is a strange and, in some respects, perplexing spectacle that is here presented to us—the organ of the Divine blessing represented by a blind old man, laid on a "couch of skins," stimulated by meat and wine, and trying to cheat God by bestowing the family blessing on the son of his own choice to the exclusion of the divinely-appointed heir. Out of such beginnings had God to educate a people worthy of Himself, and through such hazards had He to guide the spiritual blessing He designed to convey to us all.

Isaac laid a net for his own feet. By his unrighteous and timorous haste he secured the defeat of his own long-cherished scheme. It was his hasting to bless Esau which drove Rebekah to checkmate him by winning the blessing for her favourite. The shock which Isaac felt when Esau came in and the fraud was discovered is easily understood. The mortification of the old man must have been extreme when he found that he had so completely taken himself in. He was reclining in the satisfied reflection that for once he had overreached his astute Rebekah and her astute son, and in the comfortable feeling that, at last, he had accomplished his one remaining desire, when he learns from the exceeding bitter cry of Esau that he has himself been duped. It was enough to rouse the anger of the mildest and godliest of men, but Isaac does not storm and protest—"he trembles exceedingly." He recognises, by a spiritual insight quite unknown to Esau, that this is God's hand, and deliberately confirms, with his eyes open, what he had done in blindness: "I have blessed him: *Yea*, and he shall be blessed." Had he wished to deny the validity of the blessing, he had ground enough for doing so. He had not really given it: it had been stolen from him. An act must be judged by its intention, and he had been far from intending to bless Jacob. Was he to consider himself bound by what he had done under a misapprehension? He had given a blessing to one person under the impression that he was a different person; must not the blessing go to him for whom it was designed? But Isaac unhesitatingly yielded.

This clear recognition of God's hand in the matter, and quick submission to Him, reveals a habit of reflection, and a spiritual thoughtfulness, which are the good qualities in Isaac's otherwise unsatisfactory character. Before he finished his answer to Esau, he felt he was a poor feeble creature in the hand of a true and just God, who had used even his infirmity and sin to forward righteous and gracious ends. It was his sudden recognition of the frightful way in which he had been tampering with God's will, and of the grace with which God had prevented him from accomplishing a wrong destination of the inheritance, that made Isaac tremble very exceedingly.

In this humble acceptance of the disappointment of his life's love and hope, Isaac shows us the manner in which we ought to bear the consequences of our wrong-doing. The punishment of our sin often comes through the persons with whom we have to do, unintentionally on their part, and yet we are tempted to hate them because they pain and punish us, father, mother, wife, child, or whoever else. Isaac and Esau were alike disappointed. Esau only saw the supplanter, and vowed to be revenged. Isaac saw God in the matter, and trembled. So when Shimei cursed David, and his loyal retainers would have cut off his head for so doing, David said, "Let him alone, and let him curse: it may be that the Lord hath bidden him." We can bear the pain inflicted on us by men when we see that they are merely the instruments of a divine chastisement. The persons who thwart us and make our life bitter, the persons who stand between us and our dearest hopes, the persons whom we are most disposed to speak angrily and bitterly to, are often thorns planted in our path by God to keep us on the right way.

Isaac's sin propagated itself with the rapid multiplication of all sin. Rebekah overheard what passed between Isaac and Esau, and although she might have been able to wait until by fair means Jacob received the blessing, yet when she sees Isaac actually preparing to pass Jacob by and bless Esau, her fears are so excited that she cannot any longer quietly leave the matter in God's hand, but must lend her own more skilful management. It may have crossed her mind that she was justified in forwarding what she knew to be God's purpose. She saw no other way of saving God's purpose and Jacob's rights than by her interference. The emergency might have unnerved many a woman, but Rebekah is equal to the occasion. She makes the threatened exclusion of Jacob the very means for at last finally settling the inheritance upon him. She braves the indignation of Isaac and the rage of Esau, and fearless herself, and confident of success, she soon quiets the timorous and cautious objections of Jacob. She knows that for straightforward lying and acting a part she was sure of good support in Jacob. Luther says, "Had it been me, I'd have dropped the dish." But Jacob had no such tremors—could submit his hands and face to the touch of Isaac, and repeat his lie as often as needful.

An old man bedridden like Isaac becomes the subject of a number of little deceptions which may seem, and which may be, very unimportant in themselves, but which are seen to wear down the reverence due to the father of a family, and which imperceptibly sap the guileless sincerity and truthfulness of those who practise them. This overreaching of Isaac by dressing Jacob in Esau's clothes, might come in naturally as one of those daily deceptions which Rebekah was accustomed to practise on the old man whom she kept quite in her own hand, giving him as much or as little insight into the doings of the family as seemed advisable to her. It would never occur to her that she was taking God in hand; it would seem only as if she were making such use of Isaac's infirmity as she was in the daily practice of doing.

But to account for an act is not to excuse it. Underlying the conduct of Rebekah and Jacob was the conviction that they would come better speed by a little deceit of their own than by suffering God to further them in His own way—that though God would certainly not practise deception Himself, He might not object to others doing so—that in this emergency holiness was a hampering thing which might just for a little be laid aside that they might be more holy afterwards—that though no doubt in ordinary circumstances, and as a normal habit, deceit is not to be commended, yet in cases of difficulty, which call for ready wit, a prompt seizure, and delicate handling, men must be allowed to secure their ends in their own way. Their unbelief thus directly produced immorality—immorality of a very revolting kind, the defrauding of their relatives, and repulsive also because practised as if on God's side, or, as we should now say, "in the interests of religion."

To this day the method of Rebekah and Jacob is largely adopted by religious persons. It is notorious that persons whose ends are good frequently become thoroughly unscrupulous about the means they use to accomplish them. They dare not say in so many words that they may do evil that good may come, nor do they think it a tenable position in morals that the end sanctifies the means; and yet their consciousness of a justifiable and desirable end undoubtedly does blunt their sensitiveness regarding the legitimacy of the means they employ. For example, Protestant controversialists, persuaded that vehement opposition to Popery is good, and filled with the idea of accomplishing its downfall, are often guilty of gross misrepresentation, because they do not sufficiently inform themselves of the actual tenets and practices of the Church of Rome. In all controversy, religious and political, it is the same. It is always dishonest to circulate reports that you have no means of authenticating: yet how freely are such reports circulated to blacken the character of an opponent, and to prove his opinions to be dangerous. It is always dishonest to condemn opinions we have not inquired into, merely because of some fancied consequence which these opinions carry in them: yet how freely are opinions condemned by men who have never been at the trouble carefully to inquire into their truth. They do not feel the dishonesty of their position, because they have a general consciousness that they are on the side of religion, and of what has generally passed for truth. All keeping back of facts which are supposed to have an unsettling effect is but a repetition of this sin. There is no sin more hateful. Under the appearance of serving God, and maintaining His cause in the world, it insults Him by assuming that if the whole bare, undisguised truth were spoken, His cause would suffer.

The fate of all such attempts to manage God's matters by keeping things dark, and misrepresenting fact, is written for all who care to understand in the results of this scheme of Rebekah's and Jacob's. They gained nothing, and they lost a great deal, by their wicked interference. They gained nothing; for God had promised that the birthright would be Jacob's, and would have given it him in some way redounding to his credit and not to his shame. And they lost a great deal. The mother lost her son; Jacob had to flee for his life, and, for all we know, Rebekah never saw him more. And Jacob lost all the comforts of home, and all those possessions his father had accumulated. He had to flee with nothing but his staff, an outcast to begin the world for himself. From this first false step onwards to his death, he was pursued by misfortune, until his own verdict on his life was, "Few and evil have been the days of the years of my life."

Thus severely was the sin of Rebekah and Jacob punished. It coloured their whole after-life with a deep sombre hue. It was marked thus, because it was a sin by all means to be avoided. It was virtually the sin of blaming God for forgetting His promise, or of accusing Him of being unable to perform it: so that they, Rebekah and Jacob, had, forsooth, to take God's work out of His hands, and show Him how it ought to be done. The announcement of God's purpose, instead of enabling them quietly to wait for a blessing they knew to be certain, became in their unrighteous and impatient hearts actually an inducement to sin. Abraham was so bold and confident in his faith, at least latterly, that again and again he refused to take as a gift from men, and on the most honourable terms, what God had promised to give him: his grandson is so little sure of God's truth, that he will rather trust his own falsehood; and what he thinks God may forget to give him, he will steal from his own father. Some persons have especial need to consider this sin—they are tempted to play the part of Providence, to intermeddle where they ought to refrain. Sometimes just a little thing is needed to make everything go to our liking—the keeping back of one small fact, a slight variation in the way of stating the matter, is enough—things want just a little push in the right direction; it is wrong but very slightly so. And so they are encouraged to close for a moment their eyes and put to their hand.

Of all the parties in this transaction none is more to blame than Esau. He shows now how selfish and untruthful the sensual man really is, and how worthless is the generosity which is merely of impulse and not bottomed on principle. While he so furiously and bitterly blamed Jacob for supplanting him, it might surely have occurred to him that it was really he who was supplanting Jacob. He had no right, divine or human, to the inheritance. God had never said that His possession should go to the oldest, and had in this case said the express opposite. Besides, inconstant as Esau was, he could scarcely have forgotten the bargain that so pleased him at the time, and by which he had sold to his younger brother all title to his father's blessings. Jacob was to blame for seeking to win his own by craft, but Esau was more to blame for endeavouring furtively to recover what he knew to be no longer his. His bitter cry was the cry of a disappointed and enraged child, what Hosea calls the "howl" of those who seem to seek the Lord, but are really merely crying out, like animals, for corn and wine. Many that care very little for God's love will seek His favours; and every wicked wretch who has in his prosperity spurned God's offers, will, when he sees how he has cheated himself, turn to God's gifts, though not to God, with a cry. Esau would now very gladly have given a mess of pottage for the blessing that secured to its receiver "the dew of heaven, the fatness of the earth, and plenty of corn and wine." Like many another sinner, he wanted both to eat his cake and have it. He wanted to spend his youth sowing to the flesh, and have the harvest which those only can have who have sown to the spirit. He wished both of two irreconcilable things—both the red pottage and the birth right. He is a type of those who think very lightly of spiritual blessings while their appetites are strong, but afterwards bitterly complain that their whole life is filled with the results of sowing to the flesh and not to the spirit.

> "We barter life for pottage; sell true bliss
> For wealth or power, for pleasure or renown;
> Thus, Esau-like, our Father's blessing miss,
> Then wash with fruitless tears our faded crown."

The words of the New Testament, in which it is said that Esau "found no place for repentance, though he sought it carefully with tears," are sometimes misunderstood. They do not mean that he sought what we ordinarily call repentance, a change of mind about the value of the birthright. He *had* that;

it was this that made him weep. What he sought now was some means of undoing what he had done, of cancelling the deed of which he repented. His experience does not tell us that a man once sinning as Esau sinned becomes a hardened reprobate whom no good influence can impress or bring to repentance, but it says that the sin so committed leaves irreparable consequences—that no man can live a youth of folly and yet find as much in manhood and maturer years as if he had lived a careful and God-fearing youth. Esau had irrecoverably lost that which he would now have given all he had to possess; and in this, I suppose, he represents half the men who pass through this world. He warns us that it is very possible, by careless yielding to appetite and passing whim, to entangle ourselves irrecoverably for this life, if not to weaken and maim ourselves for eternity. At the time, your act may seem a very small and secular one, a mere bargain in the ordinary course, a little transaction such as one would enter into carelessly after the day's work is over, in the quiet of a summer evening or in the midst of the family circle; or it may seem so necessary that you never think of its moral qualities, as little as you question whether you are justified in breathing; but you are warned that if there be in that act a crushing out of spiritual hopes to make way for the free enjoyment of the pleasures of sense—if there be a deliberate preference of the good things of this life to the love of God—if, knowingly, you make light of spiritual blessings, and count them unreal when weighed against obvious worldly advantages—then the consequences of that act will in this life bring to you great discomfort and uneasiness, great loss and vexation, an agony of remorse, and a life-long repentance. You are warned of this, and most touchingly, by the moving entreaties, the bitter cries and tears of Esau.

But even when our life is spoiled irreparably, a hope remains for our character and ourselves—not certainly if our misfortunes embitter us, not if resentment is the chief result of our suffering; but if, subduing resentment, and taking blame to ourselves instead of trying to fix it on others, we take revenge upon the real source of our undoing, and extirpate from our own character the root of bitterness. Painful and difficult is such schooling. It calls for simplicity, and humility, and truthfulness—qualities not of frequent occurrence. It calls for abiding patience; for he who begins thus to sow to the spirit late in life, must be content with inward fruits, with peace of conscience, increase of righteousness and humility, and must learn to live without much of what all men naturally desire.

While each member of Isaac's family has thus his own plan, and is striving to fulfil his private intention, the result is, that God's purpose is fulfilled. In the human agency, such faith in God as existed was overlaid with misunderstanding and distrust of God. But notwithstanding the petty and mean devices, the short-sighted slyness, the blundering unbelief, the profane worldliness of the human parties in the transaction, the truth and mercy of God still find a way for themselves. Were matters left in our hands, we should make shipwreck even of the salvation with which we are provided. We carry into our dealings with it the same selfishness, and inconstancy, and worldliness which made it necessary: and had not God patience to bear with, as well as mercy to invite us; had He not wisdom to govern us in the use of His grace, as well as wisdom to contrive its first bestowal, we should perish with the water of life at our lips.

XXII
JACOB'S FLIGHT AND DREAM

Genesis xxvii. 41–xxviii.

"So foolish was I, and ignorant: I was as a beast before Thee. Nevertheless I am continually with Thee."—Psalm lxxiii. 22.

It is so commonly observed as to be scarcely worth again remarking, that persons who employ a great deal of craft in the management of their affairs are invariably entrapped in their own net. Life is so complicated, and every matter of conduct has so many issues, that no human brain can possibly foresee every contingency. Rebekah was a clever woman, and quite competent to outwit men like Isaac and Esau, but she had in her scheming neglected to take account of Laban, a man true brother to herself in cunning. She had calculated on Esau's resentment, and knew it would last only a few days, and this brief period she was prepared to utilize by sending Jacob out of Esau's reach to her own kith and kin, from among whom he might get a suitable wife. But she did not reckon on Laban's making her son serve fourteen years for his wife, nor upon Jacob's falling so deeply in love with Rachel as to make him apparently forget his mother.

In the first part of her scheme she feels herself at home. She is a woman who knows exactly how much of her mind to disclose, so as effectually to lead her husband to adopt her view and plan. She did not bluntly advise Isaac to send Jacob to Padan-aram, but she sowed in his apprehensive mind fears which she knew would make him send Jacob there; she suggested the possibility of Jacob's taking a wife of the daughters of Heth. She felt sure that *Isaac* did not need to be told where to send his son to find a suitable wife. So Isaac called Jacob, and said, Go to Padan-aram, to the house of thy mother's father, and take thee a wife thence. And he gave him the family blessing—God Almighty give thee the blessing of Abraham, to thee, and to thy seed with thee—so constituting him his heir, the representative of Abraham.

The effect this had on Esau is very noticeable. He sees, as the narrative tells us, a great many things, and his dull mind tries to make some meaning out of all that is passing before him. The historian seems intentionally to satirise Esau's attempt at reasoning, and the foolish simplicity of the device he fell upon. He had an idea that Jacob's obedience in going to seek a wife of another stock than he had connected himself with would be pleasing to his parents; and perhaps he had an idea that it would be possible to steal a march upon Jacob in his absence, and by a more speedily effected obedience to his parents' desire, win their preference, and perhaps move Isaac to alter his will and reverse the blessing. Though living in the chosen family, he seems to have had not the slightest idea that there was any higher will than his father's being fulfilled in their doings. He does not yet see why he himself should not be as blessed as Jacob; he cannot grasp at all the distinction that grace makes; cannot take in the idea that God has chosen a people to Himself, and that no natural advantage or force or endowment can set a man among that people, but only God's choice. Accordingly, he does not see any difference between Ishmael's family and the chosen family; they are both sprung from Abraham, both are naturally the same, and the fact that God expressly gave His inheritance past Ishmael is nothing to Esau—an act of *God* has no meaning to him. He merely sees that he has not pleased his parents as well as he might by his marriage, and his easy and yielding disposition prompts him to remedy this.

This is a fine specimen of the hazy views men have of what will bring them to a level with God's chosen. Through their crass insensibility to the high righteousness of God, there still does penetrate a perception that if they are to please Him there are certain means to be used for doing so. There are, they see, certain occupations and ways pursued by Christians, and if by themselves adopting these they can please God, they are quite willing to humour Him in this. Like Esau, they do not see their way to drop their old connections, but if by making some little additions to their habits, or forming some new connection, they can quiet this controversy that has somehow grown up between God and His children,—though, so far as they see, it is a very unmeaning controversy,—they will very gladly enter into any little arrangement for the purpose. We will not, of course, divorce the world, will not dismiss from our homes and hearts what God hates and means to destroy, will not accept God's will as our sole and absolute law, but we will so far meet God's wishes as to add to what we have adopted something that is almost as good as what God enjoins: we will make any little alterations which will not quite upset our present ways. Much commoner than hypocrisy is this dim-sighted, blundering stupidity of the really profane worldly man, who thinks he can take rank with men whose natures God has changed, by the mere imitation of some of their ways; who thinks, that as he cannot without great labour, and without too seriously endangering his hold on the world, do precisely what God requires, God may be expected to be satisfied with a something like it. Are we not aware of endeavouring at times to cloak a sin with some easy virtue, to adopt some new and apparently good habit, instead of destroying the sin we know God hates; or to offer to God, and palm upon our own conscience, a mere imitation of what God is pleased with? Do you attend Church, do you come and decorously submit to a service? That is not at all what God enjoins, though it is like it. What He means is, that you worship Him, which is a quite different employment. Do you render to God some outward respect, have you adopted some habits in deference to Him, do you even attempt some private devotion and discipline of the spirit? Still what He requires is something that goes much deeper than all that; namely, that you love Him. To conform to one or two habits of godly people is not what is required of us; but to be at heart godly.

As Jacob journeyed northwards, he came, on the second or third evening of his flight, to the hills of Bethel. As the sun was sinking he found himself toiling up the rough path which Abraham may have described to him as looking like a great staircase of rock and crag reaching from earth to sky. Slabs of rock, piled one upon another, form the whole hill-side, and to Jacob's eye, accustomed to the rolling pastures of Beersheba, they would appear almost like a structure built for superhuman uses, well founded in the valley below, and intended to reach to unknown heights. Overtaken by darkness on this rugged path, he readily finds as soft a bed and as good shelter as his shepherd-habits require, and with his head on a stone and a corner of his dress thrown over his face to preserve him from the moon, he is soon fast asleep. But in his dreams the massive staircase is still before his eyes, and it is no longer himself that is toiling up it as it leads to an unexplored hill-top above him, but the angels of God are ascending and descending upon it, and at its top is Jehovah Himself.

Thus simply does God meet the thoughts of Jacob, and lead him to the encouragement he needed. What was probably Jacob's state of mind when he lay down on that hill-side? In the first place, and as he would have said to any man he chanced to meet, he wondered what he would see when he got to the top of this hill; and still more, as he may have said to Rebekah, he wondered what reception he would meet with from Laban, and whether he would ever again see his father's tents. This vision shows him that his path leads to God, that it is He who occupies the future; and, in his dream, a voice comes to him: "I am with thee, and will keep thee in all places whither thou goest, and will bring thee again into this land." He had, no doubt, wondered much whether the blessing of his father was, after all, so valuable a possession, whether it might not have been wiser to take a share with Esau than to be driven out homeless thus. God has never spoken to him; he has heard his father speak of assurances coming to him from God, but as for him, through all the long years of his life he has never heard what he could speak of as a voice of God. But this night these doubts were silenced—there came to his soul an assurance that never departed from it. He could have affirmed he heard God saying to him: "I am the Lord God of thy father Abraham, and the God of Isaac: the land whereon thou liest, to thee will I give it." And lastly, all these thoughts probably centred in one deep feeling, that he was an outcast, a fugitive from justice. He was glad he was in so solitary a place, he was glad he was so far from Esau and from every human eye; and yet—what desolation of spirit accompanied this feeling: there was no one he could bid good-night to, no one he could spend the evening hour with in quiet talk; he was a banished man, whatever fine gloss Rebekah might put upon it, and deep down in his conscience there was that which told him he was not banished without cause. Might not God also forsake him—might not God banish him, and might he not find a curse pursuing him, preventing man or woman from ever again looking in his face with pleasure? Such fears are met by the vision. This desolate spot, unvisited by sheep or bird, has become busy with life, angels thronging the ample staircase. Here, where he thought himself lonely and outcast, he finds he has come to the very gate of heaven. His fond mother might, at that hour, have been visiting his silent tent and shedding ineffectual tears on his abandoned bed, but he finds himself in the very house of God, cared for by angels. As the darkness had revealed to him the stars shining overhead, so when the deceptive glare of waking life was dulled by sleep, he saw the actual realities which before were hidden.

No wonder that a vision which so graphically showed the open communication between earth and heaven should have deeply impressed itself on Jacob's descendants. What more effectual consolation could any poor outcast, who felt he had spoiled his life, require than the memory of this staircase reaching from the pillow of the lonely fugitive from justice up into the very heart of heaven? How could any most desolate soul feel quite abandoned so long as the memory retained the vision of the angels thronging up and down with swift service to the needy? How could it be even in the darkest hour believed that all hope was gone, and that men might but curse God and die, when the mind turned to this bridging of the interval between earth and heaven?

In the New Testament we meet with an instance of the familiarity with this vision which true Israelites enjoyed. Our Lord, in addressing Nathanael, makes use of it in a way that proves this familiarity. Under his fig-tree, whose broad leaves were used in every Jewish garden as a screen from observation, and whose branches were trained down so as to form an open-air oratory, where secret prayer might be indulged in undisturbed, Nathanael had been declaring to the Father his ways, his weaknesses, his hopes. And scarcely more astonished was Jacob when he found himself the object of this angelic ministry on the lonely hill-side, than was Nathanael when he found how one eye penetrated the leafy screen, and had read his thoughts and wishes. Apparently he had been encouraging himself with this vision, for our Lord, reading his thoughts, says: "Because I said unto thee, When thou wast under the fig-tree I saw thee, believest thou? Thou shalt see greater things than these—thou shalt see heaven opened, and the angels of God ascending and descending upon the Son of man."

This, then, is a vision for us even more than for Jacob. It has its fulfilment in the times after the Incarnation more manifestly than in previous times. The true staircase by which heavenly messengers ascend and descend is the Son of man. It is He who really bridges the interval between heaven and earth, God and man. In His person these two are united. You cannot tell whether Christ is more Divine or human, more God or man—solidly based on earth, as this massive staircase, by His real humanity, by His thirty-three years' engagement in all human functions and all experiences of this life, He is yet familiar with eternity, His name is "He that came down from heaven," and if your eye follows step by step to the heights of His person, it rests at last on what you recognise as Divine. His love it is that is wide enough to embrace God on the one hand, and the lowest sinner on the other. Truly He is the way, the stair, leading from the lowest depth of earth to the highest height of heaven. In Him you find a love that embraces you as you are, in whatever condition, however cast down and defeated, however embittered and polluted—a love that stoops tenderly to you and hopefully, and gives you once more a hold upon holiness and life, and in that very love unfolds to you the highest glory of heaven and of God.

When this comes home to a man in the hour of his need, it becomes the most arousing revelation. He springs from the troubled slumber we call life, and all earth wears a new glory and awe to him. He exclaims with Jacob, "How dreadful is this place. Surely the Lord is in this place, and I knew it not." The world that had been so bleak and empty to him, is filled with a majestic vital presence. Jacob is no longer a mere fugitive from the results of his own sin, a shepherd in search of employment, a man setting out in the world to try his fortune; he is the partner with God in the fulfilment of a Divine purpose. And such is the change that passes on every man who believes in the Incarnation, who feels himself to be connected with God by Jesus Christ; he recognises the Divine intention to uplift his life, and to fill it with new hopes and purposes. He feels that humanity is consecrated by the entrance of the Son of God into it: he feels that all human life is holy ground since the Lord Himself has passed through it. Having once had this vision of God and man united in Christ, life cannot any more be to him the poor, dreary, commonplace, wretched round of secular duties and short-lived joys and terribly punished sins it was before: but it truly becomes the very gate of heaven; from each part of it he knows there is a staircase rising to the presence of God, and that out of the region of pure holiness and justice there flow to him heavenly aids, tender guidance, and encouragement.

Do you think the idea of the Incarnation too aerial and speculative to carry with you for help in rough, practical matters? The Incarnation is not a mere idea, but a fact as substantial and solidly rooted in life as anything you have to do with. Even the shadow of it Jacob saw carried in it so much of what was real that when he was broad awake he trusted it and acted on it. It was not scattered by the chill of the morning air, nor by that fixed staring reality which external nature assumes in the gray dawn as one object after another shows itself in the same spot and form in which night had fallen upon it. There were no angels visible when he opened his eyes; the staircase was there, but it was of no heavenly substance, and if it had any secret to tell, it coldly and darkly kept it. There was no retreat for the runaway from the poor common facts of yesterday. The sky seemed as far from earth as it did yesterday, his track over the hill as lonely, his brother's wrath as real;—but other things also had become real; and as he looked back from the top of the hill on the stone he had set up, he felt the words, "I am with thee in all places whither thou goest," graven on his heart, and giving him new courage; and he knew that every footfall of his was making a Bethel, and that as he went he was carrying God through the world. The bleakest rains that swept across the hills of Bethel could never wash out of his mind the vision of bright-winged angels, as little as they could wash off the oil or wear down the stone he had set up. The brightest glare of this world's heyday of real life could not outshine and cause them to disappear; and the vision on which we hope is not one that vanishes at cock-crow, nor is He who connects us with God shy of human handling, but substantial as ourselves. He offered Himself to every kind of test, so that those who knew Him for years could say, with the most absolute confidence, "That which we have heard, which we have seen with our eyes, which we have looked upon, and our hands have handled of the Word of Life ... declare we unto you, that ye also may have fellowship with us: and truly our fellowship is with the Father, and with His Son Jesus Christ."

Jacob obeyed a good instinct when he set up as a monumental stone that which had served as his pillow while he dreamt and saw this inspiring vision. He felt that, vivid as the impression on his mind then was, it would tend to fade, and he erected this stone that in after days he might have a witness that would testify to his present assurance. One great secret in the growth of character is the art of prolonging the quickening power of right ideas, of perpetuating just and inspiring impressions. And he who despises the aid of all external helps for the accomplishment of this object is not likely to succeed. Religion, some men say, is an inward thing: it does not consist of public worship, ordinances, and so forth, but it is a state of spirit. Very true; but he knows little of human nature who fancies a state of spirit can be maintained without the aid of external reminders, presentations to eye and ear of central religious truths and facts. We have all of us had such views of truth, and such corresponding desires and purposes, as would transform us were they only permanent. But what a night has settled on our past, how little have we found skill to prolong the benefit arising from particular events or occasions. Some parts of our life, indeed, require no monument, there is nothing *there* we would ever again think of, if possible; but, alas! these, for the most part, have erected monuments of their own, to which, as with a sad fascination, our eyes are ever turning—persons we have injured, or who, somehow, so remind us of sin, that we shrink from meeting them— places to which sins of ours have attached a reproachful meaning. And these natural monuments must be imitated in the life of grace. By fixed hours of worship, by rules and habits of devotion, by public worship, and especially by the monumental ordinance of the Lord's Supper, must we cherish the memory of known truth, and deepen former impressions.

To the monument Jacob attached a vow, so that when he returned to that spot the stone might remind him of the dependence on God he now felt, of the precarious situation he was in when this vision appeared, and of all the help God had afterwards given him. He seems to have taken up the meaning of that endless chain of angels ceaselessly coming down full of blessing, and going up empty of all but desires, requests, aspirations. And if we are to live with clean conscience and with heart open to God, we must so live that the messengers who bring God's blessings to us shall not have an evil report to take back of the manner in which we have received and spent His bounty.

This whole incident makes a special appeal to those who are starting in life. Jacob was no longer a young man, but he was unmarried, and he was going to seek employment with nothing to begin the world with but his shepherd's staff, the symbol of his knowledge of a profession. Many must see in him a very exact reproduction of their own position. They have left home, and it may be they have left it not altogether with pleasant memories, and they are now launched on the world for themselves, with nothing but their staff, their knowledge of some business. The spot they have reached may seem as desolate as the rock where Jacob lay, their prospects as doubtful as his. For such an one there is absolutely no security but that which is given in the vision of Jacob—in the belief that God will be with you in all places, and that even now on that life which you are perhaps already wishing to seclude from all holy influences, the angels of God are descending to bless and restrain you from sin. Happy the man who, at the outset, can heartily welcome such a connection of his life with God: unhappy he who welcomes whatever blots out the thought of heaven, and who separates himself from all that reminds him of the good influences that throng his path. The desire of the young heart to see life and know the world is natural and innocent, but how many fancy that in seeing the lowest and poorest perversions of life they see life—how many forget that unless they keep their hearts pure they can never enter into the best and richest and most enduring of the uses and joys of human life. Even from a selfish motive and the mere desire to succeed in the world, every one starting in life would do well to consider whether he really has Jacob's blessing and is making his vow. And certainly every one who has any honour, who is governed by any of those sentiments that lead men to noble and worthy actions, will frankly meet God's offers and joyfully accept a heavenly guidance and a permanent connection with God.

Before we dismiss this vision, it may be well to look at one instance of its fulfilment, that we may understand the manner in which God fulfils His promises. Jacob's experience in Haran was not so brilliant and unexceptional as he might perhaps expect. He did, indeed, at once find a woman he could love, but he had to purchase her with seven years' toil, which ultimately became fourteen years. He did not grudge this; because it was customary, because his affections were strong, and because he was too independent to send to his father for money to buy a wife. But the bitterest disappointment awaited him. With the burning humiliation of one who has been cheated in so cruel a way, he finds himself married to Leah. He protests, but he cannot insist on his protest, nor divorce Leah; for, in point of fact, he is conscious that he is only being paid in his own coin, foiled with his own weapons. In this veiled bride brought in to him on false pretences, he sees the just retribution of his own disguise when with the hands of Esau he went in and received his father's blessing. His mouth is shut by the remembrance of his own past. But submitting to this chastisement, and recognising in it not only the craft of his uncle, but the stroke of God, that which he at first thought of as a cruel curse became a blessing. It was Leah much more than Rachel that built up the house of Israel. To this despised wife six of the tribes traced their origin, and among these was the tribe of Judah. Thus he learned the fruitfulness of God's retribution—that to be humbled by God is really to be built up, and to be punished by Him the richest blessing. Through such an experience are many persons led: when we would embrace the fruit of years of toil God thrusts into our arms something quite different from our expectation—something that not only disappoints, but that at first repels us, reminding us of acts of our own we had striven to forget. Is it with resentment you still look back on some such experience, when the reward of years of toil evaded your grasp, and you found yourself bound to what you would not have worked a day to obtain?—do you find yourself disheartened and discouraged by the way in which you seem regularly to miss the fruit of your labour? If so, no doubt it were useless to assure you that the disappointment may be more fruitful than the hope fulfilled, but it can scarcely be useless to ask you to consider whether it is not the fact that in Jacob's case what was thrust upon him *was* more fruitful than what he strove to win.

XXIII
JACOB AT PENIEL

Genesis xxxii.

"Humble yourselves in the sight of the Lord, and He shall lift you up."—James iv. 10.

Jacob had a double reason for wishing to leave Padan-aram. He believed in the promise of God to give him Canaan; and he saw that Laban was a man with whom he could never be on a thoroughly good understanding. He saw plainly that Laban was resolved to make what he could out of his skill at as cheap a rate as possible—the characteristic of a selfish, greedy, ungrateful, and therefore, in the end, ill-served master. Laban and Esau were the two men who had hitherto chiefly influenced Jacob's life. But they were very different in character. Esau could never see that there was any important difference between himself and Jacob—except that his brother was trickier. Esau was the type of those who honestly think that there is not much in religion, and that saints are but white-washed sinners. Laban, on the contrary, is almost superstitiously impressed by the distinction between God's people and others. But the chief practical issue of this impression is, not that he seeks God's friendship for himself, but that he tries to make a profitable use of God's friends. He seeks to get God's blessing, as it were, at second-hand. If men could be related to God indirectly, as if in law and not by blood, that would suit Laban. If God would admit men to his inheritance on any other terms than being sons in the direct line, if there were some relationship once removed, a kind of sons-in-law, so that mere connection with the godly, though not with God, would win His blessing, this would suit Laban.

Laban is the man who appreciates the social value of virtue, truthfulness, fidelity, temperance, godliness, but wishes to enjoy their fruits without the pain of cultivating the qualities themselves. He is scrupulous as to the character of those he takes into his employment, and seeks to connect himself in business with good men. In his domestic life, he acts on the idea which his experience has suggested to him, that persons really godly will make his home more peaceful, better regulated, safer than otherwise it might be. If he holds a position of authority, he knows how to make use, for the preservation of order and for the promotion of his own ends, of the voluntary efforts of Christian societies, of the trustworthiness of Christian officials, and of the support of the Christian community. But with all this recognition of the reality and influence of godliness, he never for one moment entertains the idea of himself becoming a godly man. In all ages there are Labans, who clearly recognise the utility and worth of a connection with God, who have been much mixed up with persons in whom that worth was very conspicuous, and who yet, at the last, "depart and return unto their place," like Jacob's father-in-law, without having themselves entered into any affectionate relations with God.

From Laban, then, Jacob was resolved to escape. And though to escape with large droves of slow-moving sheep and cattle, as well as with many women and children, seemed hopeless, the cleverness of Jacob did not fail him here. He did not get beyond reach of pursuit; he could never have expected to do so. But he stole away to such a distance from Haran as made it much easier for him to come to terms with Laban, and much more difficult for Laban to try any further device for detaining him.

But, delivered as he was from Laban, he had an even more formidable person to deal with. As soon as Laban's company disappear on the northern horizon, Jacob sends messengers south to sound Esau. His message is so contrived as to beget the idea in Esau's mind that his younger brother is a person of some importance, and yet is prepared to show greater deference to himself than formerly. But the answer brought back by the messengers is the curt and haughty despatch of the man of war to the man of peace. No notice is taken of Jacob's vaunted wealth. No proposal of terms as if Esau had an equal to deal with, is carried back. There is only the startling announcement: "Esau cometh to meet thee, and four hundred men with him." Jacob at once recognises the significance of this armed advance on Esau's part. Esau has not forgotten the wrong he suffered at Jacob's hands, and he means to show him that he is entirely in his power.

Therefore was Jacob "greatly afraid and distressed." The joy with which, a few days ago, he had greeted the host of God, was quite overcast by the tidings brought him regarding the host of Esau. Things heavenly do always look so like a mere show; visits of angels seem so delusive and fleeting; the exhibition of the powers of heaven seems so often but as a tournament painted on the sky, and so unavailable for the stern encounters that await us on earth, that one seems, even after the most impressive of such displays, to be left to fight on alone. No wonder Jacob is disturbed. His wives and dependants gather round him in dismay; the children, catching the infectious panic, cower with cries and weeping about their mothers; the whole camp is rudely shaken out of its brief truce by the news of this rough Esau, whose impetuosity and warlike ways they had all heard of and were now to experience. The accounts of the messengers would no doubt grow in alarming descriptive detail as they saw how much importance was attached to their words. Their accounts would also be exaggerated by their own unwarlike nature, and by the indistinctness with which they had made out the temper of Esau's followers, and the novelty of the equipments of war they had seen in his camp. Could we have been surprised had Jacob turned and fled when thus he was made to picture the troops of Esau sweeping from his grasp all he had so laboriously earned, and snatching the promised inheritance from him when in the very act of entering on possession? But though in fancy he already hears their rude shouts of triumph as they fall upon his defenceless band, and already sees the merciless horde dividing the spoil with shouts of derision and coarse triumph, and though all around him are clamouring to be led into a safe retreat, Jacob sees stretched before him the land that is his, and resolves that, by God's help, he shall win it. What he does is not the act of a man rendered incompetent through fear, but of one who has recovered from the first shock of alarm and has all his wits about him. He disposes his household and followers in two companies, so that each might advance with the hope that it might be the one which should not meet Esau; and having done all that his circumstances permit, he commends himself to God in prayer.

After Jacob had prayed to God, a happy thought strikes him, which he at once puts in execution. Anticipating the experience of Solomon, that "a brother offended is harder to be won than a strong city," he, in the style of a skilled tactician, lays siege to Esau's wrath, and directs against it train after train of gifts, which, like successive battalions pouring into a breach, might at length quite win his brother. This disposition of his peaceful battering trains having occupied him till sunset, he retires to the short rest of a general on the eve of battle. As soon as he judges that the weaker members of the camp are refreshed enough to begin their eventful march, he rises and goes from tent to tent awaking the sleepers, and quickly forming them into their usual line of march, sends them over the brook in the darkness, and himself is left alone, not with the depression of a man who waits for the inevitable, but with the high spirits of intense activity, and with the return of the old complacent confidence of his own superiority to his powerful but sluggish-minded brother—a confidence regained now by the certainty he felt, at least for the time, that Esau's rage could not blaze through all the relays of gifts he had sent forward. Having in this spirit seen all his camp across the brook, he himself pauses for a moment, and looks with interest at the stream before him, and at the promised land on its southern bank. This stream, too, has an interest for him as bearing a name like his own—a name that signifies the "struggler," and was given to the mountain torrent from the pain and difficulty with which it seemed to find its way through the hills. Sitting on the bank of the stream, he sees gleaming through the darkness the foam that it churned as it writhed through the obstructing rocks, or heard through the night the roar of its torrent as it leapt downwards, tortuously finding its way towards Jordan; and Jacob says, So will I, opposed though I be, win my way, by the circuitous routes of craft or by the impetuous rush of courage, into the land whither that stream is going. With compressed lips, and step as firm as when, twenty years before, he left the land, he rises to cross the brook and enter the land—he rises, and is seized in a grasp that he at once owns as formidable. But surely this silent close, as of two combatants who at once recognise one another's strength, this protracted strife, does not look like the act of a depressed man, but of one whose energies have been strung to the highest pitch, and who would have borne down the champion of Esau's host had he at that hour opposed his entrance into the land which Jacob claimed as his own, and into which, as his glove, pledging himself to follow, he had thrown all that was dear to him in the world. It was no common wrestler that would have been safe to meet him in that mood.

Why, then, was Jacob thus mysteriously held back while his household were quietly moving forward in the darkness? What is the meaning, purpose, and use of this opposition to his entrance? These are obvious from the state of mind Jacob was in. He was going forward to meet Esau under the impression that there was no other reason why he should not inherit the land but only his wrath, and pretty confident that by his superior talent, his mother-wit, he could make a tool of this stupid, generous brother of his. And the danger was, that if Jacob's device had succeeded, he would have been confirmed in these impressions, and have believed that he had won the land from Esau, with God's help certainly, but still by his own indomitable pertinacity of purpose and skill in dealing with men. Now, this was not the state of the case at all. Jacob had, by his own deceit, become an exile from the land, had been, in fact, banished for fraud; and though God had confirmed to him the covenant, and promised to him the land, yet Jacob had apparently never come to any such thorough sense of his sin and entire incompetency to win the birthright for himself, as would have made it *possible* for him to receive simply as God's gift this land which as God's gift was alone valuable. Jacob does not yet seem to have taken up the difference between inheriting a thing as God's gift, and inheriting it as the meed of his own prowess. To such a man God cannot *give* the land; Jacob cannot receive it. He is thinking only of winning it, which is not at all what God means, and which would, in fact, have annulled all the covenant, and lowered Jacob and his people to the level simply of other nations who had to win and keep their territories at their risk, and not as the blessed of God. If Jacob then is to get the land, he must take it as a gift, which he is not prepared to do. During the last twenty years he has got many a lesson which might have taught him to distrust his own management, and he had, to a certain extent, acknowledged God; but his Jacob-nature, his subtle, scheming nature, was not so easily made to stand erect, and still he is for wriggling himself into the promised land. He is coming back to the land under the impression that God needs to be managed, that even though we have His promises it requires dexterity to get them fulfilled, that a man will get into the inheritance all the readier for knowing what to veil from God and what to exhibit, when to cleave to His word with great profession of most humble and absolute reliance on Him, and when to take matters into one's own hand. Jacob, in short, was about to enter the land as Jacob, the supplanter, and that would never do; he was going to win the land from Esau by guile, or as he might; and not to receive it from God. And, therefore, just as he is going to step into it, there lays hold of him, not an armed emissary of his brother, but a far more formidable antagonist—if Jacob will win the land, if it is to be a mere trial of skill, a wrestling match, it must at least be with the right person. Jacob is met with his own weapons. He has not chosen war, so no armed opposition is made; but with the naked force of his own nature, he is prepared for any man who will hold the land against him; with such tenacity, toughness, quick presence of mind, elasticity, as nature has given him, he is confident he can win and hold his own. So the real proprietor of the land strips himself for the contest, and lets him feel, by the first hold he takes of him, that if the question be one of mere strength he shall never enter the land.

This wrestling therefore was by no means actually or symbolically prayer. Jacob was not aggressive, nor did he stay behind his company to spend the night in praying for them. It was God who came and laid hold on Jacob to prevent him from entering the land in the temper he was in, and as Jacob. He was to be taught that it was not only Esau's appeased wrath, or his own skilful smoothing down of his brother's ruffled temper, that gave him entrance; but that a nameless Being, Who came out upon him from the darkness, guarded the land, and that by His passport only could he find entrance. And henceforth, as to every reader of this history so much more to Jacob's self, the meeting with Esau and the overcoming of his opposition were quite secondary to and eclipsed by his meeting and prevailing with this unknown combatant.

This struggle had, therefore, immense significance for the history of Jacob. It is, in fact, a concrete representation of the attitude he had maintained towards God throughout his previous history; and it constitutes the turning point at which he assumes a new and satisfactory attitude. Year after year Jacob had still retained confidence in himself; he had never been thoroughly humbled, but had always felt himself able to regain the land he had lost by his sin. And in this struggle he shows this same determination and self-confidence. He wrestles on indomitably. As Kurtz, whom I follow in his interpretation of this incident, says, "All along Jacob's life had been the struggle of a clever and strong, a pertinacious and enduring, a self-confident and self-sufficient person, who was sure of the result only when he helped himself—a contest with God, who wished to break his strength and wisdom, in order to bestow upon him real strength in divine weakness, and real wisdom in divine folly." All this self-confidence culminates now, and in one final and sensible struggle, his Jacob-nature, his natural propensity to wrest what he desires and win what he aims at, from the most unwilling opponent, does its very utmost and does it in vain. His steady straining, his dexterous feints, his quick gusts of vehement assault, make no impression on this combatant and move him not one foot off his ground. Time after time his crafty nature puts out all its various resources, now letting his grasp relax and feigning defeat, and then with gathered strength hurling himself on the stranger, but all in vain. What Jacob had often surmised during the last twenty years, what had flashed through him like a sudden gleam of light when he found himself married to Leah, that he was in the hands of one against whom it is quite useless to struggle, he now again begins to suspect. And as the first faint dawn appears, and he begins dimly to make out the face, the quiet breathing of which he had felt on his own during the contest, the man with whom he wrestles touches the strongest sinew in Jacob's body, and the muscle on which the wrestler most depends shrivels at the touch and reveals to the falling Jacob how utterly futile had been all his skill and obstinacy, and how quickly the stranger might have thrown and mastered him.

All in a moment, as he falls, Jacob sees how it is with him, and Who it is that has met him thus. As the hard, stiff, corded muscle shrivelled, so shrivelled his obdurate, persistent self-confidence. And as he is thrown, yet cleaves with the natural tenacity of a wrestler to his conqueror; so, utterly humbled before this Mighty One whom now he recognises and owns, he yet cleaves to Him and entreats His blessing. It is at this touch, which discovers the Almighty power of Him with whom he has been contending, that the whole nature of Jacob goes down before God. He sees how foolish and vain has been his obstinate persistence in striving to trick God out of His blessing, or wrest it from Him, and now he owns his utter incapacity to advance one step in this way, he admits to himself that he is stopped, weakened in the way, thrown on his back, and can effect nothing, simply nothing, by what he thought would effect all; and, therefore, he passes from wrestling to praying, and with tears, as Hosea says, sobs out from the broken heart of the strong man, "I will not let thee go except thou bless me." In making this transition from the boldness and persistence of self-confidence to the boldness of faith and humility, Jacob becomes Israel—the supplanter, being baffled by his conqueror, rises a Prince. Disarmed of all other weapons, he at last finds and uses the weapons wherewith God is conquered, and with the simplicity and guilelessness now of an Israelite indeed, face to face with God, hanging helpless with his arms around Him, he supplicates the blessing he could not win.

Thus, as Abraham had to become God's heir in the simplicity of humble dependence on God; as Isaac had to lay himself on God's altar with absolute resignation, and so become the heir of God, so Jacob enters on the inheritance through the most thorough humbling. Abraham had to give up all possessions and live on God's promise; Isaac had to give up life itself; Jacob had to yield his very self, and abandon all dependence on his own ability. The new name he receives signalizes and interprets this crisis in his life. He enters his land not as Jacob, but as Israel. The man who crossed the Jabbok was not the same as he who had cheated Esau and outwitted Laban and determinedly striven this morning with the angel. He was Israel, God's prince, entering on the land freely bestowed on him by an authority none could resist; a man who had learned that in order to receive from God, one must ask.

Very significant to Jacob in his after life must have been the lameness consequent on this night's struggle. He, the wrestler, had to go halting all his days. He who had carried all his weapons in his own person, in his intelligent watchful eye and tough right arm, he who had felt sufficient for all emergencies and a match for all men, had now to limp along as one who had been worsted and baffled and could not hide his shame from men. So it sometimes happens that a man never recovers the severe handling he has received at some turning point in his life. Often there is never again the same elastic step, the same free and confident bearing, the same apparent power, the same appearance to our fellow-men of completeness in our life; but, instead of this, there is a humble decision which, if it does not walk with so free a gait, yet knows better what ground it is treading and by what right. To the end some men bear the marks of the heavy stroke by which God first humbled them. It came in a sudden shock that broke their health, or in a disappointment which nothing now given can ever quite obliterate the trace of, or in circumstances painfully and permanently altered. And the man has to say with Jacob, I shall never now be what I might have been; I was resolved to have my own way, and though God in His mercy did not suffer me to destroy myself, yet to drive me from my purpose He was forced to use a violence, under the effects of which I go halting all my days, saved and whole, yet maimed to the end of time. I am not ashamed of the mark, at least when I think of it as God's signature I am able to glory in it, but it never fails to remind me of a perverse wilfulness I am ashamed of. With many men God is forced to such treatment; if any of us are under it, God forbid we should mistake its meaning and lie prostrate and despairing in the darkness instead of clinging to Him Who has smitten and will heal us.

For the treatment which Jacob received at Peniel must not be set aside as singular or exceptional. Sometimes God interposes between us and a greatly-desired possession which we have been counting upon as our right and as the fair and natural consequence of our past efforts and ways. The expectation of this possession has indeed determined our movements and shaped our life for some time past, and it would not only be assigned to us by men as fairly ours, but God also has Himself seemed to encourage us to win it. Yet when it is now within sight, and when we are rising to pass the little stream which seems alone to separate us from it, we are arrested by a strong, an irresistible hand. The reason is, that God wishes us to be in such a state of mind that we shall receive it as His gift, so that it becomes ours by an indefeasible title.

Similarly, when advancing to a spiritual possession, such checks are not without their use. Many men look with longing to what is eternal and spiritual, and they resolve to win this inheritance. And this resolve they often make as if its accomplishment depended solely on their own endurance. They leave almost wholly out of account that the possibility of their entering the state they long for is not decided by their readiness to pass through any ordeal, spiritual or physical, which may be required of them, but by God's willingness to give it. They act as if by taking advantage of God's promises, and by passing through certain states of mind and prescribed duties, they could, irrespective of God's present attitude towards them and constant love, win eternal happiness. In the life of such persons there must therefore come a time when their own spiritual energy seems all to collapse in that painful, utter way in which, when the body is exhausted, the muscles are suddenly found to be cramped and heavy and no longer responsive to the will. They are made to feel that a spiritual dislocation has taken place, and that their eagerness to enter life everlasting no longer stirs the active energies of the soul.

In that hour the man learns the most valuable truth he can learn, that it is God Who is wishing to save him, not he who must wrest a blessing from an unwilling God. Instead of any longer looking on himself as against the world, he takes his place as one who has the whole energy of God's will at his back, to give him rightful entrance into all blessedness. So long as Jacob was in doubt whether it was not some kind of man that was opposing him, he wrestled on; and our foolish ways of dealing with God terminate, when we recognise that He is not such an one as ourselves. We naturally act as if God had some pleasure in thwarting us—as if we could, and even ought to, maintain a kind of contest with God. We deal with Him as if He were opposed to our best purposes and grudged to advance us in all good, and as if He needed to be propitiated by penitence and cajoled by forced feelings and sanctimonious demeanour. We act as if we could make more way were God not in our way, as if our best prospects began in our own conception and we had to win God over to our views. If God is unwilling, then there is an end: no device nor force will get us past Him. If He is willing, why all this unworthy dealing with Him, as if the whole idea and accomplishment of salvation did not proceed from Him?

XXIV
JACOB'S RETURN

Genesis xxxv.

"As for me, when I came from Padan, Rachel died by me in the land of Canaan in the way."—Gen. xlviii. 7.

The words of the Wrestler at the brook Jabbok, "Let me go, for the day breaketh," express the truth that spiritual things will not submit themselves to sensible tests. When we seek to let the full daylight, by which we discern other objects, stream upon them, they elude our grasp. When we fancy we are on the verge of having our doubts for ever scattered, and our suppositions changed into certainties, the very approach of clear knowledge and demonstration seems to drive those sensitive spiritual presences into darkness. As Pascal remarked, and remarked as the mouth-piece of all souls that have earnestly sought for God, the world only gives us indications of the presence of a God Who conceals Himself. It is, indeed, one of the most mysterious characteristics of our life in this world, that the great Existence which originates and embraces all other Beings, should Himself be so silent and concealed: that there should be need of subtle arguments to prove His existence, and that no argument ever conceived has been found sufficiently cogent to convince all men. One is always tempted to say, how easy to end all doubt, how easy for God so to reveal Himself as to make unbelief impossible, and give to all men the glad consciousness that they have a God.

The reason of this "reserve" of God must lie in the nature of things. The greatest forces in nature are silent and unobtrusive and incomprehensible. Without the law of gravitation the universe would rush into ruin, but who has ever seen this force? Its effects are everywhere visible, but itself is shrouded in darkness and cannot be comprehended. So much more must the Infinite Spirit remain unseen and baffling all comprehension. "No man hath seen God at any time" must ever remain true. To ask for God's name, therefore, as Jacob did, is a mistake. For almost every one supposes that when he knows the name of a thing, he knows also its nature. The giving of a name, therefore, tends to discourage enquiry, and to beget an unfounded satisfaction as if, when we know what a thing is called, we know what it is.

The craving, therefore, which we all feel in common with Jacob—to have all mystery swept from between us and God, and to see Him face to face, so that we may know Him as we know our friends—is a craving which cannot be satisfied. You cannot ever know God as He is. Your mind cannot comprehend a Being who is pure Spirit, inhabiting no body, present with you here but present also hundreds of millions of miles away, related to time and to space and to matter in ways utterly impossible for you to comprehend.

What is possible, God has done. He has made Himself known in Christ. We are assured, on testimony that stands every kind of test, that in Him, if nowhere else, we find God. And yet even by Christ this same law of reserve if not concealment was observed. Not only did He forbid men and devils to proclaim who He was, but when men, weary of their own doubts and debatings, impatiently challenged him, "If thou be the Christ tell us plainly," He declined to do so. For really men must grow to the knowledge of Him. Even a human face cannot be known by once or twice seeing it; the practised artist often misses the expression best loved by the intimate friend, or by the relative whose own nature interprets to him the face in which he sees himself reflected. Much more can the child of God only attain to the knowledge of his Father's face by first of all *being* a child of God, and then by gradually growing up into His likeness.

But though God's operation is in darkness the results of it are in the light. "As Jacob passed over Peniel, the *sun rose* upon him, and he halted upon his thigh." As Jacob's company halted when they missed him, and as many anxious eyes were turned back into the darkness, they were unable still to see him; and even when the darkness began to scatter, and they saw dimly and far off a human figure, the sharpest eyes among them declare it cannot be Jacob, for the gait and walk, which alone they can judge by at that distance and in that light, are not his. But when at last the first ray of sunlight streams on him from over the hills of Gilead, all doubt is at an end; it *is* Jacob, but halting on his thigh. And he himself finds it is not a strain which the walking of a few paces will ease, nor a night cramp which will pass off, nor a mere dream which would vanish in broad day, but a real permanent lameness which he must explain to his company. Has he missed a step on the bank in the darkness, or stumbled or slipped on the slippery stones of the ford? It is a far more real thing to him than any such accident. So, however others may discredit the results of a work on the soul which they have not seen—however they may say of the first and most obvious results, "This is but a sickness of soul which the rising sun will dispel; a feigned peculiarity of walk which will be forgotten in the bustle of the day's work"—it is not so, but every contact with real life makes it more obvious that when God touches a man the result is real. And as Jacob's household and children in all generations counted that sinew which shrank sacred, and would not eat of it, so surely should we be reverential towards God's work in the soul of our neighbour, and respect even those peculiarities which are often the most obvious first-fruits of conversion, and which make it difficult for us to walk in the same comfort with these persons, and keep step with them as easily as once we did. A reluctance to live like other good people, an inability to share their innocent amusements, a distaste for the very duties of this life, a harsh or reserved bearing towards unconverted persons, an awkwardness in speaking of their religious experience, as well as an awkwardness in applying it to the ordinary circumstances of their life,—these and many other of the results of God's work on the soul should not be rudely dealt with, but respected; for though not in themselves either seemly or beneficial, they are evidence of God's touch.

After this contest with the angel, the meeting of Jacob with Esau has no separate significance. Jacob succeeds with his brother because already he has prevailed with God. He is on a satisfactory footing now with the Sovereign who alone can bestow the land and judge betwixt him and his brother. Jacob can no longer suppose that the chief obstacle to his advance is the resentment of Esau. He has felt and submitted to a stronger hand than Esau's. Such schooling we all need; and get, if we will take it. Like Jacob, we have to make our way to our end through numberless human interferences and worldly obstacles. Some of these we have to flee from, as Jacob from Laban; others we must meet and overcome, as our Esaus. Our own sin or mistake has put us under the power of some whose influence is disastrous; others, though we are not under their power at all, yet, consciously or unconsciously to themselves, continually cross our path and thwart us, keep us back and prevent us from effecting what we desire, and from shaping things about us according to our own ideas. And there will, from time to time, be present to our minds obvious ways in which we could defeat the opposition of these persons, and by which we fancy we could triumph over them. And what we are here taught is, that we need look for no triumph, and it is a pity for us if we win a triumph over any human opposition, however purely secular and unchristian, without first having prevailed with God in the matter. He comes in between us and all men and things, and, laying His hand on us, arrests us from further progress till we have to the very bottom and in every part adjusted the affair with Him—and then, standing right with Him, we can very easily, or at least we *can*, get right with all things. And it should be a suggestive and fruitful thought to the most of us that, in all cases in which we sin against our brother, God presents Himself as the champion of the wronged party. One day or other we must meet not the strongest putting of all those cases in which we have erred as the offended party could himself put them, but we must meet them as put by the Eternal Advocate of justice and right, who saw our spirit, our merely selfish calculating, our base motive, our impure desire, our unrighteous deed. Gladly would Jacob have met the mightiest of Esau's host in place of this invincible opponent, and it is this same Mighty One, this same watchful guardian of right Who threw Himself in Jacob's way, Who has His eye on us, Who has tracked us through all our years, and Who will certainly one time appear in our path as the champion of every one we have wronged, of every one whose soul we have put in jeopardy, of every one to whom we have not done what God intended we should do, of every one whom we have attempted merely to make use of; and in stating their case and showing us what justice and duty would have required of us, He will make us feel, what we cannot feel till He Himself convinces us, that, in all our dealings with men, wherein we have wronged them we have wronged Him.

The narrative now prepares to leave Jacob and make room for Joseph. It brings him back to Bethel, thereby completing the history of his triumph over the difficulties with which his life had been so thickly studded. The interest and much of the significance of a man's life come to an end when position and success are achieved. The remaining notices of Jacob's experience are of a sorrowful kind; he lives under a cloud until at the close the sun shines out again. We have seen him in his youth making experiments in life; in his prime founding a family and winning his way by slow and painful steps to his own place in the world; and now he enters on the last stage of his life, a stage in which signs of breaking up appear almost as soon as he attains his aim and place in life.

After all that had happened to Jacob, we should have expected him to make for Bethel as rapidly as his unwieldy company could be moved forwards. But the pastures that had charmed the eye of his grandfather captivated Jacob as well. He bought land at Shechem, and appeared willing to settle there. The vows which he had uttered with such fervour when his future was precarious are apparently quite forgotten, or more probably neglected, now that danger seems past. To go to Bethel involved the abandonment of admirable pastures, and the introduction of new religious views and habits into his family life. A man who has large possessions, difficult and precarious relations to sustain with the world, and a household unmanageable from its size, and from the variety of dispositions included in it, requires great independence and determination to carry out domestic reform on religious grounds. Even a slight change in our habits is often delayed because we are shy of exposing to observation fresh and deep convictions on religious subjects. Besides, we forget our fears and our vows when the time of hardship passes away; and that which, as young men, we considered almost hopeless, we at length accept as our right, and omit all remembrance and gratitude. A spiritual experience that is separated from your present by twenty years of active life, by a foreign residence, by marriage, by the growing up of a family around you, by other and fresher spiritual experiences, is apt to be very indistinctly remembered. The obligations you then felt and owned have been overlaid and buried in the lapse of years. And so it comes that a low tone is introduced into your life, and your homes cease to be model homes.

Out of this condition Jacob was roughly awakened. Sinning by unfaithfulness and softness towards his family, he is, according to the usual law, punished by family disaster of the most painful kind. The conduct of Simeon and Levi was apparently due quite as much to family pride and religious fanaticism as to brotherly love or any high moral view. In them first we see how the true religion, when held by coarse and ungodly men, becomes the root of all evil. We see the first instance of that fanaticism which so often made the Jews a curse rather than a blessing to other nations. Indeed, it is but an instance of the injustice, cruelty, and violence that at all times result where men suppose that they themselves are raised to quite peculiar privileges and to a position superior to their fellows, without recognising also that this position is held by the grace of a holy God and for the good of their fellows.

Jacob is now compelled to make a virtue of necessity. He flees to Bethel to escape the vengeance of the Shechemites. To such serious calamities do men expose themselves by arguing with conscience and by refusing to live up to their engagements. How can men be saved from living merely for sheep-feeding and cattle-breeding and trade and enjoyment? how can they be saved from gradually expelling from their character all principle and all high sentiment that conflicts with immediate advantage and present pleasure, save by such irresistible blows as here compelled Jacob to shift his camp? He has spiritual perception enough left to see what is meant. The order is at once issued: "Put away the strange gods that are among you, and be clean, and change your garments: and let us arise, and go up to Bethel; and I will make there an altar unto God, who answered me in the day of my distress, and was with me in the way which I went." Thus frankly does he acknowledge his error, and repair, so far as he can, the evil he has done. Thus decidedly does he press God's command on those whom he had hitherto encouraged or connived at. Even from his favourite Rachel he takes her gods and buries them. The fierce Simeon and Levi, proud of the blood with which they had washed out their sister's stain, are ordered to cleanse their garments and show some seemly sorrow, if they can.

If years go by without any such incident occurring in our life as drives us to a recognition of our moral laxity and deterioration, and to a frank and humble return to a closer walk with God, we had need to strive to awaken ourselves and ascertain whether we are living up to old vows and are really animated by thoroughly worthy motives. It was when Jacob came back to the very spot where he had lain on the open hill-side, and pointed out to his wives and children the stone he had set up to mark the spot, that he felt humbled as he cast his eye over the flocks and tents he now owned. And if you can, like Jacob, go back to spots in your life which were very woful and perplexed, years even when all continued dreary, dark, and hopeless, when friendlessness and poverty, bereavement or disease, laid their chilling, crushing hands upon you, times when you could not see what possible good there was for you in the world; and if now all this is solved, and your condition is in the most striking contrast to what you can remember, it becomes you to make acknowledgment to God such as you may have made to your friends, such acknowledgment as makes it plain that you are touched by His kindness. The acknowledgment Jacob made was sensible and honest. He put away the gods which had divided the worship of his family. In our life there is probably that which constantly tends to usurp an undue place in our regard; something which gives us more pleasure than the thought of God, or from which we really expect a more palpable benefit than we expect from God, and which, therefore, we cultivate with far greater assiduity. How easily, if we really wish to be on a clear footing with God, can we discover what things should be cast revengefully from us, buried and stamped upon and numbered with the things of the past. Are there not in your life any objects for the sake of which you sacrifice that nearness to God, and that sure hold of Him you once enjoyed? Are you not conscious of any pursuits, or hopes, or pleasures, or employments which practically have the effect of making you indifferent to spiritual advancement, and which make you shy of Bethel—shy of all that sets clear before you your indebtedness to God, and your own past vows and resolves?

"But," continues the narrative, "*but* Deborah, Rebekah's nurse, died;" that is, although Jacob and his house were now living in the fear of God, that did not exempt them from the ordinary distresses of family life. And among these, one that falls on us with a chastening and mild sadness all its own, occurs when there passes from the family one of its oldest members, and one who has by the delicate tact of love gained influence over all, and has by the common consent become the arbiter and mediator, the confidant and counsellor of the family. They, indeed, are the true salt of the earth whose own peace is so deep and abiding, and whose purity is so thorough and energetic, that into their ear we can disburden the troubled heart or the guilty conscience, as the wildest brook disturbs not and the most polluted fouls not the settled depths of the all-cleansing ocean. Such must Deborah have been, for the oak under which she was buried was afterwards known as "the oak of weeping." Specially must Jacob himself have mourned the death of her whose face was the oldest in his remembrance, and with whom his mother and his happy early days were associated. Very dear to Jacob, as to most men, were those who had been connected with and could tell him of his parents, and remind him of his early years. Deborah, by treating him still as a little boy, perhaps the only one who now called him by the pet name of childhood, gave him the pleasantest relief from the cares of manhood and the obsequious deportment of the other members of his household towards him. So that when she went a great blank was made to him: no longer was the wise and happy old face seen in her tent door to greet him of an evening; no longer could he take refuge in the peacefulness of her old age from the troubles of his lot: she being gone, a whole generation was gone, and a new stage of life was entered on.

But a heavier blow, the heaviest that death could inflict, soon fell upon him. She who had been as God's gift and smile to him since ever he had left Bethel at the first is taken from him now that he is restored to God's house. The number of his sons is completed, and the mother is removed. Suddenly and unexpectedly the blow fell, as they were journeying and fearing no ill. Notwithstanding the confident and cheering, though ambiguous, assurances of those about her, she had that clear knowledge of her own state which, without contradicting, simply put aside such assurances, and, as her soul was departing, feebly named her son Benoni, Son of my sorrow. She felt keenly what was, to a nature like hers, the very anguish of disappointment. She was never to feel the little creature stirring in her arms with personal human life, nor see him growing up to manhood as the son of his father's right hand. It was this sad death of Rachel's which made her the typical mother in Israel. It was not an unclouded, merely prosperous life which could fitly have foreshadowed the lives of those by whom the promised seed was to come; and least of all of the virgin to whom it was said, "A sword shall pierce through thine own soul also." It was the wail of Rachel that poetical minds among the Jews heard from time to time mourning their national disasters—"Rachel weeping" for her children, when by captivity they were separated from their mother country, or when, by the sword of Herod, the mothers of Bethlehem were bereaved of their babes. But it was also observed that that which brought this anguish on the mothers of Bethlehem was the birth there of the last Son of Israel, the blossom of this long-growing plant, suddenly born after a long and barren period, the son of Israel's right hand.

Still another death is registered in this chapter. It took place twelve years after Joseph went into Egypt, but is set down here for convenience. Esau and Jacob are, for the last time, brought together over their dead father—and for the last time, as they see that family likeness which comes out so strikingly in the face of the dead, do they feel drawn with brotherly affection to greet one another as sons of one father. In the dead Isaac, too, they find an object of veneration more impressive than they had found in the living father: the infirmities of age are exchanged for the mystery and majesty of death; the man has passed out of reach of pity, of contempt; the shrill, uncontrolled treble is no longer heard, there are no weak, plaintive movements, no childishness; but a solemn, august silence, a silence that seems to bid onlookers be still and refrain from disturbing the first communings of the departed spirit with things unseen.

The tenderness of these two brothers towards one another and towards their father was probably quickened by remorse when they met at his deathbed. They could not, perhaps, think that they had hastened his end by causing him anxieties which age has not strength to throw off; but they could not miss the reflection that the life now closed and finally sealed up might have been a much brighter life had they acted the part of dutiful, loving sons. Scarcely can one of our number pass from among us without leaving in our minds some self-reproach that we were not more kindly towards him, and that now he is beyond our kindness; that our opportunity for being brotherly towards *him* is for ever gone. And when we have very manifestly erred in this respect, perhaps there are among all the stings of a guilty conscience few more bitterly piercing than this. Many a son who has stood unmoved by the tears of a living mother—his mother by whom he lives, who has cherished him as her own soul, who has forgiven and forgiven and forgiven him, who has toiled and prayed, and watched for him—though he has hardened himself against her looks of imploring love and turned carelessly from her entreaties and burst through all the fond cords and snares by which she has sought to keep him, has yet broken down before the calm, unsolicitous, resting face of the dead. Hitherto he has not listened to her pleadings, and now she pleads no more. Hitherto she has heard no word of pure love from him, and now she hears no more. Hitherto he has done nothing for her of all that a son may do, and now there is nothing he can do. All the goodness of her life gathers up and stands out at once, and the time for gratitude is past. He sees suddenly, as by the withdrawal of a veil, all that that worn body has passed through for him, and all the goodness these features have expressed, and now they can never light up with joyful acceptance of his love and duty. Such grief as this finds its one alleviation in the knowledge that we may follow those who have gone before us; that we may yet make reparation. And when we think how many we have let pass without those frank, human, kindly offices we might have rendered, the knowledge that we also shall be gathered to our people comes in as very cheering. It is a grateful thought that there is a place where we shall be able to live rightly, where selfishness will not intrude and spoil all, but will leave us free to be to our neighbour all that we ought to be and all that we would be.

XXV
JOSEPH'S DREAMS

Genesis xxxvii.

"Surely the wrath of man shall praise thee."—Psalm lxxvi. 10.

The migration of Israel from Canaan to Egypt was a step of prime importance in the history. Great difficulties surrounded it, and very extraordinary means were used to bring it about. The preparatory steps occupied about twenty years, and nearly a fourth of the Book of Genesis is devoted to this period. This migration was a new idea. So little was it the result of an accidental dearth, or of any of those unforeseen calamities which cause families to emigrate from our own country, that God had forewarned Abraham himself that it must be. But only when it was becoming matter of actual experience and of history did God make known the precise object to be accomplished by it. This He makes known to Jacob as he passes from Canaan; and as, in abandoning the land he had so painfully won, his heart sinks, he is sustained by the assurance, "Fear not to go down into Egypt; I will there make thee a great nation."

The meaning of the step and the suitableness of the time and of the place to which Israel migrated, are apparent. For more than two hundred years now had Abraham and his descendants been wandering as pilgrims, and as yet there were no signs of God's promise being kept to them. That promise had been of a land and of a seed. Great fecundity had been promised to the race; but instead of that there had been a remarkable and perplexing barrenness, so that after two centuries one tent could contain the whole male population. In Jacob's time the population began to increase, but just in proportion as this part of the promise showed signs of fulfilment did the other part seem precarious. For, in proportion to their increase, the family became hostile to the Canaanites, and how should they ever get past that critical point in their history at which they would be strong enough to excite the suspicion, jealousy, and hatred of the indigenous tribes, and yet not strong enough to defend themselves against this enmity? Their presence was tolerated, just as our countrymen tolerated the presence of French refugees, on the score of their impotence to do harm. They were placed in a quite anomalous position; a single family who had continued for two hundred years in a land which they could only seem in jest to call theirs, dwelling as guests amid the natives, maintaining peculiar forms of worship and customs. Collision with the inhabitants seemed unavoidable as soon as their real character and pretensions oozed out, and as soon as it seemed at all likely that they really proposed to become owners and masters in the land. And, in case of such collision, what could be the result, but that which has ever followed where a few score men, brave enough to be cut down where they stood, have been exposed to mass after mass of fierce and blood-thirsty barbarians? A small number of men have often made good their entrance into lands where the inhabitants greatly outnumbered them, but these have commonly been highly disciplined troops, as in the case of the handful of Spaniards who seized Mexico and Peru; or they have been backed by a power which could aid with vast resources, as when the Romans held this country, or when the English lad in India left his pen on his desk and headed his few resolute countrymen, and held his own against unnumbered millions. It may be argued that if even Abraham with his own household swept Canaan clear of invaders, it might now have been possible for his grandson to do as much with increased means at his disposal. But, not to mention that every man has not the native genius for command and military enterprise which Abraham had, it must be taken into account that a force which is quite sufficient for a marauding expedition or a night attack, is inadequate for the exigencies of a campaign of several years' duration. The war which Jacob must have waged, had hostilities been opened, must have been a war of extermination, and such a war must have desolated the house of Israel if victorious, and, more probably by far, would have quite annihilated it.

It is to obviate these dangers, and to secure that Israel grow without let or hindrance, that Jacob's household is removed to a land where protection and seclusion would at once be secured to them. In the land of Goshen, secured from molestation partly by the influence of Joseph, but much more by the caste-prejudices of the Egyptians, and their hatred of all foreigners, and shepherds in particular, they enjoyed such prosperity and attained so rapidly the magnitude of a nation that some, forgetful alike of the promise of God and of the natural advantages of Israel's position, have refused to credit the accounts given us of the increase in their population. In a land so roomy, so fertile, and so secluded as that in which they were now settled, they had every advantage for making the transition from a family to a nation. Here they were preserved from all temptation to mingle with neighbours of a different race, and so lose their special place as a people called out by God to stand alone. The Egyptians would have scorned the marriages which the

Canaanites passionately solicited. Here the very contempt in which they were held proved to be their most valuable bulwark. And if Christians have any of the wisdom of the serpent, they will often find in the contempt or exclusiveness of worldly men a convenient barrier, preventing them, indeed, from enjoying some privileges, but at the same time enabling them, without molestation, to pursue their own way. I believe young people especially feel put about by the deprivations which they have to suffer in order to save their religious scruples; they are shut off from what their friends and associates enjoy, and they perceive that they are not so well liked as they would be had they less desire to live by conscience and by God's will. They feel ostracized, banished, frowned upon, laid under disabilities; but all this has its compensations: it forms for them a kind of Goshen where they may worship and increase, it runs a fence around them which keeps them apart from much that tempts and from much that enfeebles.

The residence of Israel in Egypt served another important purpose. By contact with the most civilised people of antiquity they emerged from the semi-barbarous condition in which they had previously been living. Going into Egypt mere shepherds, as Jacob somewhat plaintively and deprecatingly says to Pharaoh; not even possessed, so far as we know, of the fundamental arts on which civilisation rests, unable to record in writing the revelations God made, or to read them if recorded; having the most rudimentary ideas of law and justice, and having nothing to keep them together and give them form and strength, save the one idea that God meant to confer on them great distinction; they were transferred into a land where government had been so long established and law had come to be so thoroughly administered that life and property were as safe as among ourselves to-day, where science had made such advances that even the weather-beaten and time-stained relics of it seem to point to regions into which even the bold enterprise of modern investigation has not penetrated, and where all the arts needful for life were in familiar use, and even some practised which modern times have as yet been unable to recover. To no better school could the barbarous sons of Bilhah and Zilpah have been sent; to no more fitting discipline could the lawless spirits of Reuben, Simeon, and Levi have been subjected. In Egypt, where human life was sacred, where truth was worshipped as a deity, and where law was invested with the sanctity which belonged to what was supposed to have descended from heaven, they were brought under influences similar to those which ancient Rome exerted over conquered races.

The unwitting pioneer of this great movement was a man in all respects fitted to initiate it happily. In Joseph we meet a type of character rare in any race, and which, though occasionally reproduced in Jewish history, we should certainly not have expected to meet with at so early a period. For what chiefly strikes one in Joseph is a combination of grace and power, which is commonly looked upon as the peculiar result of civilising influences, knowledge of history, familiarity with foreign races, and hereditary dignity. In David we find a similar flexibility and grace of character, and a similar personal superiority. We find the same bright and humorous disposition helping him to play the man in adverse circumstances; but we miss in David Joseph's self-control and incorruptible purity, as we also miss something of his capacity for difficult affairs of state. In Daniel this latter capacity is abundantly present, and a facility equal to Joseph's in dealing with foreigners, and there is also a certain grace or nobility in the Jewish Vizier; but Joseph had a surplus of power which enabled him to be cheerful and alert in doleful circumstances, which Daniel would certainly have borne manfully but probably in a sterner and more passive mood. Joseph, indeed, seemed to inherit and happily combine the highest qualities of his ancestors. He had Abraham's dignity and capacity, Isaac's purity and power of self-devotion, Jacob's cleverness and buoyancy and tenacity. From his mother's family he had personal beauty, humour, and management.

A young man of such capabilities could not long remain insensible to his own powers or indifferent to his own destiny. Indeed, the conduct of his father and brothers towards him must have made him self-conscious, even though he had been wholly innocent of introspection. The force of the impression he produced on his family may be measured by the circumstance that the princely dress given him by his father did not excite his brothers' ridicule but their envy and hatred. In this dress there was a manifest suitableness to his person, and this excited them to a keen resentment of the distinction. So too they felt that his dreams were not the mere whimsicalities of a lively fancy, but were possessed of a verisimilitude which gave them importance. In short, the dress and the dreams were insufferably exasperating to the brothers, because they proclaimed and marked in a definite way the feeling of Joseph's superiority which had already been vaguely rankling in their consciousness. And it is creditable to Joseph that this superiority should first have emerged in connection with a point of conduct. It was in moral stature that the sons of Bilhah and Zilpah felt that they were outgrown by the stripling whom they carried with them as their drudge. Neither are we obliged to suppose that Joseph was a gratuitous tale-bearer, or that when he carried their evil report to his father he was actuated by a prudish, censorious, or in any way unworthy spirit. That he very well knew how to hold his tongue no man ever gave more adequate proof; but he that understands that there is a time to keep silence necessarily sees also that there is a time to speak. And no one can tell what torture that pure young soul may have endured in the remote pastures, when left alone to withstand day after day the outrage of these coarse and unscrupulous men. An elder brother, if he will, can more effectually guard the innocence of a younger brother than any other relative can, but he can also inflict a more exquisite torture.

Joseph, then, could not but come to think of his future and of his destiny in this family. That his father should make a pet of him rather than of Benjamin, he would refer to the circumstance that he was the oldest son of the wife of his choice, of her whom first he had loved, and who had no rival while he lived. To so charming a companion as Joseph must always have been, Jacob would naturally impart all the traditions and hopes of the family. In him he found a sympathetic and appreciative listener, who wiled him on to endless narrative, and whose imaginativeness quickened his own hopes and made the future seem grander and the world more wide. And what Jacob had to tell could fall into no kindlier soil than the opening mind of Joseph. No hint was lost, every promise was interpreted by some waiting aspiration. And thus, like every youth of capacity, he came to have his day-dreams. These day-dreams, though derided by those who cannot see the Cæsar in the careless trifler, and though often awkward and even offensive in their expression, are not always the mere discontented cravings of youthful vanity, but are frequently instinctive gropings towards the position which the nature is fitted to fill. "Our wishes," it has been said, "are the forefeeling of our capabilities;" and certainly where there is any special gift or genius in a man, the wish of his youth is predictive of the attainment of manhood. Whims, no doubt, there are, passing phases through which natural growth carries us, flutterings of the needle when too near some powerful influence; yet amidst all variations the true direction will be discernible and ultimately will be dominant. And it is a great art to discover what we are fit for, so that we may settle down to our own work, or patiently wait for our own place, without enviously striving to rob every other man of his crown and so losing our own. It is an art that saves us much fretting and disappointment and waste of time, to understand early in life what it is we can accomplish, and what precisely we mean to be at; "to recognise in our personal gifts or station, in the circumstances and complications of our life, in our relations to others, or to the world—the will of God teaching us what we are, and for what we ought to live." How much of life often is gone before its possessor sees the use he can put it to, and ceases to beat the air! How much of life is an ill-considered but passionate striving after what can never be attained, or a vain imitation of persons who have quite different talents and opportunities from ourselves, and who are therefore set to quite another work than ours.

It was because Joseph's dreams embodied his waking ambition that they were of importance. Dreams become significant when they are the concentrated essence of the main stream of the waking thoughts, and picturesquely exhibit the tendency of the character. "In a dream," says Elihu, "in a vision of the night, when deep sleep falleth upon men, in slumberings upon the bed; then He openeth the ears of men, and sealeth their instruction, that He may withdraw man from his purpose." This is precisely the use of dreams: our tendencies, unbridled by reason and fact, run on to results; the purposes which the business and other good influences of the day have kept down act themselves out in our dreams, and we see the character unimpeded by social checks, and as it would be were it unmodified by the restraints and efforts and external considerations of our conscious hours. Our vanity, our pride, our malice, our impurity, our deceit, our every evil passion, has free play, and shows us its finished result, and in so vivid and true though caricatured a form that we are startled and withdrawn from our purpose. The evil thought we have suffered to creep about our heart seems in our dreams to become a deed, and we wake in horror and thank God we can yet refrain. Thus the poor woman, who in utter destitution was beginning to find her child a burden, dreamt she had drowned it, and woke in horror at the fancied sound of the plunge—woke to clasp her little one to her breast with the thrill of a grateful affection that never again gave way. So that while no man is so foolish as to expect instruction from every dream any more than from every thought that visits his waking mind, yet every one who has been accumulating some knowledge of himself is aware that he has drawn a large part of this from his unconscious hours. As the naturalist would know but a small part of the animal kingdom by studying the creatures that show themselves in the daylight, so there are moles and bats of the spirit that exhibit themselves most freely in the darkness; and there are jungles and waste places in the character which, if you look on them only in the sunshine, may seem safe and lovely, but which at night show themselves to be full of all loathsome and savage beasts.

With the simplicity of a guileless mind, and with the natural proneness of members of one family to tell in the morning the dreams they have had, Joseph tells to the rest what seems to himself interesting, if not very suggestive. Possibly he thought very little of his dream till he saw how much importance his brothers attached to it. Possibly there might be discernible in his tone and look some mixture of youthful arrogance. And in his relation of the second dream, there was discernible at least a confidence that it would be realised, which was peculiarly intolerable to his brothers, and to his father seemed a dangerous symptom that called for rebuke. And yet "his father observed the saying;" as a parent has sometimes occasion to check his child, and yet, having done so, feels that that does not end the matter; that his boy and he are in somewhat different spheres, so that while he was certainly justified in punishing such and such a manifestation of his character, there is yet something behind that he does not quite understand, and for which possibly punishment may not be exactly the suitable award.

We fall into Jacob's mistake when we refuse to acknowledge as genuine and God-inspired any religious experience which we ourselves have not passed through, and which appears in a guise that is not only unfamiliar, but that is in some particulars objectionable. Up to the measure of our own religious experience, we recognise as genuine, and sympathise with, the parallel experience of others; but when they rise above us and get beyond us, we begin to speak of them as visionaries, enthusiasts, dreamers. We content ourselves with pointing again and again to the blots in their manner, and refuse to read the future through the ideas they add to our knowledge. But the future necessarily lies, not in the definite and finished attainment, but in the indefinite and hazy and dream-like germs that have yet growth in them. The future is not with Jacob, the rebuker, but with the dreaming, and, possibly, somewhat offensive Joseph. It was certainly a new element Joseph introduced into the experience of God's people. He saw, obscurely indeed, but with sufficient clearness to make him thoughtful, that the man whom God chooses and makes a blessing to others is so far advanced above his fellows that they lean upon him and pay him homage as if he were in the place of God to them. He saw that his higher powers were to be used for his brethren, and that the high destiny he somehow felt to be his was to be won by doing service so essential that his family would bow before him and give themselves into his hand. He saw this, as every man whose love keeps pace with his talent sees it, and he so far anticipated the dignity of Him who, in the deepest self-sacrifice, assumed a position and asserted claims which enraged His brethren and made even His believing mother marvel. Joseph knew that the welfare of his family rested not with the Esau-like good-nature of Reuben, still less with the fanatical ferocity of Simeon and Levi, not with the servile patience of Issachar, nor with the natural force and dignity of Judah, but with some deeper qualities which, if he himself did not yet possess, he at least valued and aspired to.

Whatever Joseph thought of the path by which he was to reach the high dignity which his dreams foreshadowed, he was soon to learn that the path was neither easy nor short. Each man thinks that, for himself at least, an exceptional path will be broken out, and that without difficulties and humiliations he will inherit the kingdom. But it cannot be so. And as the first step a lad takes towards the attainment of his position often involves him in trouble and covers him with confusion, and does so even although he ultimately finds that it was the only path by which he could have reached his goal; so, that which was really the first step towards Joseph's high destiny, no doubt seemed to him most calamitous and fatal. It certainly did so to his brothers, who thought that they were effectually and for ever putting an end to Joseph's pretensions. "Behold, this dreamer cometh; come now therefore, and let us slay him, and we shall see what will become of his dreams." They were, however, so far turned from their purpose by Reuben as to put him in a pit, meaning to leave him to die; and, doubtless, they thought themselves lenient in doing so. The less violent the death inflicted, the less of murder seems to be in it; so that he who slowly kills the body by only wounding the affections often counts himself no murderer at all, because he strikes no blood-shedding blow, and can deceive himself into the idea that it is the working of his victim's own spirit that is doing the damage.

The tank into which Joseph's brethren cast him was apparently one of those huge reservoirs excavated by shepherds in the East, that they may have a supply of water for their flocks in the end of the dry season, when the running waters fail them. Being so narrow at the mouth that they can be covered by a single stone, they gradually widen and form a large subterranean room; and the facility they thus afford for the confinement of prisoners was from the first too obvious not to be commonly taken advantage of. In such a place was Joseph left to die: under the ground, sinking in mire, his flesh creeping at the touch of unseen slimy creatures, in darkness, alone; that is to say, in a species of confinement which tames the most reckless and maddens the best balanced spirits, which shakes the nerve of the calmest, and has sometimes left the blankness of idiocy in masculine understandings. A few wild cries that ring painfully round his prison show him he need expect no help from without; a few wild and desperate beatings round the shelving walls of rock show him there is no possibility of escape; he covers his face, or casts himself on the floor of his dungeon to escape within himself, but only to find this also in vain, and to rise and renew efforts he knows to be fruitless. Here, then, is what has come of his fine dreams. With shame he now remembers the beaming confidence with which he had related them; with bitterness he thinks of the bright life above him, from which these few feet cut him so absolutely off, and of the quick termination that has been put to all his hopes.

Into such tanks do young persons especially get cast; finding themselves suddenly dropped out of the lively scenery and bright sunshine in which they have been living, down into roomy graves where they seem left to die at leisure. They had conceived a way of being useful in the world; they had found an aim or a hope; they had, like Joseph, discerned their place and were making towards it, when suddenly they seem to be thrown out and are left to learn that the world can do very well without them, that the sun and moon and the eleven stars do not drop from their courses or make wail because of their sad condition. High aims and commendable purposes are not so easily fulfilled as they fancied. The faculty and desire in them to be of service are not recognised. Men do not make room for them, and God seems to disregard the hopes He has excited in them. The little attempt at living they have made seems only to have got themselves and others into trouble. They begin to think it a mistake their being in the world at all; they curse the day of their birth. Others are enjoying this life, and seem to be making something of it, having found work that suits and develops them; but, for their own part, they cannot get fitted into life at any point, and are excluded from the onward movement of the world. They are again and again flung back, until they fear they are not to see the fulfilment of any one bright dream that has ever visited them, and that they are never, never at all, to live out the life it is in them to live, or find light and scope for maturing those germs of the rich human nature that they feel within them.

All this is in the way to attainment. This or that check, this long burial for years, does not come upon you merely because stoppage and hindrance have been useful to others, but because your advancement lies through these experiences. Young persons naturally feel strongly that life is all before them, that this life is, in the first place, their concern, and that God must be proved sufficient for this life, able to bring them to their ideal. And the first lesson they have to learn is, that mere youthful confidence and energy are not the qualities that overcome the world. They have to learn that humility, and the ambition that seeks great things, but not for ourselves, are the qualities really indispensable. But do men become humble by being told to become so, or by knowing they ought to be so? God must make us humble by the actual experience we meet with in our ordinary life. Joseph, no doubt, knew very well, what his aged grandfather must often have told him, that a man must die before he begins to live. But what could an ambitious, happy youth make of this, till he was thrown into the pit and left there? as truly passing through the bitterness of death as Isaac had passed through it, and as keenly feeling the pain of severance from the light of life. Then, no doubt, he thought of Isaac, and of Isaac's God, till between himself and the impenetrable dungeon-walls the everlasting arms seemed to interpose, and through the darkness of his death-like solitude the face of Jacob's God appeared to beam upon him, and he came to feel what we must, by some extremity, all be made to feel, that it was not in this world's life but in God he lived, that nothing could befall him which God did not will, and that what God had for him to do, God would enable him to do.

The heartless barbarity with which the brethren of Joseph sat down to eat and drink the very dainties he had brought them from his father, while they left him, as they thought, to starve, has been regarded by all later generations as the height of hard-hearted indifference. Amos, at a loss to describe the recklessness of his own generation, falls back upon this incident, and cries woe upon those "that drink wine in bowls, and anoint themselves with the chief ointment, but they are not grieved for the affliction of Joseph." We reflect, if we do not substantially reproduce, their sin when we are filled with animosity against those who usher in some higher kind of life, effort, or worship, than we ourselves as yet desire or are fit for, and which, therefore, reflects shame on our incapacity; and when we would fain, without using violence, get rid of such persons. There are often schemes set on foot by better men than ourselves, against which somehow our spirit rises, yet which, did we consider, we should at the most say with the cautious Gamaliel, Let us beware of doing anything to hinder this, let us see whether, perchance, it be not of God. Sometimes there are in families individuals who do not get the encouragement in well-doing they might expect in a Christian family, but are rather frowned upon and hindered by the other members of it, because they seem to be inaugurating a higher style of religion than the family is used to, and to be reflecting from their own conduct a condemnation of what has hitherto been current.

This treatment, who among us has not extended to Him who in His whole experience so closely resembles Joseph? So long as Christ is to us merely, as it were, the pet of the family, the innocent, guileless, loving Being on whom we can heap pretty epithets, and in whom we find play for our best affections, to whom it is easier to show ourselves affectionate and well-disposed than to the brothers who mingle with us in all our pursuits; so long as He remains to us as a child whose demands it is a relaxation to fulfil, we fancy that we are giving Him our hearts, and that He, if any, has our love. But when He declares to us His dreams, and claims to be our Lord, to whom with most absolute homage we must bow, who has a right to rule and means to rule over us, who will have His will done by us and not our own, then the love we fancied seems to pass into something like aversion. His purposes we would fain believe to be the idle fancies of a dreamer which He Himself does not expect us to pay much heed to. And if we do not resent the absolute surrender of ourselves to Him which He demands, if the bowing down of our fullest sheaves and brightest glory to Him is too little understood by us to be resented; if we think such dreams are not to come true, and that He does not mean much by demanding our homage, and therefore do not resent the demand; yet possibly we can remember with shame how we have "anointed ourselves with the chief ointment," lain listlessly enjoying some of those luxuries which our Brother has brought us from the Father's house, and yet let Himself and His cause be buried out of sight—enjoyed the good name of Christian, the pleasant social refinements of a Christian land, even the peace of conscience which the knowledge of the Christian's God produces, and yet turned away from the deeper emotions which His personal entreaties stir, and from those self-sacrificing efforts which His cause requires if it is to prosper.

There are, too, unstable Reubens still, whom something always draws aside, and who are ever out of the way when most needed; who, like him, are on the other side of the hill when Christ's cause is being betrayed; who still count their own private business that which must be done, and God's work that which may be done—work for themselves necessary, and God's work only voluntary and in the second place. And there are also those who, though they would be honestly shocked to be charged with murdering Christ's cause, can yet leave it to perish.

XXVI
JOSEPH IN PRISON

Genesis xxxix.

"Blessed is the man that endureth temptation: for when he is tried, he shall receive the crown of life."—James i. 12.

Dramatists and novelists who make it their business to give accurate representations of human life, proceed upon the understanding that there is a plot in it, and that if you take the beginning or middle without the end, you must fail to comprehend these prior parts. And a plot is pronounced good in proportion as, without violating truth to nature, it brings the leading characters into situations of extreme danger or distress, from which there seems no possible exit, and in which the characters themselves may have fullest opportunity to display and ripen their individual excellences. A life is judged poor and without significance, certainly unworthy of any longer record than a monumental epitaph may contain, if there be in it no critical passages, no emergencies when all anticipation of the next step is baffled, or when ruin seems certain. Though it has been brought to a successful issue, yet, to make it worthy of our consideration, it must have been brought to this issue through hazard, through opposition, contrary to many expectations that were plausibly entertained at the several stages of its career All men, in short, are agreed that the value of a human life consists very much in the hazards and conflicts through which it is carried; and yet we resent God's dealing with us when it comes to be our turn to play the hero, and by patient endurance and righteous endeavour to bring our lives to a successful issue. How flat and tame would this narrative have read had Joseph by easy steps come to the dignity he at last reached through a series of misadventures that called out and ripened all that was manly and strong and tender in his character. And take out of your own life all your difficulties, all that ever pained, agitated, depressed you, all that disappointed or postponed your expectations, all that suddenly called upon you to act in trying situations, all that thoroughly put you to the proof—take all this away, and what do you leave, but a blank insipid life that not even yourself can see any interest in?

And when we speak of Joseph's life as typical, we mean that it illustrates on a great scale and in picturesque and memorable situations principles which are obscurely operative in our own experience. It pleases the fancy to trace the incidental analogies between the life of Joseph and that of our Lord. As our Lord, so Joseph was the beloved of his father, sent by him to visit his brethren, and see after their well-being, seized and sold by them to strangers, and thus raised to be their Saviour and the Saviour of the world. Joseph in prison pronouncing the doom of one of his fellow-prisoners and the exaltation of the other, suggests the scene on Calvary where the one fellow-sufferer was taken, the other left. Joseph's contemporaries had of course no idea that his life foreshadowed the life of the Redeemer, yet they must have seen, or ought to have seen, that the deepest humiliation is often the path to the highest exaltation, that the deliverer sent by God to save a people may come in the guise of a slave, and that false accusations, imprisonment, years of suffering, do not make it impossible nor even unlikely that he who endures all these may be God's chosen Son.

In Joseph's being lifted out of the pit only to pass into slavery, many a man of Joseph's years has seen a picture of what has happened to himself. From a position in which they have been as if buried alive, young men not uncommonly emerge into a position preferable certainly to that out of which they have been brought, but in which they are compelled to work beyond their strength, and *that* for some superior in whom they have no special interest. Grinding toil, and often cruel insult, are their portion; and no necklace heavy with tokens of honour that afterwards may be allotted them can ever quite hide the scars made by the iron collar of the slave. One need not pity them over much, for they are young and have a whole lifetime of energy and power of resistance in their spirit. And yet they will often call themselves slaves, and complain that all the fruit of their labour passes over to others and away from themselves, and all prospect of the fulfilment of their former dreams is quite cut off. That which haunts their heart by day and by night, that which they seem destined and fit for, they never get time nor liberty to work out and attain. They are never viewed as proprietors of themselves, who may possibly have interests of their own and hopes of their own.

In Joseph's case there were many aggravations of the soreness of such a condition. He had not one friend in the country. He had no knowledge of the language, no knowledge of any trade that could make him valuable in Egypt—nothing, in short, but his own manhood and his faith in God. His introduction to Egypt was of the most dispiriting kind. What could he expect from strangers, if his own brothers had found him so obnoxious? Now when a man is thus galled and stung by injury, and has learned how little he can depend upon finding good faith and common justice in the world, his character will show itself in the attitude he assumes towards men and towards life generally. A weak nature, when it finds itself thus deceived and injured, will sullenly surrender all expectation of good, and will vent its spleen on the world by angry denunciations of the heartless and ungrateful ways of men. A proud nature will gather itself up from every blow, and determinedly work its way to an adequate revenge. A mean nature will accept its fate, and while it indulges in cynical and spiteful observations on human life, will greedily accept the paltriest rewards it can secure. But the supreme healthiness of Joseph's nature resists all the infectious influences that emanate from the world around him, and preserves him from every kind of morbid attitude towards the world and life. So easily did he throw off all vain regrets and stifle all vindictive and morbid feelings, so readily did he adjust himself to and so heartily enter into life as it presented itself to him, that he speedily rose to be overseer in the house of Potiphar. His capacity for business, his genial power of devoting himself to other men's interests, his clear integrity, were such, that this officer of Pharaoh's could find no more trustworthy servant in all Egypt—"he left all that he had in Joseph's hand: and he knew not ought he had, save the bread which he did eat."

Thus Joseph passed safely through a critical period of his life—the period during which men assume the attitude towards life and their fellow-men which they commonly retain throughout. Too often we accept the weapons with which the world challenges us, and seek to force our way by means little more commendable than the injustice and coldness we ourselves resent. Joseph gives the first great evidence of moral strength by rising superior to this temptation, to which almost all men in one degree or other succumb. You can hear him saying, deep down in his heart and almost unconsciously to himself: If the world is full of hatred, there is all the more need that at least one man should forgive and love; if men's hearts are black with selfishness, ambition, and lust, all the more reason for me to be pure and to do my best for all whom my service can reach; if cruelty, lying, and fraud meet me at every step, all the more am I called to conquer these by integrity and guilelessness.

His capacity, then, and power of governing others, were no longer dreams of his own, but qualities with which he was accredited by those who judged dispassionately and from the bare actual results. But this recognition and promotion brought with it serious temptation. So capable a person was he that a year or two had brought him to the highest post he could expect as a slave. His advancement, therefore, only brought his actual attainment into more painful contrast with the attainment of his dreams. As this sense of disappointment becomes more familiar to his heart, and threatens, under the monotonous routine of his household work, to deepen into a habit, there suddenly opens to him a new and unthought-of path to high position. An intrigue with Potiphar's wife might lead to the very advancement he sought. It might lift him out of the condition of a slave. It may have been known to him that other men had not scrupled so to promote their own interests. Besides, Joseph was young, and a nature like his, lively and sympathetic, must have felt deeply that in his position he was not likely to meet such a woman as could command his cordial love. That the temptation was in any degree to the sensual side of his nature there is no evidence whatever. For all that the narrative says, Potiphar's wife may not have been attractive in person. She *may* have been; and as she used persistently, "day by day," every art and wile by which she could lure Joseph to her mind, in some of his moods and under such circumstances as she would study to arrange he may have felt even this element of the temptation. But it is too little observed, and especially by young men who have most need to observe it, that in such temptations it is not only what is sensual that needs to be guarded against, but also two much deeper-lying tendencies—the craving for loving recognition, and the desire to respond to the feminine love for admiration and devotion. The latter tendency may not seem dangerous, but I am sure that if an analysis could be made of the broken hearts and shame-crushed lives around us, it would be found that a large proportion of misery is due to a kind of uncontrolled and mistaken chivalry. Men of masculine make are prone to show their regard for women. This regard, when genuine and manly, will show itself in purity of sympathy and respectful attention. But when this regard is debased by a desire to please and ingratiate oneself, men are precipitated into the unseemly expressions of a spurious manhood. The other craving—the craving for love—acts also in a somewhat latent way. It is this craving which drives men to seek to satisfy themselves with the expressions of love, as if thus they could secure love itself. They do not distinguish between the two; they do not recognise that what they most deeply desire is love, rather than the expression of it; and they awake to find that precisely in so far as they have accepted the expression without the sentiment, in so far have they put love itself beyond their reach.

This temptation was, in Joseph's case, aggravated by his being in a foreign country, unrestrained by the expectations of his own family, or by the eye of those he loved. He had, however, that which restrained him, and made the sin seem to him an impossible wickedness, the thought of which he could not, for a moment, entertain. "Behold, my master wotteth not what is with me in the house, and he hath committed all that he hath to my hand; there is none greater in this house than I; neither hath he kept back anything from me but thee, because thou art his wife: how then can I do this great wickedness, and sin against God?" Gratitude to the man who had pitied him in the slave market, and shown a generous confidence in a comparative stranger, was, with Joseph, a stronger sentiment than any that Potiphar's wife could stir in him. One can well believe it. We know what enthusiastic devotedness a young man of any worth delights to give to his superior who has treated him with justice, generosity, and confidence; who himself occupies a station of importance in public life; and who, by a dignified graciousness of demeanour, can make even the slave feel that he too is a man, and that through his slave's dress his proper manhood and worth are recognised. There are few stronger sentiments than the enthusiasm or quiet fidelity that can thus be kindled, and the influence such a superior wields over the young mind is paramount. To disregard the rights of his master seemed to Joseph a great wickedness and sin against God. The treachery of the sin strikes him; his native discernment of the true rights of every party in the case cannot, for a moment, be hoodwinked. He is not a man who can, even in the excitement of temptation, overlook the consequences his sin may have on others. Not unsteadied by the flattering solicitations of one so much above him in rank, nor sullied by the contagion of her vehement passion; neither afraid to incur the resentment of one who so regarded him, nor kindled to any impure desire by contact with her blazing lust; neither scrupling thoroughly to disappoint her in himself, nor to make her feel her own great guilt, he flung from him the strong inducements that seemed to net him round and entangle him as his garment did, and tore himself, shocked and grieved, from the beseeching hand of his temptress.

The incident is related not because it was the most violent temptation to which Joseph was ever exposed, but because it formed a necessary link in the chain of circumstances that brought him before Pharaoh. And however strong this temptation may have been, more men would be found who could thus have spoken to Potiphar's wife than who could have kept silence when accused by Potiphar. For his purity you will find his equal, one among a thousand; for his mercy scarcely one. For there is nothing more intensely trying than to live under false and painful accusations, which totally misrepresent and damage your character; which effectually bar your advancement, and which yet you have it in your power to disprove. Joseph, feeling his indebtedness to Potiphar, contents himself with the simple averment that he himself is innocent. The word is on his tongue that can put a very different face on the matter, but rather than utter that word, Joseph will suffer the stroke that otherwise must fall on his master's honour; will pass from his high place and office of trust, through the jeering or possibly compassionating slaves, branded as one who has betrayed the frankest confidence, and is fitter for the dungeon than the stewardship of Potiphar. He is content to lie under the cruel suspicion that he had in the foulest way wronged the man whom most he should have regarded, and whom in point of fact he did enthusiastically serve. There was one man in Egypt whose good-will he prized, and this man now scorned and condemned him, and this for the very act by which Joseph had proved most faithful and deserving.

And even after a long imprisonment, when he had now no reputation to maintain, and when such a little bit of court scandal as he could have retailed would have been highly palatable and possibly useful to some of those polished ruffians and adventurers who made their dungeon ring with questionable tales, and with whom the free and levelling intercourse of prison life had put him on the most familiar footing, and when they twitted and taunted him with his supposed crime, and gave him the prison sobriquet that would most pungently embody his villainy and failure, and when it might plausibly have been pleaded by himself that such a woman should be exposed, Joseph uttered no word of recrimination, but quietly endured, knowing that God's providence could allow him to be merciful; protesting, when needful, that he himself was innocent, but seeking to entangle no one else in his misfortune.

It is this that has made the world seem so terrible a place to many—that the innocent must so often suffer for the guilty, and that, without appeal, the pure and loving must lie in chains and bitterness, while the wicked live and see good days. It is this that has made men most despairingly question whether there be indeed a God in heaven Who knows who the real culprit is, and yet suffers a terrible doom slowly to close around the innocent; Who sees where the guilt lies, and yet moves no finger nor speaks the word that would bring justice to light, shaming the secure triumph of the wrongdoer, and saving the bleeding spirit from its agony. It was this that came as the last stroke of the passion of our Lord, that He was numbered among the transgressors; it was this that caused or materially increased the feeling that God had deserted Him; and it was this that wrung from Him the cry which once was wrung from David, and may well have been wrung from Joseph, when, cast into the dungeon as a mean and treacherous villain, whose freedom was the peril of domestic peace and honour, he found himself again helpless and forlorn, regarded now not as a mere worthless lad, but as a criminal of the lowest type. And as there always recur cases in which exculpation is impossible just in proportion as the party accused is possessed of honourable feeling, and where silent acceptance of doom is the result not of convicted guilt, but of the very triumph of self-sacrifice, we must beware of over-suspicion and injustice. There is nothing in which we are more frequently mistaken than in our suspicions and harsh judgments of others.

"But the Lord was with Joseph, and allowed him mercy, and gave him favour in the sight of the keeper of the prison." As in Potiphar's house, so in the king's house of detention, Joseph's fidelity and serviceableness made him seem indispensable, and by sheer force of character he occupied the place rather of governor than of prisoner. The discerning men he had to do with, accustomed to deal with criminals and suspects of all shades, very quickly perceived that in Joseph's case justice was at fault, and that he was a mere scape-goat. Well might Potiphar's wife, like Pilate's, have had warning dreams regarding the innocent person who was being condemned; and probably Potiphar himself had suspicion enough of the true state of matters to prevent him from going to extremities with Joseph, and so to imprison him more out of deference to the opinion of his household, and for the sake of appearances, than because Joseph alone was the object of his anger. At any rate, such was the vitality of Joseph's confidence in God, and such was the light-heartedness that sprang from his integrity of conscience, that he was free from all absorbing anxiety about himself, and had leisure to amuse and help his fellow-prisoners, so that such promotion as a gaol could afford he won, from a dungeon to a chain, from a chain to his word of honour. Thus even in the unlatticed dungeon the sun and moon look in upon him and bow to him; and while his sheaf seems at its poorest, all rust and mildew, the sheaves of his masters do homage.

After the arrival of two such notable criminals as the chief butler and baker of Pharaoh—the chamberlain and steward of the royal household—Joseph, if sometimes pensive, must yet have had sufficient entertainment at times in conversing with men who stood by the king, and were familiar with the statesmen, courtiers, and military men who frequented the house of Potiphar. He had now ample opportunity for acquiring information which afterwards stood him in good stead, for apprehending the character of Pharaoh, and for making himself acquainted with many details of his government, and with the general condition of the people. Officials in disgrace would be found much more accessible and much more communicative of important information than officials in court favour could have been to one in Joseph's position.

It is not surprising that three nights before Pharaoh's birthday these functionaries of the court should have recalled in sleep such scenes as that day was wont to bring round, nor that they should vividly have seen the parts they themselves used to play in the festival. Neither is it surprising that they should have had very anxious thoughts regarding their own fate on a day which was chosen for deciding the fate of political or courtly offenders. But it is remarkable that they having dreamed these dreams Joseph should have been found willing to interpret them. One desires some evidence of Joseph's attitude towards God during this period when God's attitude towards him might seem doubtful, and especially one would like to know what Joseph by this time thought of his juvenile dreams, and whether in the prison his face wore the same beaming confidence in his own future which had smitten the hearts of his brothers with impatient envy of the dreamer. We seek some evidence, and here we find it. Joseph's willingness to interpret the dreams of his fellow-prisoners proves that he still believed in his own, that among his other qualities he had this characteristic also of a steadfast and profound soul, that he "reverenced as a man the dreams of his youth." Had he not done so, and had he not yet hoped that somehow God would bring truth out of them, he would surely have said: Don't you believe in dreams; they will only get you into difficulties. He would have said what some of us could dictate from our own thoughts: I won't meddle with dreams any more; I am not so young as I once was; doctrines and principles that served for fervent romantic youth seem puerile now, when I have learned what human life actually is; I can't ask this man, who knows the world and has held the cup for Pharaoh, and is aware what a practical shape the king's anger takes, to cherish hopes similar to those which often seem so remote and doubtful to myself. My religion has brought me into trouble: it has lost me my situation, it has kept me poor, it has made me despised, it has debarred me from enjoyment. Can I ask this man to trust to inward whisperings which seem to have so misled me? No, no; let every man bear his own burden. If he wishes to become religious, let not me bear the responsibility. If he will dream, let him find some other interpreter.

This casual conversation, then, with his fellow-prisoners was for Joseph one of those perilous moments when a man holds his fate in his hand, and yet does not know that he is specially on trial, but has for his guidance and safe-conduct through the hazard only the ordinary safeguards and lights by the aid of which he is framing his daily life. A man cannot be forewarned of trial, if the trial is to be a fair test of his habitual life. He must not be called to the lists by the herald's trumpet warning him to mind his seat and grasp his weapon; but must be suddenly set upon if his habit of steadiness and balance is to be tested, and the warrior-instinct to which the right weapon is ever at hand. As Joseph, going the round of his morning duty and spreading what might stir the appetite of these dainty courtiers, noted the gloom on their faces, had he not been of a nature to take upon himself the sorrows of others, he might have been glad to escape from their presence, fearful lest he should be infected by their depression, or should become an object on which they might vent their ill-humour. But he was girt with a healthy cheerfulness that could bear more than his own burden; and his pondering of his own experience made him sensitive to all that affected the destinies of other men.

Thus Joseph in becoming the interpreter of the dreams of other men became the fulfiller of his own. Had he made light of the dreams of his fellow-prisoners because he had already made light of his own, he would, for aught we can see, have died in the dungeon. And, indeed, what hope is left for a man, and what deliverance is possible, when he makes light of his own most sacred experience, and doubts whether after all there was any Divine voice in that part of his life which once he felt to be full of significance? Sadness, cynical worldliness, irritability, sour and isolating selfishness, rapid deterioration in every part of the character—these are the results which follow our repudiation of past experience and denial of truth that once animated and purified us; when, at least, this repudiation and denial are not themselves the results of our advance to a higher, more animating, and more purifying truth. We cannot but leave behind us many "childish things," beliefs that we now recognise as mere superstitions, hopes and fears which do not move the maturer mind; we cannot but seek always to be stripping ourselves of modes of thinking which have served their purpose and are out of date, but we do so only for the sake of attaining freer movement in all serviceable and righteous conduct, and more adequate covering for the permanent weaknesses of our own nature— "not for that we would be unclothed, but clothed upon," that truth partial and dawning may be swallowed up in the perfect light of noon. And when a supposed advance in the knowledge of things spiritual robs us of all that sustains true spiritual life in us, and begets an angry contempt of our own past experience and a proud scorning of the dreams that agitate other men; when it ministers not at all to the growth in us of what is tender and pure and loving and progressive, but hardens us to a sullen or coarsely riotous or coldly calculating character, we cannot but question whether it is not a delusion rather than a truth that has taken possession of us.

If it is fanciful, it is yet almost inevitable, to compare Joseph at this stage of his career to the great Interpreter who stands between God and us, and makes all His signs intelligible. Those Egyptians could not forbear honouring Joseph, who was able to solve to them the mysteries on the borders of which the Egyptian mind continually hovered, and which it symbolized by its mysterious sphinxes, its strange chambers of imagery, its unapproachable divinities. And we bow before the Lord Jesus Christ, because He can read our fate and unriddle all our dim anticipations of good and evil, and make intelligible to us the visions of our own hearts. There is that in us, as in these men, from which a skilled eye could already read our destiny. In the eye of One who sees the end from the beginning, and can distinguish between the determining influences of character and the insignificant manifestations of a passing mood, we are already designed to our eternal places. And it is in Christ alone your future is explained. You cannot understand your future without taking Him into your confidence. You go forward blindly to meet you know not what, unless you listen to His interpretation of the vague presentiments that visit you. Without Him what can we make of those suspicions of a future judgment, or of those yearnings after God, that hang about our hearts? Without Him what can we make of the idea and hope of a better life than we are now living, or of the strange persuasion that all will yet be well—a persuasion that seems so groundless, and which yet will not be shaken off, but finds its explanation in Christ? The excess of side light that falls across our path from the present seems only to make the future more obscure and doubtful, and from Him alone do we receive any interpretation of ourselves that even seems to be satisfying. Our fellow-prisoners are often seen to be so absorbed in their own affairs that it is vain to seek light from them; but He, with patient, self-forgetting friendliness, is ever disengaged, and even elicits, by the kindly and interrogating attitude He takes towards us, the utterance of all our woes and perplexities. And it is because He has had dreams Himself that He has become so skilled an interpreter of ours. It is because in His own life He had His mind hard pressed for a solution of those very problems which baffle us, because He had for Himself to adjust God's promise to the ordinary and apparently casual and untoward incidents of a human life, and because He had to wait long before it became quite clear how one Scripture after another was to be fulfilled by a course of simple confiding obedience—it is because of this experience of His own, that He can now enter into and rightly guide to its goal every longing we cherish.

XXVII
PHARAOH'S DREAMS

Genesis xli.

"Thus saith the Lord, that frustrateth the tokens of the liars, and maketh diviners mad; that confirmeth the word of His servant, and performeth the counsel of His messengers: that saith of Cyrus, He is My shepherd, and shall perform all My pleasure."—Isa. xliv. 25, 28.

The preceding act in this great drama—the act comprising the scenes of Joseph's temptation, unjust imprisonment, and interpretation of his fellow-prisoners' dreams—was written for the sake of explaining how Joseph came to be introduced to Pharaoh. Other friendships may have been formed in the prison, and other threads may have been spun which went to make up the life of Joseph, but this only is pursued. For a time, however, there seemed very little prospect that this would prove to be the thread on which his destiny hung. Joseph made a touching appeal to the Chief Butler: "yet did not the Chief Butler remember Joseph, but forgat him." You can see him in the joy of his release affectionately pressing Joseph's hand as the king's messengers knocked off his fetters. You can see him assuring Joseph, by his farewell look, that he might trust him; mistaking mere elation at his own release for warmth of feeling towards Joseph, though perhaps even already feeling just the slightest touch of awkwardness at being seen on such intimate terms with a Hebrew slave. How could he, when in the palace of Pharaoh and decorated with the insignia of his office and surrounded by courtiers, break through the formal etiquette of the place? What with the pleasant congratulations of old friends, and the accumulation of business since he had been imprisoned, and the excitement of restoration from so low and hopeless to so high and busy a position, the promise to Joseph is obliterated from his mind. If it once or twice recurs to his memory, he persuades himself he is waiting for a good opening to mention Joseph. It would perhaps be unwarrantable to say that he admits the idea that he is in no way indebted to Joseph, since all that Joseph had done was to interpret, but by no means to determine, his fate.

The analogy which we could not help seeing between Joseph's relation to his fellow-prisoners, and our Lord's relation to us, pursues us here. For does not the bond between us and Him seem often very slender, when once we have received from Him the knowledge of the King's good-will, and find ourselves set in a place of security? Is not Christ with many a mere stepping-stone for their own advancement, and of interest only so long as they are in anxiety about their own fate? Their regard for Him seems abruptly to terminate as soon as they are ushered to freer air. Brought for a while into contact with Him, the very peace and prosperity which that intercourse has introduced them to become opiates to dull their memory and their gratitude. They have received all they at present desire, they have no more dreams, their life has become so plain and simple and glad that they need no interpreter. They seem to regard Him no more than an official is regarded who is set to discharge to all comers some duty for which he is paid; who mingles no love with his work, and from whom they would receive the same benefits whether he had any personal interest in them or no. But there is no Christianity where there is no loving remembrance of Christ. If your contact with Him has not made Him your Friend whom you can by no possibility forget, you have missed the best result of your introduction to Him. It makes one think meanly of the Chief Butler that such a personality as Joseph's had not more deeply impressed him—that everything he heard and saw among the courtiers did not make him say to himself: There is a friend of mine, in prison hard by, that for beauty, wisdom, and vivacity would more than match the finest of you all. And it says very little for us if we can have known anything of Christ without seeing that in Him we have what is nowhere else, and without finding that He has become the necessity of our life to whom we turn at every point.

But, as things turned out, it was perhaps as well for Joseph that his promising friend did forget him. For, supposing the Chief Butler had overcome his natural reluctance to increase his own indebtedness to Pharaoh by interceding for a friend, supposing he had been willing to risk the friendship of the Captain of the Guard by interfering in so delicate a matter, and supposing Pharaoh had been willing to listen to him, what would have been the result? Probably that Joseph would have been sold away to the quarries, for certainly he could not have been restored to Potiphar's house; or, at the most, he might have received his liberty, and a free pass out of Egypt. That is to say, he would have obtained liberty to return to sheep-shearing and cattle-dealing and checkmating his brother's plots. In any probable case his career would have tended rather towards obscurity than towards the fulfilment of his dreams.

There seems equal reason to congratulate Joseph on his friend's forgetfulness, when we consider its probable effects, not on his career, but on his character. When he was left in prison after so sudden and exciting an incursion of the outer world as the king's messengers would make, his mind must have run chiefly in two lines of thought. Naturally he would feel some envy of the man who was being restored; and when day after day passed and more than the former monotony of prison routine palled on his spirit; when he found how completely he was forgotten, and how friendless and lone a creature he was in that strange land where things had gone so mysteriously against him; when he saw before him no other fate than that which he had seen befall so many a slave thrown into a dungeon at his master's pleasure and never more heard of, he must have been sorely tempted to hate the whole world, and especially those brethren who had been the beginning of all his misfortunes. Had there been any selfishness in solution in Joseph's character, this is the point at which it would have quickly crystallized into permanent forms. For nothing more certainly elicits and confirms selfishness than bad treatment. But from his conduct on his release, we see clearly enough that through all this trying time his heroism was not only that of the strong man who vows that though the whole world is against him the day will come when the world shall have need of him, but of the saint of God in whom suffering and injustice leave no bitterness against his fellows, nor even provoke one slightest morbid utterance.

But another process must have been going on in Joseph's mind at the same time. He must have felt that it was a very serious thing that he had been called upon to do in interpreting God's will to his fellow-prisoners. No doubt he fell into it quite naturally and aptly, because it was liker his proper vocation, and more of his character could come out in it than in anything he had yet done. Still, to be mixed up thus with matters of life and death concerning other people, and to have men of practical ability and experience and high position listening to him as to an oracle, and to find that in very truth a great power was committed to him, was calculated to have *some* considerable result one way or other on Joseph. And these two years of unrelieved and sobering obscurity cannot but be considered most opportune. For one of two things is apt to follow the world's first recognition of a man's gifts. He is either induced to pander to the world's wonder and become artificial and strained in all he does, so losing the spontaneity and naturalness and sincerity which characterise the best work; or he is awed and steadied. And whether the one or the other result follow, will depend very much on the other things that are happening to him. In Joseph's case it was probably well that after having made proof of his powers he was left in such circumstances as would not only give him time for reflection, but also give a humble and believing turn to his reflections. He was not at once exalted to the priestly caste, nor enrolled among the wise men, nor put in any position in which he would have been under constant temptation to display and trifle with his power; and so he was led to the conviction that deeper even than the joy of receiving the recognition and gratitude of men was the abiding satisfaction of having done the thing God had given him to do.

These two years, then, during which Joseph's active mind must necessarily have been forced to provide food for itself, and have been thrown back upon his past experience, seem to have been of eminent service in maturing his character. The self-possessed dignity and ease of command which appear in him from the moment when he is ushered into Pharaoh's presence have their roots in these two years of silence. As the bones of a strong man are slowly, imperceptibly knit, and gradually take the shape and texture they retain throughout; so during these years there was silently and secretly consolidating a character of almost unparalleled calmness and power. One has no words to express how tantalizing it must have been to Joseph to see this Egyptian have his dreams so gladly and speedily fulfilled, while he himself, who had so long waited on the true God, was left waiting still, and now so utterly unbefriended that there seemed no possible way of ever again connecting himself with the world outside the prison walls. Being pressed thus for an answer to the question, What does God mean to make of my life? he was brought to see and to hold as the most important truth for him, that the first concern is, that God's purposes be accomplished; the second, that his own dreams be fulfilled. He was enabled, as we shall see in the sequel, to put God truly in the first place, and to see that by forwarding the interests of other men, even though they were but light-minded chief butlers at a foreign court, he might be as serviceably furthering the purposes of God, as if he were forwarding his own interests. He was compelled to seek for some principle that would sustain and guide him in the midst of much disappointment and perplexity, and he found it in the conviction that the essential thing to be accomplished in this world, and to which every man must lay his shoulder, is God's purpose. Let that go on, and all else that should go on will go on. And he further saw that he best fulfils God's purpose who, without anxiety and impatience, does the duty of the day, and gives himself without stint to the "charities that soothe and heal and bless."

His perception of the breadth of God's purpose, and his profound and sympathetic and active submission to it, were qualities too rare not to be called into influential exercise. After two years he is suddenly summoned to become God's interpreter to Pharaoh. The Egyptian king was in the unhappy though not uncommon position of having a revelation from God which he could not read, intimations and presentiments he could not interpret. To one man is given the revelation, to another the interpretation. The official dignity of the king is respected, and to him is given the revelation which concerns the welfare of the whole people. But to read God's meaning in a revelation requires a spiritual intelligence trained to sympathy with His purposes, and such a spirit was found in Joseph alone.

The dreams of Pharaoh were thoroughly Egyptian. The marvel is, that a symbolism so familiar to the Egyptian eye should not have been easily legible to even the most slenderly gifted of Pharaoh's wise men. "In my dream," says the king, "behold, I stood upon the bank of the river: and, behold, there came up out of the river seven kine," and so on. Every land or city is proud of its river, but none has such cause to be so as Egypt of its Nile. The country is accurately as well as poetically called "the gift of Nile." Out of the river do really come good or bad years, fat or lean kine. Wholly dependent on its annual rise and overflow for the irrigating and enriching of the soil, the people worship it and love it, and at the season of its overflow give way to the most rapturous expressions of joy. The cow also was revered as the symbol of the earth's productive power. If then, as Joseph avers, God wished to show to Pharaoh that seven years of plenty were approaching, this announcement could hardly have been made plainer in the language of dreams than by showing to Pharaoh seven well-favoured kine coming up out of the bountiful river to feed on the meadow made richly green by its waters. If the king had been sacrificing to the river, such a sight, familiar as it was to the dwellers by the Nile, might well have been accepted by him as a promise of plenty in the land. But what agitated Pharaoh, and gave him the shuddering presentiment of evil which accompanies some dreams, was the sequel. "Behold, seven other kine came up after them, poor and very ill-favoured and lean-fleshed, such as I never saw in all the land of Egypt for badness: and the lean and the ill-favoured kine did eat up the first seven fat kine: and when they had eaten them up it could not be known that they had eaten them; but they were still ill-favoured, as at the beginning," —a picture which to the inspired dream-reader represented seven years of famine so grievous, that the preceding plenty should be swallowed up and not be known. A similar image occurred to a writer who, in describing a more recent famine in the same land, says: "The year presented itself as a monster whose wrath must annihilate all the resources of life and all the means of subsistence."

It tells in favour of the court magicians and wise men that not one of them offered an interpretation of dreams to which it would certainly not have been difficult to attach some tolerably feasible interpretation. Probably these men were as yet sincere devotees of astrology and occult science, and not the mere jugglers and charlatans their successors seem to have become. When men cannot make out the purpose of God regarding the future of the race, it is not wonderful that they should endeavour to catch the faintest, most broken echo of His voice to the world, wherever they can find it. Now there is a wide region, a borderland between the two worlds of spirit and of matter, in which are found a great many mysterious phenomena which cannot be explained by any known laws of nature, and through which men fancy they get nearer to the spiritual world. There are many singular and startling appearances, coincidences, forebodings, premonitions which men have always been attracted towards, and which they have considered as open ways of communication between God and man. There are dreams, visions, strange apprehensions, freaks of memory, and other mental phenomena, which, when all classed together, assorted, and skilfully applied to the reading of the future, once formed quite a science by itself. When men have no word from God to depend upon, no knowledge at all of where either the race or individuals are going to, they will eagerly grasp at anything that even seems to shed a ray of light on their future. We for the most part make light of that whole category of phenomena, because we have a more sure word of prophecy by which, as with a light in a dark place, we can tell where our next step should be, and what the end shall be. But invariably in heathen countries, where no guiding Spirit of God was believed in, and where the absence of His revealed will left numberless points of duty doubtful and all the future dark, there existed in lieu of this a class of persons who, under one name or other, undertook to satisfy the craving of men to see into the future, to forewarn them of danger, and advise them regarding matters of conduct and affairs of state.

At various points of the history of God's revelation these professors of occult science appear. In each case a profound impression is made by the superior wisdom or power displayed by the "wise men" of God. But in reading the accounts we have of these collisions between the wisdom of God and that of the magicians, a slight feeling of uneasiness sometimes enters the mind. You may feel that these wonders of Joseph, Moses, and Daniel have a romantic air about them, and you feel, perhaps, a slight scruple in granting that God would lend Himself to such displays—displays so completely out of date in our day. But we are to consider not only that there is nothing of the kind more certain than that dreams do sometimes even now impart most significant warning to men; but, also, that the time in which Joseph lived was the childhood of the world, when God had neither spoken much to men, nor could speak much, because as yet they had not learned His language, but were only being slowly taught it by signs suited to their capacity. If these men were to receive any knowledge beyond what their own unaided efforts could attain, they must be taught in a language they understood. They could not be dealt with as if they had already attained a knowledge and a capacity which could only be theirs many centuries after; they must be dealt with by signs and wonders which had perhaps little moral teaching in them, but yet gave evidence of God's nearness and power such as they could and did understand. God thus stretched out His hand to men in the darkness, and let them feel His strength before they could look on His face and understand His nature.

It is the existence at the court of Pharaoh of this highly respected class of dream-interpreters and wise men, which lends significance to the conduct of Joseph when summoned into the royal presence. Such wisdom as he displayed in reading Pharaoh's visions was looked upon as attainable by means within the reach of any man who had sufficient faculty for the science. And the first idea in the minds of the courtiers would probably have been, had Joseph not solemnly protested against it, that he was an adept where they were apprentices and bunglers, and that his success was due purely to professional skill. This was of course perfectly well known to Joseph, who for a number of years had been familiar with the ideas prevalent at the court of Pharaoh; and he might have argued that there could be no great harm in at least effecting his deliverance from an unjust imprisonment by allowing Pharaoh to suppose that it was to him he was indebted for the interpretation of his dreams. But his first word to Pharaoh is a self-renouncing exclamation: "Not in me: *God* shall give Pharaoh an answer of peace." Two years had elapsed since anything had occurred which looked the least like the fulfilment of his own dreams, or gave him any hope of release from prison; and now, when measuring himself with these courtiers and feeling able to take his place with the best of them, getting again a breath of free air and feeling once more the charm of life, and having an opening set before his young ambition, being so suddenly transferred from a place where his very existence seemed to be forgotten to a place where Pharaoh himself and all his court eyed him with the intensest interest and anxiety, it is significant that he should appear regardless of his own fate, but jealously careful of the glory of God. Considering how jealous men commonly are of their own reputation, and how impatiently eager to receive all the credit that is due to them for their own share in any good that is doing, and considering of what essential importance it seemed that Joseph should seize this opportunity of providing for his own safety and advancement, and should use this as the tide in his affairs that led to fortune, his words and bearing before Pharaoh undoubtedly disclose a deeply in-wrought fidelity to God, and a magnanimous patience regarding his own personal interests.

For it is extremely unlikely that in proposing to Pharaoh to set a man over this important business of collecting corn to last through the years of famine, it presented itself to Joseph as a conceivable result that he should be the person appointed—he a Hebrew, a slave, a prisoner, cleaned but for the nonce, could not suppose that Pharaoh would pass over all those tried officers and ministers of state around him and fix upon a youth who was wholly untried, and who might, by his different race and religion, prove obnoxious to the people. Joseph may have expected to make interest enough with Pharaoh to secure his freedom, and possibly some subordinate berth where he could hopefully begin the world again; but his only allusion to himself is of a depreciatory kind, while his reference to God is marked with a profound conviction that this is God's doing, and that to Him is due whatever is due. Well may the Hebrew race be proud of those men like Joseph and Daniel, who stood in the presence of foreign monarchs in a spirit of perfect fidelity to God, commanding the respect of all, and clothed with the dignity and simplicity which that fidelity imparted. It matters not to Joseph that there may perhaps be none in that land who can appreciate his fidelity to God or understand his motive. It matters not what he may lose by it, or what he could gain by falling in with the notions of those around him. He himself knows the real state of the case, and will not act untruly to his God, even though for years he seems to have been forgotten by Him. With Daniel he says in spirit, "Let thy gifts be to thyself, and give thy rewards to another. As for me, this secret is not revealed to me for any wisdom that I have more than any living, but that the interpretation may be known to the king, and that thou mayest know the thoughts of thine heart. He that revealeth secrets maketh known to thee what shall come to pass." There is something particularly noble and worthy of admiration in a man thus standing alone and maintaining the fullest allegiance to God, without ostentation, and with a quiet dignity and naturalness that show he has a great fund of strength behind.

That we do not misjudge Joseph's character or ascribe to him qualities which were invisible to his contemporaries, is apparent from the circumstance that Pharaoh and his advisers, with little or no hesitation, agreed that to no man could they more safely entrust their country in this emergency. The mere personal charm of Joseph might have won over those experienced advisers of the crown to make compensation for his imprisonment by an unusually handsome reward, but no mere attractiveness of person and manner, nor even the unquestionable guilelessness of his bearing, could have induced them to put such an affair as this into his hands. Plainly they were impressed with Joseph; almost supernaturally impressed, and felt God through him. He stood before them as one mysteriously appearing in their emergency, sent out of unthought-of quarters to warn and save them. Happily there was as yet no jealousy of the God of the Hebrews, nor any exclusiveness on the part of the chosen people: Pharaoh and Joseph alike felt that there was one God over all and through all. And it was Joseph's self-abnegating sympathy with the purposes of this Supreme God that made him a transparent medium, so that in his presence the Egyptians felt themselves in the presence of God. It is so always. Influence in the long run belongs to those who rid their minds of all private aims, and get close to the great centre in which all the race meets and is cared for. Men feel themselves safe with the unselfish, with persons in whom they meet principle, justice, truth, love, God. We are unattractive, useless, uninfluential, just because we are still childishly craving a private and selfish good. We know that a life which does not pour itself freely into the common stream of public good is lost in dry and sterile sands. We know that a life spent upon self is contemptible, barren, empty, yet how slowly do we come to the attitude of Joseph, who watched for the fulfilment of God's purposes, and found his happiness in forwarding what God designed for the people.

XXVIII
JOSEPH'S ADMINISTRATION

Gen. xli. 37–57, and xlvii. 13–26.

"He made him lord of his house, and ruler of all his substance: To bind his princes at his pleasure; and teach his senators wisdom."—Psalm. cv. 21, 22.

"Many a monument consecrated to the memory of some nobleman gone to his long home, who during life had held high rank at the court of Pharaoh, is decorated with the simple but laudatory inscription, 'His ancestors were unknown people'"—so we are told by our most accurate informant regarding Egyptian affairs. Indeed, the tales we read of adventurers in the East, and the histories which recount how some dynasties have been founded, are sufficient evidence that, in other countries besides Egypt, sudden elevation from the lowest to the highest rank is not so unusual as amongst ourselves. Historians have recently made out that in one period of the history of Egypt there are traces of a kind of Semitic mania, a strong leaning towards Syrian and Arabian customs, phrases, and persons. Such manias have occurred in most countries. There was a period in the history of Rome when everything that had a Greek flavour was admired; an Anglo-mania once affected a portion of the French population, and reciprocally, French manners and ideas have at times found a welcome among ourselves. It is also clear that for a time Lower Egypt was under the dominion of foreign rulers who were in race more nearly allied to Joseph than to the native population. But there is no need that so complicated a question as the exact date of this foreign domination be debated here, for there was that in Joseph's bearing which would have commended him to any sagacious monarch. Not only did the court accept him as a messenger from God, but they could not fail to recognise substantial and serviceable human qualities alongside of what was mysterious in him. The ready apprehension with which he appreciated the magnitude of the danger, the clear-sighted promptitude with which he met it, the resource and quiet capacity with which he handled a matter involving the entire condition of Egypt, showed them that they were in the presence of a true statesman. No doubt the confidence with which he described the best method of dealing with the emergency was the confidence of one who was convinced he was speaking for God. This was the great distinction they perceived between Joseph and ordinary dream-interpreters. It was not guesswork with him. The same distinction is always apparent between revelation and speculation. Revelation speaks with authority; speculation gropes its way, and when wisest is most diffident. At the same time Pharaoh was perfectly right in his inference: "Forasmuch as God hath shewed thee all this, there is none so discreet and wise as thou art." He believed that God had chosen him to deal with this matter because he was wise in heart, and he believed his wisdom would remain because God had chosen him.

At length, then, Joseph saw the fulfilment of his dreams within his reach. The coat of many colours with which his father had paid a tribute to the princely person and ways of the boy, was now replaced by the robe of state and the heavy gold necklace which marked him out as second to Pharaoh. Whatever nerve and self-command and humble dependence on God his varied experience had wrought in him were all needed when Pharaoh took his hand and placed his own ring on it, thus transferring all his authority to him, and when turning from the king he received the acclamations of the court and the people, bowed to by his old masters, and acknowledged the superior of all the dignitaries and potentates of Egypt. Only once besides, so far as the Egyptian inscriptions have yet been deciphered, does it appear that any subject was raised to be Regent or Viceroy with similar powers. Joseph is, as far as possible, naturalised as an Egyptian. He receives a name easier of pronunciation than his own, at least to Egyptian tongues—Zaphnath-Paaneah, which, however, was perhaps only an official title meaning "Governor of the district of the place of life," the name by which one of the Egyptian counties or states was known. The king crowned his liberality and completed the process of naturalisation by providing him with a wife, Asenath, the daughter of Potipherah, priest of On. This city was not far from Avaris or Haouar, where Joseph's Pharaoh, Ra-apepi II., at this time resided. The worship of the sun-god, Ra, had its centre at On (or Heliopolis, as it was called by the Greeks), and the priests of On took precedence of all Egyptian priests. Joseph was thus connected with one of the most influential families in the land, and if he had any scruples about marrying into an idolatrous family, they were too insignificant to influence his conduct, or leave any trace in the narrative.

His attitude towards God and his own family was disclosed in the names which he gave to his children. In giving names which had a meaning at all, and not merely a taking sound, he showed that he understood, as well he might, that every human life has a significance and expresses some principle or fact. And in giving names which recorded his acknowledgment of God's goodness, he showed that prosperity had as little influence as adversity to move him from his allegiance to the God of his fathers. His first son he called Manasseh, *Making to forget*, "for God," said he, "hath made me forget all my toil and all my father's house"—not as if he were now so abundantly satisfied in Egypt that the thought of his father's house was blotted from his mind, but only that in this child the keen longings he had felt for kindred and home were somewhat alleviated. He again found an object for his strong family affection. The void in his heart he had so long felt was filled by the little babe. A new home was begun around him. But this new affection would not weaken, though it would alter the character of, his love for his father and brethren. The birth of this child would really be a new tie to the land from which he had been stolen. For, however ready men are to spend their own life in foreign service, you see them wishing that their children should spend their days among the scenes with which their own childhood was familiar.

In the naming of his second son Ephraim he recognises that God had made him fruitful in the most unlikely way. He does not leave it to us to interpret his life, but records what he himself saw in it. It has been said: "To get at the truth of any history is good; but a man's own history—when he reads that truly, ... and knows what he is about and has been about, it is a Bible to him." And now that Joseph, from the height he had reached, could look back on the way by which he had been led to it, he cordially approved of all that God had done. There was no resentment, no murmuring. He would often find himself looking back and thinking, Had I found my brothers where I thought they were, had the pit not been on the caravan-road, had the merchants not come up so opportunely, had I not been sold at all or to some other master, had I not been imprisoned, or had I been put in another ward—had any one of the many slender links in the chain of my career been absent, how different might my present state have been. How plainly I now see that all those sad mishaps that crushed my hopes and tortured my spirit were steps in the only conceivable path to my present position.

Many a man has added his signature to this acknowledgment of Joseph's, and confessed a providence guiding his life and working out good for him through injuries and sorrows, as well as through honours, marriages, births. As in the heat of summer it is difficult to recall the sensation of winter's bitter cold, so the fruitless and barren periods of a man's life are sometimes quite obliterated from his memory. God has it in His power to raise a man higher above the level of ordinary happiness than ever he has sunk below it; and as winter and spring-time, when the seed is sown, are stormy and bleak and gusty, so in human life seed-time is not bright as summer nor cheerful as autumn; and yet it is then, when all the earth lies bare and will yield us nothing, that the precious seed is sown: and when we confidently commit our labour or patience of to-day to God, the land of our affliction, now bare and desolate, will certainly wave for us, as it has waved for others, with rich produce whitened to the harvest.

There is no doubt then that Joseph had learned to recognise the providence of God as a most important factor in his life. And the man who does so, gains for his character all the strength and resolution that come with a capacity for waiting. He saw, most legibly written on his own life, that God is never in a hurry. And for the resolute adherence to his seven-years' policy such a belief was most necessary. Nothing, indeed, is said of opposition or incredulity on the part of the Egyptians. But was there ever a policy of such magnitude carried out in any country without opposition or without evilly-disposed persons using it as a weapon against its promoter? No doubt during these years he had need of all the personal determination as well as of all the official authority he possessed. And if, on the whole, remarkable success attended his efforts, we must ascribe this partly to the unchallengeable justice of his arrangements, and partly to the impression of commanding genius Joseph seems everywhere to have made. As with his father and brethren he was felt to be superior, as in Potiphar's house he was quickly recognised, as in the prison no prison-garb or slave-brand could disguise him, as in the court his superiority was instinctively felt, so in his administration the people seem to have believed in him.

And if, on the whole and in general, Joseph was reckoned a wise and equitable ruler, and even adored as a kind of saviour of the world, it would be idle in us to canvass the wisdom of his administration. When we have not sufficient historical material to apprehend the full significance of any policy, it is safe to accept the judgment of men who not only knew the facts, but were themselves so deeply involved in them that they would certainly have felt and expressed discontent had there been ground for doing so. The policy of Joseph was simply to economize during the seven years of abundance to such an extent that provision might be made against the seven years of famine. He calculated that one-fifth of the produce of years so extraordinarily plenteous would serve for the seven scarce years. This fifth he seems to have bought in the king's name from the people, buying it, no doubt, at the cheap rates of abundant years. When the years of famine came, the people were referred to Joseph; and, till their money was gone, he sold corn to them, probably not at famine prices. Next he acquired their cattle, and finally, in exchange for food, they yielded to him both their lands and their persons. So that the result of the whole was, that the people who would otherwise have perished were preserved, and in return for this preservation they paid a tax or rent on their farm-lands to the amount of one-fifth of their produce. The people ceased to be proprietors of their own farms, but they were not slaves with no interest in the soil, but tenants sitting at easy rents—a fair enough exchange for being preserved in life. This kind of taxation is eminently fair in principle, securing, as it does, that the wealth of the king and government shall vary with the prosperity of the whole land. The chief difficulty that has always been experienced in working it, has arisen from the necessity of leaving a good deal of discretionary power in the hands of the collectors, who have generally been found not slow to abuse this power.

The only semblance of despotism in Joseph's policy is found in the curious circumstance that he interfered with the people's choice of residence, and shifted them from one end of the land to another. This may have been necessary not only as a kind of seal on the deed by which the lands were conveyed to the king, and as a significant sign to them that they were mere tenants, but also Joseph probably saw that for the interests of the country, if not of agricultural prosperity, this shifting had become necessary for the breaking up of illegal associations, nests of sedition, and sectional prejudices and enmities which were endangering the community.[1] Modern experience supplies us with instances in which, by such a policy, a country might be regenerated and a seven years' famine hailed as a blessing if, without famishing the people, it put them unconditionally into the hands of an able, bold, and beneficent ruler. And this was a policy which could be much better devised and executed by a foreigner than by a native.

Egypt's indebtedness to Joseph was, in fact, two-fold. In the first place he succeeded in doing what many strong governments have failed to do: he enabled a large population to survive a long and severe famine. Even with all modern facilities for transport and for making the abundance of remote countries available for times of scarcity, it has not always been found possible to save our own fellow-subjects from starvation. In a prolonged famine which occurred in Egypt during the middle ages, the inhabitants, reduced to the unnatural habits which are the most painful feature of such times, not only ate their own dead, but kidnapped the living on the streets of Cairo and consumed them in secret. One of the most touching memorials of the famine with which Joseph had to deal is found in a sepulchral inscription in Arabia. A flood of rain laid bare a tomb in which lay a woman having on her person a profusion of jewels which represented a very large value. At her head stood a coffer filled with treasure, and a tablet with this inscription: "In Thy name, O God, the God of Himyar, I, Tayar, the daughter of Dzu Shefar, sent my steward to Joseph, and he delaying to return to me, I sent my handmaid with a measure of silver to bring me back a measure of flour; and not being able to procure it, I sent her with a measure of gold; and not being able to procure it, I sent her with a measure of pearls; and not being able to procure it, I commanded them to be ground; and finding no profit in them, I am shut up here." If this inscription is genuine—and there seems no reason to call it in question—it shows that there is no exaggeration in the statement of our narrator that the famine was very grievous in other lands as well as in Egypt. And, whether genuine or not, one cannot but admire the grim humour of the starving woman getting herself buried in the jewels which had suddenly dropped to less than the value of a loaf of bread.

But besides being indebted to Joseph for their preservation, the Egyptians owed to him an extension of their influence; for, as all the lands round about became dependent on Egypt for provision, they must have contracted a respect for the Egyptian administration. They must also have added greatly to Egypt's wealth and during those years of constant traffic many commercial connections must have been formed which in future years would be of untold value to Egypt. But above all, the permanent alterations made by Joseph on their tenure of land, and on their places of abode, may have convinced the most sagacious of the Egyptians that it was well for them that their money had failed, and that they had been compelled to yield themselves unconditionally into the hands of this remarkable ruler. It is the mark of a competent statesman that he makes temporary distress the occasion for permanent benefit; and from the confidence Joseph won with the people, there seems every reason to believe that the permanent alterations he introduced were considered as beneficial as certainly they were bold.

And for our own spiritual uses it is this point which seems chiefly important. In Joseph is illustrated the principle that, in order to the attainment of certain blessings, unconditional submission to God's delegate is required. If we miss this, we miss a large part of what his history exhibits, and it becomes a mere pretty story. The prominent idea in his dreams was that he was to be worshipped by his brethren. In his exaltation by Pharaoh, the absolute authority given to him is again conspicuous: "Without thee shall no man lift up hand or foot in all the land of Egypt." And still the same autocracy appears in the fact that not one Egyptian who was helpful to him in this matter is mentioned; and no one has received such exclusive possession of a considerable part of Scripture, so personal and outstanding a place. All this leaves upon the mind the impression that Joseph becomes a benefactor, and in his degree a saviour, to men by becoming their absolute master. When this was hinted in his dreams at first his brothers fiercely resented it. But when they were put to the push by famine, both they and the Egyptians recognised that he was appointed by God to be their saviour, while at the same time they markedly and consciously submitted themselves to him. Men may always be expected to recognise that he who can save them alive in famine has a right to order the bounds of their habitation; and also that in the hands of one who, from disinterested motives, has saved them, they are likely to be quite as safe as in their own. And if we are all quite sure of this, that men of great political sagacity can regulate our affairs with tenfold the judgment and success that we ourselves could achieve, we cannot wonder that in matters still higher, and for which we are notoriously incompetent, there should be One into whose hands it is well to commit ourselves—One whose judgment is not warped by the prejudices which blind all mere natives of this world, but who, separate from sinners yet naturalised among us, can both detect and rectify everything in our condition which is less than perfect. If there are certainly many cases in which explanations are out of the question, and in which the governed, if they are wise, will yield themselves to a trusted authority, and leave it to time and results to justify his measures, any one, I think, who anxiously considers our spiritual condition must see that here too obedience is for us the greater part of wisdom, and that, after all speculation and efforts at sufficing investigation, we can still do no better than yield ourselves absolutely to Jesus Christ. He alone understands our whole position; He alone speaks with the authority that commands confidence, because it is felt to be the authority of the truth. We feel the present pressure of famine; we have discernment enough, some of us, to know we are in danger, but we cannot penetrate deeply either into the cause or the possible consequences of our present state. But Christ—if we may continue the figure—legislates with a breadth of administrative capacity which includes not only our present distress but our future condition, and, with the boldness of one who is master of the whole case, requires that we put ourselves wholly into His hand. He takes the responsibility of all the changes we make in obedience to Him, and proposes so to relieve us that the relief shall be permanent, and that the very emergency which has thrown us upon His help shall be the occasion of our transference not merely out of the present evil, but into the best possible form of human life.

From this chapter, then, in the history of Joseph, we may reasonably take occasion to remind ourselves, first, that in all things pertaining to God unconditional submission to Christ is necessarily required of us. Apart from Christ we cannot tell what are the necessary elements of a permanently happy state; nor, indeed, even whether there is any such state awaiting us. There is a great deal of truth in what is urged by unbelievers to the effect that spiritual matters are in great measure beyond our cognizance, and that many of our religious phrases are but, as it were, thrown out in the direction of a truth but do not perfectly represent it. No doubt we are in a provisional state, in which we are not in direct contact with the absolute truth, nor in a final attitude of mind towards it; and certain representations of things given in the Word of God may seem to us not to cover the whole truth. But this only compels the conclusion that for us Christ is the way, the truth, and the life. To probe existence to the bottom is plainly not in our power. To say precisely what God is, and how we are to carry ourselves towards Him, is possible only to him who has been with God and is God. To submit to the Spirit of Christ, and to live under those influences and views which formed His life, is the only method that promises deliverance from that moral condition which makes spiritual vision impossible.

We may remind ourselves, secondly, that this submission to Christ should be consistently adhered to in connection with those outward occurrences in our life which give us opportunity of enlarging our spiritual capacity. There can be little doubt that there would be presented to Joseph many a plan for the better administration of this whole matter, and many a petition from individuals craving exemption from the seemingly arbitrary and certainly painful and troublesome edict regulating change of residence. Many a man would think himself much wiser than the minister of Pharaoh in whom was the Spirit of God. When we act in a similar manner, and take upon us to specify with precision the changes we should like to see in our condition, and the methods by which these changes might best be accomplished, we commonly manifest our own incompetence. The changes which the strong hand of Providence enforces, the dislocation which our life suffers from some irresistible blow, the necessity laid upon us to begin life again and on apparently disadvantageous terms, are naturally resented; but these things being certainly the result of some unguardedness, improvidence, or weakness in our past state, are necessarily the means most appropriate for disclosing to us these elements of calamity and for securing our permanent welfare. We rebel against such perilous and sweeping revolutions as the basing of our life on a new foundation demands; we would disregard the appointments of Providence if we could; but both our voluntary consent to the authority of Christ and the impossibility of resisting His providential arrangements, prevent us from refusing to fall in with them, however needless and tyrannical they seem, and however little we perceive that they are intended to accomplish our permanent well-being. And it is in after years, when the pain of severance from old friends and habits is healed, and when the discomfort of adapting ourselves to a new kind of life is replaced by peaceful and docile resignation to new conditions, that we reach the clear perception that the changes we resented have in point of fact rendered harmless the seeds of fresh disaster, and rescued us from the results of long bad government. He who has most keenly felt the hardship of being diverted from his original course in life, will in after life tell you that had he been allowed to hold his own land, and remain his own master in his old loved abode, he would have lapsed into a condition from which no worthy harvest could be expected. If a man only wishes that his own conceptions of prosperity be realised, then let him keep his land in his own hand and work his material irrespective of God's demands; for certainly if he yields himself to God, his own ideas of prosperity will not be realised. But if he suspects that God may have a more liberal conception of prosperity and may understand better than he what is eternally beneficial, let him commit himself and all his material of prosperity without doubting into God's hand, and let him greedily obey all God's precepts; for in neglecting one of these, he so far neglects and misses what God would have him enter into.

FOOTNOTES:

[1] "It happened very often that the inhabitants of one district threatened an attack on the occupants of another on account of some dispute about divine or human questions. The hostile feelings of the opponents not unfrequently broke out into a hard struggle, and it required the whole armed power of the king to extinguish at its first outburst the flaming torch of war, kindled by domineering chiefs of nomes or ambitious priests."—Brugsch, *History of Egypt*, i. 16.

XXIX
VISITS OF JOSEPH'S BRETHREN

Gen. xlii.–xliv.

"Fear not: for am I in the place of God? But as for you, ye thought evil against me; but God meant it unto good."—Gen. 1. 19, 20.

The purpose of God to bring Israel into Egypt was accomplished by the unconscious agency of Joseph's natural affection for his kindred. Tenderness towards home is usually increased by residence in a foreign land; for absence, like a little death, sheds a halo round those separated from us. But Joseph could not as yet either re-visit his old home or invite his father's family into Egypt. Even, indeed, when his brothers first appeared before him, he seems to have had no immediate intention of inviting them as a family to settle in the country of his adoption, or even to visit it. If he had cherished any such purpose or desire he might have sent down wagons at once, as he at last did, to bring his father's household out of Canaan. Why, then, did he proceed so cautiously? Whence this mystery, and disguise, and circuitous compassing of his end? What intervened between the first and last visit of his brethren to make it seem advisable to disclose himself and invite them? Manifestly there had intervened enough to give Joseph insight into the state of mind his brethren were in, enough to satisfy him they were not the men they had been, and that it was safe to ask them and would be pleasant to have them with him in Egypt. Fully alive to the elements of disorder and violence that once existed among them, and having had no opportunity of ascertaining whether they were now altered, there was no course open but that which he adopted of endeavouring in some unobserved way to discover whether twenty years had wrought any change in them.

For effecting this object he fell on the expedient of imprisoning them, on pretence of their being spies. This served the double purpose of detaining them until he should have made up his mind as to the best means of dealing with them, and of securing their retention under his eye until some display of character might sufficiently certify him of their state of mind. Possibly he adopted this expedient also because it was likely deeply to move them, so that they might be expected to exhibit not such superficial feelings as might have been elicited had he set them down to a banquet and entered into conversation with them over their wine, but such as men are surprised to find in themselves, and know nothing of in their lighter hours. Joseph was, of course, well aware that in the analysis of character the most potent elements are only brought into clear view when the test of severe trouble is applied, and when men are thrown out of all conventional modes of thinking and speaking.

The display of character which Joseph awaited he speedily obtained. For so new an experience to these free dwellers in tents as imprisonment under grim Egyptian guards worked wonders in them. Men who have experienced such treatment aver that nothing more effectually tames and breaks the spirit: it is not the being confined for a definite time with the certainty of release in the end, but the being shut up at the caprice of another on a false and absurd accusation; the being cooped up at the will of a stranger in a foreign country, uncertain and hopeless of release. To Joseph's brethren so sudden and great a calamity seemed explicable only on the theory that it was retribution for the great crime of their life. The uneasy feeling which each of them had hidden in his own conscience, and which the lapse of twenty years had not materially alleviated, finds expression: "And they said one to another, We are verily guilty concerning our brother, in that we saw the anguish of his soul, when he besought us, and we would not hear; therefore is this distress come upon us." The similarity of their position to that in which they had placed their brother stimulates and assists their conscience. Joseph, in the anguish of his soul, had protested his innocence, but they had not listened; and now their own protestations are treated as idle wind by this Egyptian. Their own feelings, representing to them what they had caused Joseph to suffer, stir a keener sense of their guilt than they seem ever before to have reached. Under this new light they see their sin more clearly, and are humbled by the distress into which it has brought them.

When Joseph sees this, his heart warms to them. He may not yet be quite sure of them. A prison-repentance is perhaps scarcely to be trusted. He sees they would for the moment deal differently with him had they the opportunity, and would welcome no one more heartily than himself, whose coming among them had once so exasperated them. Himself keen in his affections, he is deeply moved, and his eyes fill with tears as he witnesses their emotion and grief on his account. Fain would he relieve them from their remorse and apprehension—why, then, does he forbear? Why does he not at this juncture disclose himself? It has been satisfactorily proved that his brethren counted their sale of him the great crime of their life. Their imprisonment has elicited evidence that that crime had taken in their conscience the capital place, the place which a man finds some one sin or series of sins will take, to follow him with its appropriate curse, and hang over his future like a cloud—a sin of which he thinks when any strange thing happens to him, and to which he traces all disaster—a sin so iniquitous that it seems capable of producing any results however grievous, and to which he has so given himself that his life seems to be concentrated there, and he cannot but connect with it all the greater ills that happen to him. Was not this, then, security enough that they would never again perpetrate a crime of like atrocity? Every man who has almost at all observed the history of sin in himself, will say that most certainly it was quite insufficient security against their ever again doing the like. Evidence that a man is conscious of his sin, and, while suffering from its consequences, feels deeply its guilt, is not evidence that his character is altered.

And because we believe men so much more readily than God, and think that they do not require, for form's sake, such needless pledges of a changed character as God seems to demand, it is worth observing that Joseph, moved as he was even to tears, felt that common prudence forbade him to commit himself to his brethren without further evidence of their disposition. They had distinctly acknowledged their guilt, and in his hearing had admitted that the great calamity that had befallen them was no more than they deserved; yet Joseph, judging merely as an intelligent man who had worldly interests depending on his judgment, could not discern enough here to justify him in supposing that his brethren were changed men. And it might sometimes serve to expose the insufficiency of our repentance were clear-seeing men the judges of it, and did they express their opinion of its trustworthiness. We may think that God is needlessly exacting when He requires evidence not only of a changed mind about past sin, but also of such a mind being now in us as will preserve us from future sin; but the truth is, that no man whose common worldly interests were at stake would commit himself to us on any less evidence. God, then, meaning to bring the house of Israel into Egypt in order to make progress in the Divine education He was giving to them, could not introduce them into that land in a state of mind which would negative all the discipline they were there to receive.

These men then had to give evidence that they not only saw, and in some sense repented of, their sin, but also that they had got rid of the evil passion which had led to it. This is what God means by repentance. Our sins are in general not so microscopic that it requires very keen spiritual discernment to perceive them. But to be quite aware of our sin, and to acknowledge it, is not to repent of it. Everything falls short of thorough repentance which does not prevent us from committing the sin anew. We do not so much desire to be accurately informed about our past sins, and to get right views of our past selves; we wish to be no longer sinners, we wish to pass through some process by which we may be separated from that in us which has led us into sin. Such a process there is, for these men passed through it.

The test which revealed the thoroughness of his brothers' repentance was unintentionally applied by Joseph. When he hid his cup in Benjamin's sack, all that he intended was to furnish a pretext for detaining Benjamin, and so gratifying his own affection. But, to his astonishment, his trick effected far more than he intended; for the brothers, recognising now their brotherhood, circled round Benjamin, and, to a man, resolved to go back with him to Egypt. We cannot argue from this that Joseph had misapprehended the state of mind in which his brothers were, and in his judgment of them had been either too timorous or too severe; nor need we suppose that he was hampered by his relations to Pharaoh, and therefore unwilling to connect himself too closely with men of whom he might be safer to be rid; because it was this very peril of Benjamin's that matured their brotherly affection. They themselves could not have anticipated that they would make such a sacrifice for Benjamin. But throughout their dealings with this mysterious Egyptian, they felt themselves under a spell, and were being gradually, though perhaps unconsciously, softened, and in order to complete the change passing upon them, they but required some such incident as this of Benjamin's arrest. This incident seemed by some strange fatality to threaten them with a renewed perpetration of the very crime they had committed against Rachel's other son. It threatened to force them to become again the instrument of bereaving their father of his darling child, and bringing about that very calamity which they had pledged themselves should never happen. It was an incident, therefore, which, more than any other, was likely to call out their family love.

The scene lives in every one's memory. They were going gladly back to their own country with corn enough for their children, proud of their entertainment by the lord of Egypt; anticipating their father's exultation when he heard how generously they had been treated and when he saw Benjamin safely restored, feeling that in bringing him back they almost compensated for having bereaved him of Joseph. Simeon is revelling in the free air that blew from Canaan and brought with it the scents of his native land, and breaks into the old songs that the strait confinement of his prison had so long silenced—all of them together rejoicing in a scarcely hoped-for success; when suddenly, ere the first elation is spent, they are startled to see the hasty approach of the Egyptian messenger, and to hear the stern summons that brought them to a halt, and boded all ill. The few words of the just Egyptian, and his calm, explicit judgment, "Ye have done evil in so doing," pierce them like a keen blade—that they should be suspected of robbing one who had dealt so generously with them; that all Israel should be put to shame in the sight of the stranger! But they begin to feel relief as one brother after another steps forward with the boldness of innocence; and as sack after sack is emptied, shaken, and flung aside, they already eye the steward with the bright air of triumph; when, as the very last sack is emptied, and as all breathlessly stand round, amid the quick rustle of the corn, the sharp rattle of metal strikes on their ear, and the gleam of silver dazzles their eyes as the cup rolls out in the sunshine. This, then, is the brother of whom their father was so careful that he dared not suffer him out of his sight! This is the precious youth whose life was of more value than the lives of all the brethren, and to keep whom a few months longer in his father's sight Simeon had been left to rot in a dungeon! This is how he repays the anxiety of the family and their love, and this is how he repays the extraordinary favour of Joseph! By one rash childish act had this fondled youth, to all appearance, brought upon the house of Israel irretrievable disgrace, if not complete extinction. Had these men been of their old temper, their knives had very speedily proved that their contempt for the deed was as great as the Egyptian's; by violence towards Benjamin they might have cleared themselves of all suspicion of complicity; or, at the best, they might have considered themselves to be acting in a fair and even lenient manner if they had surrendered the culprit to the steward, and once again carried back to their father a tale of blood. But they were under the spell of their old sin. In all disaster, however innocent they now were, they saw the retribution of their old iniquity; they seem scarcely to consider whether Benjamin was innocent or guilty, but as humbled, God-smitten men, "they rent their clothes, and laded every man his ass, and returned to the city."

Thus Joseph in seeking to gain *one* brother found eleven—for now there could be no doubt that they were very different men from those brethren who had so heartlessly sold into slavery their father's favourite—men now with really brotherly feelings, by penitence and regard for their father so wrought together into one family, that this calamity, intended to fall only on one of their number, did in falling on him fall on them all. So far from wishing now to rid themselves of Rachel's son and their father's favourite, who had been put by their father in so prominent a place in his affection, they will not even give him up to suffer what seemed the just punishment of his theft, do not even reproach him with having brought them all into disgrace and difficulty, but, as humbled men who knew they had greater sins of their own to answer for, went quietly back to Egypt, determined to see their younger brother through his misfortune or to share his bondage with him. Had these men not been thoroughly changed, thoroughly convinced that at all costs upright dealing and brotherly love should continue; had they not possessed that first and last of Christian virtues, love to their brother, then nothing could so certainly have revealed their want of it as this apparent theft of Benjamin's. It seemed in itself a very likely thing that a lad accustomed to plain modes of life, and whose character it was to "ravin as a wolf," should, when suddenly introduced to the gorgeous Egyptian banqueting-house with all its sumptuous furnishings, have coveted some choice specimen of Egyptian art, to carry home to his father as proof that he could not only bring himself back in safety, but scorned to come back from any expedition empty-handed. It was not unlikely either that, with his mother's own superstition, he might have conceived the bold design of robbing this Egyptian, so mysterious and so powerful, according to his brothers' account, and of breaking that spell which he had thrown over them; he may thus have conceived the idea of achieving for himself a reputation in the family, and of once for all redeeming himself from the somewhat undignified, and to one of his spirit somewhat uncongenial, position of the youngest of a family. If, as is possible, he had let any such idea ooze out in talking with his brethren as they went down to Egypt, and only abandoned it on their indignant and urgent remonstrance, then when the cup, Joseph's chief treasure according to his own account, was discovered in Benjamin's sack, the case must have looked sadly against him even in the eyes of his brethren. No protestations of innocence in a particular instance avail much when the character and general habits of the accused point to guilt. It is quite possible, therefore, that the brethren, though willing to believe Benjamin, were yet not so thoroughly convinced of his innocence as they would have desired. The fact that they themselves had found their money returned in their sacks, made for Benjamin; yet in most cases, especially where circumstances corroborate it, an accusation even against the innocent takes immediate hold and cannot be summarily and at once got rid of.

Thus was proof given that the house of Israel was now in truth one family. The men who, on very slight instigation, had without compunction sold Joseph to a life of slavery, cannot now find it in their heart to abandon a brother who, to all appearance, was worthy of no better life than that of a slave, and who had brought them all into disgrace and danger. Judah had no doubt pledged himself to bring the lad back without scathe to his father, but he had done so without contemplating the possibility of Benjamin becoming amenable to Egyptian law. And no one can read the speech of Judah—one of the most pathetic on record—in which he replies to Joseph's judgment that Benjamin alone should remain in Egypt, without perceiving that he speaks not as one who merely seeks to redeem a pledge, but as a good son and a good brother. He speaks, too, as the mouth-piece of the rest, and as he had taken the lead in Joseph's sale, so he does not shrink from standing forward and accepting the heavy responsibility which may now light upon the man who represents these brethren. His former faults are redeemed by the courage, one may say heroism, he now shows. And as he spoke, so the rest felt. They could not bring themselves to inflict a new sorrow on their aged father; neither could they bear to leave their young brother in the hands of strangers. The passions which had alienated them from one another, and had threatened to break up the family, are subdued. There is now discernible a common feeling that binds them together, and a common object for which they willingly sacrifice themselves. They are, therefore, now prepared to pass into that higher school to which God called them in Egypt. It mattered little what strong and equitable laws they found in the land of their adoption, if they had no taste for upright living; it mattered little what thorough national organization they would be brought into contact with in Egypt, if in point of fact they owned no common brotherhood, and were willing rather to live as units and every man for himself than for any common interest. But now they were prepared, open to teaching, and docile.

To complete our apprehension of the state of mind into which the brethren were brought by Joseph's treatment of them, we must take into account the assurance he gave them, when he made himself known to them, that it was not they but God who had sent him into Egypt, and that God had done this for the purpose of preserving the whole house of Israel. At first sight this might seem to be an injudicious speech, calculated to make the brethren think lightly of their guilt, and to remove the just impressions they now entertained of the unbrotherliness of their conduct to Joseph. And it might have been an injudicious speech to impenitent men; but no further view of sin can lighten its heinousness to a really penitent sinner. Prove to him that his sin has become the means of untold good, and you only humble him the more, and more deeply convince him that while he was recklessly gratifying himself and sacrificing others for his own pleasure, God has been mindful of others, and, pardoning him, has blessed them. God does not need our sins to work out His good intentions, but we give Him little other material; and the discovery that through our evil purposes and injurious deeds God has worked out His beneficent will, is certainly not calculated to make us think more lightly of our sin or more highly of ourselves.

Joseph in thus addressing his brethren did, in fact, but add to their feelings the tenderness that is in all religious conviction, and that springs out of the consciousness that in all our sin there has been with us a holy and loving Father, mindful of His children. This is the final stage of penitence. The knowledge that God has prevented our sin from doing the harm it might have done, does relieve the bitterness and despair with which we view our life, but at the same time it strengthens the most effectual bulwark between us and sin—love to a holy, over-ruling God. This, therefore, may always be safely said to penitents: Out of your worst sin God can bring good to yourself or to others, and good of an apparently necessary kind; but good of a permanent kind can result from your sin only when you have truly repented of it, and sincerely wish you had never done it. Once this repentance is really wrought in you, then, though your life can never be the same as it might have been had you not sinned, it may be, in some respects, a more richly developed life, a life fuller of humility and love. You can never have what you sold for your sin; but the poverty your sin has brought may excite within you thoughts and energies more valuable than what you have lost, as these men lost a brother but found a Saviour. The wickedness that has often made you bow your head and mourn in secret, and which is in itself unutterable shame and loss, may, in God's hand, become food against the day of famine. You cannot ever have the enjoyments which are possible only to those whose conscience is laden with no evil remembrances, and whose nature, uncontracted and unwithered by familiarity with sin, can give itself to enjoyment with the abandonment and fearlessness reserved for the innocent. No more at all will you have that fineness of feeling which only ignorance of evil can preserve; no more that high and great conscientiousness which, once broken, is never repaired; no more that respect from other men which for ever and instinctively departs from those who have lost self-respect. But you may have a more intelligent sympathy with other men and a keener pity for them; the experience you have gathered too late to save yourself may put it in your power to be of essential service to others. You cannot win your way back to the happy, useful, evenly-developed life of the comparatively innocent, but the life of the true-hearted penitent is yet open to you. Every beat of your heart now may be as if it throbbed against a poisoned dagger, every duty may shame you, every day bring weariness and new humiliation, but let no pain or discouragement avail to defraud you of the good fruits of true reconciliation to God and submission to His lifelong discipline. See that you lose not both lives, the life of the comparatively innocent and the life of the truly penitent.

XXX
THE RECONCILIATION

Gen. xlv.

"By faith Joseph, when he died, made mention of the departing of the children of Israel; and gave commandment concerning his bones."—Heb. xi. 22.

It is generally by some circumstance or event which perplexes, troubles, or gladdens us, that new thoughts regarding conduct are presented to us, and new impulses communicated to our life. And the circumstances through which Joseph's brethren passed during the famine not only subdued and softened them to a genuine family feeling, but elicited in Joseph himself a more tender affection for them than he seems at first to have cherished. For the first time since his entrance into Egypt did he feel, when Judah spoke so touchingly and effectively, that the family of Israel was one; and that he himself would be reprehensible did he make further breaches in it by carrying out his intention of detaining Benjamin. Moved by Judah's pathetic appeal, and yielding to the generous impulse of the moment, and being led by a right state of feeling to a right judgment regarding duty, he claimed his brethren as brethren, and proposed that the whole family be brought into Egypt.

The scene in which the sacred writer describes the reconciliation of Joseph and his brothers is one of the most touching on record;—the long estrangement so happily terminated; the caution, the doubts, the hesitation on Joseph's part, swept away at last by the resistless tide of long pent-up emotion; the surprise and perplexity of the brethren as they dared now to lift their eyes and scrutinize the face of the governor, and discerned the lighter complexion of the Hebrew, the features of the family of Jacob, the expression of their own brother; the anxiety with which they wait to know how he means to repay their crime, and the relief with which they hear that he bears them no ill-will—everything, in short, conduces to render this recognition of the brethren interesting and affecting. That Joseph, who had controlled his feeling in many a trying situation, should now have "wept aloud," needs no explanation. Tears always express a mingled feeling; at least the tears of a man do. They may express grief, but it is grief with some remorse in it, or it is grief passing into resignation. They may express joy, but it is joy born of long sorrow, the joy of deliverance, joy that can now afford to let the heart weep out the fears it has been holding down. It is as with a kind of breaking of the heart, and apparent unmanning of the man, that the human soul takes possession of its greatest treasures; unexpected success and unmerited joy humble a man; and as laughter expresses the surprise of the intellect, so tears express the amazement of the soul when it is stormed suddenly by a great joy. Joseph had been hardening himself to lead a solitary life in Egypt, and it is with all this strong self-sufficiency breaking down within him that he eyes his brethren. It is his love for them making its way through all his ability to do without them, and sweeping away as a flood the bulwarks he had built round his heart,—it is this that breaks him down before them, a man conquered by his own love, and unable to control it. It compels him to make himself known, and to possess himself of its objects, those unconscious brethren. It is a signal instance of the law by which love brings all the best and holiest beings into contact with their inferiors, and, in a sense, puts them in their power, and thus eternally provides that the superiority of those that are high in the scale of being shall ever be at the service of those who in themselves are not so richly endowed. The higher any being is, the more love is in him: that is to say, the higher he is, the more surely is he bound to all who are beneath him. If God is highest of all, it is because there is in Him sufficiency for all His creatures, and love to make it universally available.

It is one of our most familiar intellectual pleasures to see in the experience of others, or to read, a lucid and moving account of emotions identical with those which have once been our own. In reading an account of what others have passed through, our pleasure is derived mainly from two sources—either from our being brought, by sympathy with them and in imagination, into circumstances we ourselves have never been placed in, and thus artificially enlarging our sphere of life, and adding to our experience feelings which could not have been derived from anything we ourselves have met with; or, from our living over again, by means of their experience, a part of our life which had great interest and meaning to us. It may be excusable, therefore, if we divert this narrative from its original historical significance, and use it as the mirror in which we may see reflected an important passage or crisis in our own spiritual history. For though some may find in it little that reflects their own experience, others cannot fail to be reminded of feelings with which they were very familiar when first they were introduced to Christ, and acknowledged by Him.

1. The modes in which our Lord makes Himself known to men are various as their lives and characters. But frequently the forerunning choice of a sinner by Christ is discovered in such gradual and ill-understood dealings as Joseph used with those brethren. It is the closing of a net around them. They do not see what is driving them forward, nor whither they are being driven; they are anxious and ill at ease; and not comprehending what ails them, they make only ineffectual efforts for deliverance. There is no recognition of the hand that is guiding all this circuitous and mysterious preparatory work, nor of the eye that affectionately watches their perplexity, nor are they aware of any friendly ear that catches each sigh in which they seem hopelessly to resign themselves to the relentless past from which they cannot escape. They feel that they are left alone to make what they can now of the life they have chosen and made for themselves; that there is floating behind and around them a cloud bearing the very essence exhaled from their past, and ready to burst over them; a phantom that is yet real, and that belongs both to the spiritual and material world, and can follow them in either. They seem to be doomed men—men who are never at all to get disentangled from their old sin.

If any one is in this baffled and heartless condition, fearing even good lest it turn to evil in his hand; afraid to take the money that lies in his sack's mouth, because he feels there is a snare in it; if any one is sensible that life has become unmanageable in his hands, and that he is being drawn on by an unseen power which he does not understand, then let him consider in the scene before us how such a condition ends or may end. It took many months of doubt, and fear, and mystery to bring those brethren to such a state of mind as made it advisable for Joseph to disclose himself, to scatter the mystery, and relieve them of the unaccountable uneasiness that possessed their minds. And your perplexity will not be allowed to last longer than it is needful. But it is often needful that we should first learn that in sinning we have introduced into our life a baffling, perplexing element, have brought our life into connection with inscrutable laws which we cannot control, and which we feel may at any moment destroy us utterly. It is not from carelessness on Christ's part that His people are not always and from the first rejoicing in the assurance and appreciation of His love. It is His carefulness which lays a restraining hand on the ardour of His affection. We see that this burst of tears on Joseph's part was genuine, we have no suspicion that he was feigning an emotion he did not feel; we believe that his affection at last could not be restrained, that he was fairly overcome,—can we not trust Christ for as genuine a love, and believe that His emotion is as deep? We are, in a word, reminded by this scene, that there is always in Christ a greater love seeking the friendship of the sinner than there is in the sinner seeking for Christ. The search of the sinner for Christ is always a dubious, hesitating, uncertain groping; while on Christ's part there is a clear-seeing, affectionate solicitude which lays joyful surprises along the sinner's path, and enjoys by anticipation the gladness and repose which are prepared for him in the final recognition and reconcilement.

2. In finding their brother again, those sons of Jacob found also their own better selves which they had long lost. They had been living in a lie, unable to look the past in the face, and so becoming more and more false. Trying to leave their sin behind them, they always found it rising in the path before them, and again they had to resort to some new mode of laying this uneasy ghost. They turned away from it, busied themselves among other people, refused to think of it, assumed all kinds of disguise, professed to themselves that they had done no great wrong; but nothing gave them deliverance—there was their old sin quietly waiting for them in their tent door when they went home of an evening, laying its hand on their shoulder in the most unlooked-for places, and whispering in their ear at the most unwelcome seasons. A great part of their mental energy had been spent in deleting this mark from their memory, and yet day by day it resumed its supreme place in their life, holding them under arrest as they secretly felt, and keeping them reserved to judgment.

So, too, do many of us live as if yet we had not found the life eternal, the kind of life that we can always go on with—rather as those who are but making the best of a life which can never be very valuable, nor ever perfect. There seem voices calling us back, assuring us we must yet retrace our steps, that there are passages in our past with which we are not done, that there is an inevitable humiliation and penitence awaiting us. It is through that we can alone get back to the good we once saw and hoped for; there were right desires and resolves in us once, views of a well-spent life which have been forgotten and pressed out of remembrance, but all these rise again in the presence of Christ. Reconciled to Him and claimed by Him, all hope is renewed within us. If He makes Himself known to us, if He claims connection with us, have we not here the promise of all good? If He, after careful scrutiny, after full consideration of all the circumstances, bids us claim as our brother Him to whom all power and glory are given, ought not this to quicken within us everything that is hopeful, and ought it not to strengthen us for all frank acknowledgment of the past and true humiliation on account of it?

3. A third suggestion is made by this narrative. Joseph commanded from his presence all who might be merely curious spectators of his burst of feeling, and might, themselves unmoved, criticise this new feature of the governor's character. In all love there is a similar reserve. The true friend

of Christ, the man who is profoundly conscious that between himself and Christ there is a bond unique and eternal, longs for a time when he may enjoy greater liberty in uttering what he feels towards his Lord and Redeemer, and when, too, Christ Himself shall by telling and sufficient signs put it for ever beyond doubt that this love is more than responded to. Words sufficiently impassioned have indeed been put into our lips by men of profound spiritual feeling, but the feeling continually weighs upon us that some more palpable mutual recognition is desirable between persons so vitally and peculiarly knit together as Christ and the Christian are. Such recognition, indubitable and reciprocal, must one day take place. And when Christ Himself shall have taken the initiative, and shall have caused us to understand that we are verily the objects of His love, and shall have given such expression to His knowledge of us as we cannot now receive, we on our part shall be able to reciprocate, or at least to accept, this greatest of possessions, the brotherly love of the Son of God. Meanwhile this passage in Joseph's history may remind us that behind all sternness of expression there may pulsate a tenderness that needs thus to disguise itself; and that to those who have not yet recognised Christ, He is better than He seems. Those brethren no doubt wonder now that even twenty years' alienation should have so blinded them. The relaxation of the expression from the sternness of an Egyptian governor to the fondness of family love, the voice heard now in the familiar mother tongue, reveal the brother; and they who have shrunk from Christ as if He were a cold official, and who have never lifted their eyes to scrutinize His face, are reminded that He can so make Himself known to them that not all the wealth of Egypt would purchase from them one of the assurances they have received from Him.

The same warm tide of feeling which carried away all that separated Joseph from his brethren bore him on also to the decision to invite his father's entire household into Egypt. We are reminded that the history of Joseph in Egypt is an episode, and that Jacob is still the head of the house, maintaining its dignity and guiding its movements. The notices we get of him in this latter part of his history are very characteristic. The indomitable toughness of his youth remained with him in his old age. He was one of those old men who maintain their vigour to the end, the energy of whose age seems to shame and overtax the prime of common men; whose minds are still the clearest, their advice the safest, their word waited for, their perception of the actual state of affairs always in advance of their juniors, more modern and fully abreast of the times in their ideas than the latest born of their children. Such an old age we recognise in Jacob's half-scornful chiding of the helplessness of his sons even after they had heard that there was corn in Egypt. "Why look ye one upon another? Behold! I have heard that there is corn in Egypt;

get ye down thither and buy for us from thence." Jacob, the man who had wrestled through life and bent all things to his will, cannot put up with the helpless dejection of this troop of strong men, who have no wit to devise an escape for themselves, and no resolution to enforce upon the others any device that may occur to them. Waiting still like children for some one else to help them, having strength to endure but no strength to undertake the responsibility of advising in an emergency, they are roused by their father, who has been eyeing this condition of theirs with some curiosity and with some contempt, and now breaks in upon it with his "Why look ye one upon another?" It is the old Jacob, full of resources, prompt and imperturbable, equal to every turn of fortune, and never knowing how to yield.

Even more clearly do we see the vigour of Jacob's old age when he comes in contact with Joseph. For many years Joseph had been accustomed to command; he had unusual natural sagacity and a special gift of insight from God, but he seems a child in comparison with Jacob. When he brings his two sons to get their grandfather's blessing, Jacob sees what Joseph has no inkling of, and peremptorily declines to follow the advice of his wise son. With all Joseph's sagacity there were points in which his blind father saw more clearly than he. Joseph, who could teach the Egyptian senators wisdom, standing thus at a loss even to understand his father, and suggesting in his ignorance futile corrections, is a picture of the incapacity of natural affection to rise to the wisdom of God's love, and of the finest natural discernment to anticipate God's purposes or supply the place of a lifelong experience.

Jacob's warm-heartedness has also survived the chills and shocks of a long lifetime. He clings now to Benjamin as once he clung to Joseph. And as he had wrought for Rachel fourteen years, and the love he bare to her made them seem but a few days, so for twenty years now had he remembered Joseph who had inherited this love, and he shows by his frequent reference to him that he was keeping his word and going down to the grave mourning for his son. To such a man it must have been a severe trial indeed to be left alone in his tents, deprived of all his twelve sons; and we hear his old faith in God steadying the voice that yet trembles with emotion as he says, "If I be bereaved of my children, I am bereaved." It was a trial not, indeed, so painful as that of Abraham when he lifted the knife over the life of his only son; but it was so similar to it as inevitably to suggest it to the mind. Jacob also had to yield up all his children, and to feel, as he sat solitary in his tent, how utterly dependent upon God he was for their restoration; that it was not he but God alone who could build the house of Israel.

The anxiety with which he gazed evening after evening towards the setting sun, to descry the returning caravan, was at last relieved. But his joy was not altogether unalloyed. His sons brought with them a summons to shift the patriarchal encampment into Egypt—a summons which evidently nothing would have induced Jacob to respond to had it not come from his long-lost Joseph, and had it not thus received what he felt to be a divine sanction. The extreme reluctance which Jacob showed to the journey, we must be careful to refer to its true source. The Asiatics, and especially shepherd tribes, move easily. One who thoroughly knows the East says: "The Oriental is not afraid to go far, if he has not to cross the sea; for, once uprooted, distance makes little difference to him. He has no furniture to carry, for, except a carpet and a few brass pans, he uses none. He has no trouble about meals, for he is content with parched grain, which his wife can cook anywhere, or dried dates, or dried flesh, or anything obtainable which will keep. He is, on a march, careless where he sleeps, provided his family are around him—in a stable, under a porch, in the open air. He never changes his clothes at night, and he is profoundly indifferent to everything that the Western man understands by 'comfort.'" But there was in Jacob's case a peculiarity. He was called upon to abandon, for an indefinite period, the land which God had given him as the heir of His promise. With very great toil and not a little danger had Jacob won his way back to Canaan from Mesopotamia; on his return he had spent the best years of his life, and now he was resting there in his old age, having seen his children's children, and expecting nothing but a peaceful departure to his fathers. But suddenly the wagons of Pharaoh stand at his tent-door, and while the parched and bare pastures bid him go to the plenty of Egypt, to which the voice of his long-lost son invites him, he hears a summons which, however trying, he cannot disregard.

Such an experience is perpetually reproduced. Many are they who having at length received from God some long-expected good are quickly summoned to relinquish it again. And while the waiting for what seems indispensable to us is trying, it is tenfold more so to have to part with it when at last obtained, and obtained at the cost of much besides. That particular arrangement of our worldly circumstances which we have long sought, we are almost immediately thrown out of. That position in life, or that object of desire, which God Himself seems in many ways to have encouraged us to seek, is taken from us almost as soon as we have tasted its sweetness. The cup is dashed from our lips at the very moment when our thirst was to be fully slaked. In such distressing circumstances we cannot *see* the end God is aiming at; but of this we may be certain, that He does not wantonly annoy, or relish our discomfiture, and that when we are compelled to resign what is partial, it is that we may one day enjoy what is complete, and that if for the present we have to forego much comfort and delight, this is only an absolutely necessary step towards our permanent establishment in all that can bless and prosper us.

It is this state of feeling which explains the words of Jacob when introduced to Pharaoh. A recent writer, who spent some years on the banks of the Nile and on its waters, and who mixed freely with the inhabitants of Egypt, says: "Old Jacob's speech to Pharaoh really made me laugh, because it is so exactly like what a Fellah says to a Pacha, 'Few and evil have the days of the years of my life been,' Jacob being a most prosperous man, but it is manners to say all that." But Eastern manners need scarcely be called in to explain a sentiment which we find repeated by one who is generally esteemed the most self-sufficing of Europeans. "I have ever been esteemed," Goethe says, "one of Fortune's chiefest favourites; nor will I complain or find fault with the course my life has taken. Yet, truly, there has been nothing but toil and care; and I may say that, in all my seventy-five years, I have never had a month of genuine comfort. It has been the perpetual rolling of a stone, which I have always had to raise anew." Jacob's life had been almost ceaseless disquiet and disappointment. A man who had fled his country, who had been cheated into a marriage, who had been compelled by his own relative to live like a slave, who was only by flight able to save himself from a perpetual injustice, whose sons made his life bitter,—one of them by the foulest outrage a father could suffer, two of them by making him, as he himself said, to stink in the nostrils of the inhabitants of the land he was trying to settle in, and all of them by conspiring to deprive him of the child he most dearly loved—a man who at last, when he seemed to have had experience of every form of human calamity, was compelled by famine to relinquish the land for the sake of which he had endured all and spent all, might surely be forgiven a little plaintiveness in looking back upon his past. The wonder is to find Jacob to the end unbroken, dignified, and clear-seeing, capable and commanding, loving and full of faith.

Cordial as the reconciliation between Joseph and his brethren seemed, it was not as thorough as might have been desired. So long, indeed, as Jacob lived, all went well; but "when Joseph's brethren saw that their father was dead, they said, Joseph will peradventure hate us, and will certainly requite us all the evil which we did unto him." No wonder Joseph wept when he received their message. He wept because he saw that he was still misunderstood and distrusted by his brethren; because he felt, too, that had they been more generous men themselves, they would more easily have believed in his forgiveness; and because his pity was stirred for these men, who recognised that they were so completely in the power of their younger brother. Joseph had passed through severe conflicts of feeling about them, had been at great expense both of emotion and of outward good on their account, had risked his position in order to be able to serve them, and here is his reward! They supposed he had been but biding his time, that his apparent forgetfulness of their injury had been the crafty restraint of a deep-seated resentment; or, at best, that he had been unconsciously influenced by regard for his father, and now, when that influence was removed, the helpless condition of his brethren might tempt him to retaliate. This exhibition of a craven and suspicious spirit is unexpected, and must have been profoundly saddening to Joseph. Yet here, as elsewhere, he is magnanimous. Pity for them turns his thoughts from the injustice done to himself. He comforts them, and speaks kindly to them, saying, Fear ye not; I will nourish you and your little ones.

Many painful thoughts must have been suggested to Joseph by this conduct. If, after all he had done for his brethren, they had not yet learned to love him, but met his kindness with suspicion, was it not probable that underneath his apparent popularity with the Egyptians there might lie envy, or the cold acknowledgment that falls far short of love? This sudden disclosure of the real feeling of his brethren towards him must necessarily have made him uneasy about his other friendships. Did every one merely make use of him, and did no one give him pure love for his own sake? The people he had saved from famine, was there one of them that regarded him with anything resembling personal affection? Distrust seemed to pursue Joseph from first to last. First his own family misunderstood and persecuted him. Then his Egyptian master had returned his devoted service with suspicion and imprisonment. And now again, after sufficient time for testing his character might seem to have elapsed, he was still looked upon with distrust by those who of all others had best reason to believe in him. But though Joseph had through all his life been thus conversant with suspicion, cruelty, falsehood, ingratitude, and blindness, though he seemed doomed to be always misread, and to have his best deeds made the ground of accusation against him, he remained not merely unsoured, but equally ready as ever to be of service to all. The finest natures may be disconcerted and deadened by universal distrust; characters not naturally unamiable are sometimes embittered by suspicion; and persons who are in the main high-minded do stoop, when stung by such treatment, to rail at the world, or to question all generous emotion, steadfast friendship, or unimpeachable integrity. In Joseph there is nothing of this. If ever man had a right to complain of being unappreciated, it was he; if ever man was tempted to give up making sacrifices for his relatives, it was he. But through all this he bore himself with manly generosity, with simple and persistent faith, with a dignified respect for himself and for other men. In the ingratitude and injustice he had to endure, he only found opportunity for a deeper unselfishness, a more God-like forbearance. And that such may be the outcome of the sorest parts of human experience we have one day or other need to remember. When our good is evil spoken of, our motives suspected, our most sincere sacrifices scrutinized by an ignorant and malicious spirit, our most substantial and well-judged acts of kindness received with suspicion, and the love that is in them quite rejected, it is then we have opportunity to show that to us belongs the Christian temper that can pardon till seventy times seven, and that can persist in loving where love meets no response, and benefits provoke no gratitude.

How Joseph spent the years which succeeded the famine we have no means of knowing; but the closing act of his life seemed to the narrator so significant as to be worthy of record. "Joseph said unto his brethren, I die: and God will surely visit you, and bring you out of this land unto the land which he sware to Abraham, to Isaac, and to Jacob. And Joseph took an oath of the children of Israel, saying, God will surely visit you, and ye shall carry up my bones from hence." The Egyptians must have chiefly been struck by the simplicity of character which this request betokened. To the great benefactors of our country, the highest award is reserved to be given after death. So long as a man lives, some rude stroke of fortune or some disastrous error of his own may blast his fame; but when his bones are laid with those who have served their country best, a seal is set on his life, and a sentence pronounced which the revision of posterity rarely revokes. Such honours were customary among the Egyptians; it is from their tombs that their history can now be written. And to none were such honours more accessible than to Joseph. But after a life in the service of the state he retains the simplicity of the Hebrew lad. With the magnanimity of a great and pure soul, he passed uncontaminated through the flatteries and temptations of court-life; and, like Moses, "esteemed the reproach of Christ greater riches than the treasures of Egypt." He has not indulged in any affectation of simplicity, nor has he, in the pride that apes humility, declined the ordinary honours due to a man in his position. He wears the badges of office, the robe and the gold necklace, but these things do not reach his spirit. He has lived in a region in which such honours make no deep impression; and in his death he shows where his heart has been. The small voice of God, spoken centuries ago to his forefathers, deafens him to the loud acclaim with which the people do him homage.

By later generations this dying request of Joseph's was looked upon as one of the most remarkable instances of faith. For many years there had been no new revelation. The rising generations that had seen no man with whom God had spoken, were little interested in the land which was said to be theirs, but which they very well knew was infested by fierce tribes who, on at least one occasion during this period, inflicted disastrous defeat on one of the boldest of their own tribes. They were, besides, extremely attached to the country of their adoption; they luxuriated in its fertile meadows and teeming gardens, which kept them supplied at little cost of labour with delicacies unknown on the hills of Canaan. This oath, therefore, which Joseph made them swear, may have revived the drooping hopes of the small remnant who had any of his own spirit. They saw that he, their most sagacious man, lived and died in full assurance that God would visit His people. And through all the terrible bondage they were destined to suffer, the bones of Joseph, or rather his embalmed body, stood as the most eloquent advocate of God's faithfulness, ceaselessly reminding the despondent generations of the oath which God would yet enable them to fulfil. As often as they felt inclined to give up all hope and the last surviving Israelitish peculiarity, there was the unburied coffin remonstrating; Joseph still, even when dead, refusing to let his dust mingle with Egyptian earth.

And thus, as Joseph had been their pioneer who broke out a way for them into Egypt, so did he continue to hold open the gate and point the way back to Canaan. The brethren had sold him into this foreign land, meaning to bury him for ever; he retaliated by requiring that the tribes should restore him to the land from which he had been expelled. Few men have opportunity of showing so noble a revenge; fewer still, having the opportunity, would so have used it. Jacob had been carried up to Canaan as soon as he was dead: Joseph declines this exceptional treatment, and prefers to share the fortunes of his brethren, and will then only enter on the promised land when all his people can go with him. As in life, so in death, he took a large view of things, and had no feeling that the world ended in him. His career had taught him to consider national interests; and now, on his death-bed, it is from the point of view of his people that he looks at the future.

Several passages in the life of Joseph have shown us that where the Spirit of Christ is present, many parts of the conduct will suggest, if they do not actually resemble, acts in the life of Christ. The attitude towards the future in which Joseph sets his people as he leaves them, can scarcely fail to suggest the attitude which Christians are called to assume. The prospect which the Hebrews had of fulfilling their oath grew increasingly faint, but the difficulties in the way of its performance must only have made them more clearly see that they depended on God for entrance on the promised inheritance. And so may the difficulty of our duties as Christ's followers measure for us the amount of grace God has provided for us. The commands that make you sensible of your weakness, and bring to light more clearly than ever how unfit for good you are, are witnesses to you that God will visit you and enable you to fulfil the oath He has required you to take. The children of Israel could not suppose that a man so wise as Joseph had ended his life with a childish folly, when he made them swear this oath, and could not but renew their hope that the day would come when his wisdom would be justified by their ability to discharge it. Neither ought it to be beyond our belief that, in requiring from us such and such conduct, our Lord has kept in view our actual condition and its possibilities, and that His commands are our best guide towards a state of permanent felicity. He that aims always at the performance of the oath he has taken, will assuredly find that God will not stultify Himself by failing to support him.

XXXI
THE BLESSINGS OF THE TRIBES

Genesis xlviii. and xlix.

Jacob's blessing of his sons marks the close of the patriarchal dispensation. Henceforth the channel of God's blessing to man does not consist of one person only, but of a people or nation. It is still *one seed*, as Paul reminds us, a unit that God will bless, but this unit is now no longer a single person—as Abraham, Isaac, or Jacob—but one people, composed of several parts, and yet one whole; equally representative of Christ, as the patriarchs were, and of equal effect every way in receiving God's blessing and handing it down until Christ came. The Old Testament Church, quite as truly as the New, formed one whole with Christ. Apart from Him it had no meaning, and would have had no existence. It was the promised seed, always growing more and more to its perfect development in Christ. As the promise was kept to Abraham when Isaac was born, and as Isaac was truly the promised seed—in so far as he was a part of the series that led on to Christ, and was given in fulfilment of the promise that promised Christ to the world—so all through the history of Israel we must bear in mind that in them God is fulfilling this same promise, and that they are the promised seed in so far as they are one with Christ. And this interprets to us all those passages of the prophets regarding which men have disputed whether they are to be applied to Israel or to Christ: passages in which God addresses Israel in such words as, "Behold My servant," "Mine elect," and so forth, and in the interpretation of which it has been thought sufficient proof that they do not apply to Christ, to prove that they do apply to Israel; whereas, on the principle just laid down, it might much more safely be argued that because they apply to Israel, therefore they apply to Christ. And it is at this point—where Israel distributes among his sons the blessing which heretofore had all lodged in himself—that we see the first multiplication of Christ's representatives; the mediation going on no longer through individuals, but through a nation; and where individuals are still chosen by God, as commonly they are, for the conveyance of God's communications to earth, these individuals, whether priests or prophets, are themselves but the official representatives of the nation.

As the patriarchal dispensation ceases, it secures to the tribes all the blessing it has itself contained. Every father desires to leave to his sons whatever he has himself found helpful, but as they gather round his dying bed, or as he sits setting his house in order, and considering what portion is appropriate for each, he recognises that to some of them it is quite useless to bequeath the most valuable parts of his property, while in others he discerns a capacity which promises the improvement of all that is entrusted to it. And from the earliest times the various characters of the tribes were destined to modify the blessing conveyed to them by their father. The blessing of Israel is now distributed, and each receives what each can take; and while in some of the individual tribes there may seem to be very little of blessing at all, yet, taken together, they form a picture of the common outstanding features of human nature, and of that nature as acted upon by God's blessing, and forming together one body or Church. A peculiar interest attaches to the history of some nations, and is not altogether absent from our own, from the precision with which we can trace the character of families, descending often with the same unmistakable lineaments from father to son for many generations.[2] One knows at once to what families to look for restless and turbulent spirits, ready for conspiracy and revolution; and one knows also where to seek steady and faithful loyalty, public-spiritedness, or native ability. And in Israel's national character there was room for the great distinguishing features of the tribes, and to show the richness and variety with which the promise of God could fulfil itself wherever it was received. The distinguishing features which Jacob depicts in the blessings of his sons are necessarily veiled under the poetic figures of prophecy, and spoken of as they would reveal themselves in worldly matters; but these features were found in all the generations of the tribes, and displayed themselves in things spiritual also. For a man has not two characters, but one; and what he is in the world, that he is in his religion. In our own country, it is seen how the forms of worship, and even the doctrines believed, and certainly the modes of religious thought and feeling, depend on the natural character, and the natural character on the local situation of the respective sections of the community. No doubt in a country like ours, where men so constantly migrate from place to place, and where one common literature tends to mould us all to the same way of thinking, you do get men of all kinds in every place; yet even among ourselves the character of a place is generally still visible, and predominates over all that mingles with it. Much more must this character have been retained in a country where each man could trace his ancestry up to the father of the tribe, and cultivated with pride the family characteristics, and had but little intercourse, either literary or personal, with other minds and other manners. As we know by dialect and by the manners of the people when we pass into a new country, so must the Israelite have known by the eye and ear when he had crossed the county frontier, when he was conversing with a Benjamite, and when with a descendant of Judah. We are not therefore to suppose that any of these utterances of Jacob are mere geographical predictions, or that they depict characteristics which might appear in civil life, but not in religion and the Church, or that they would die out with the first generation.

In these blessings, therefore, we have the history of the Church in its most interesting form. In these sons gathered round him, the patriarch sees his own nature reflected piece by piece, and he sees also the general outline of all that must be produced by such natures as these men have. The whole destiny of Israel is here in germ, and the spirit of prophecy in Jacob sees and declares it. It has often been remarked[3] that as a man draws near to death, he seems to see many things in a much clearer light, and especially gets glimpses into the future, which are hidden from others.

"The soul's dark cottage, battered and decayed,
Lets in new light through chinks that time hath made."

Being nearer to eternity, he instinctively measures things by its standard, and thus comes nearer a just valuation of all things before his mind, and can better distinguish reality from appearance. Jacob has studied these sons of his for fifty years, and has had his acute perception of character painfully enough called to exercise itself on them. He has all his life long had a liking for analysing men's inner life, knowing that, when he understands that, he can better use them for his own ends; and these sons of his own have cost him thought enough over and above that sometimes penetrating interest which a father will take in the growth of a son's character; and now he knows them thoroughly, understands their temptations, their weaknesses, their capabilities, and, as a wise head of a house, can, with delicate and unnoticed skill, balance the one against the other, ward off awkward collisions, and prevent the evil from destroying the good. This knowledge of Jacob prepares him for being the intelligent agent by whom God predicts in outline the future of His Church.

One cannot but admire, too, the faith which enables Jacob to apportion to his sons the blessings of a land which had not been much of a resting-place to himself, and regarding the occupation of which his sons might have put to him some very difficult questions. And we admire this dignified faith the more on reflecting that it has often been very grievously lacking in our own case—that we have felt almost ashamed of having so little of a present tangible kind to offer, and of being obliged to speak only of invisible and future blessings; to set a spiritual consolation over against a worldly grief; to point a man whose fortunes are ruined to an eternal inheritance; or to speak to one who knows himself quite in the power of sin of a remedy which has often seemed illusory to ourselves. Some of us have got so little comfort or strength from religion ourselves, that we have no heart to offer it to others; and most of us have a feeling that we should seem to trifle were we to offer invisible aid against very visible calamity. At least we feel that we are doing a daring thing in making such an offer, and can scarce get over the desire that we had something to speak of which sight could appreciate, and which did not require the exercise of faith. Again and again the wish rises within us that to the sick man we could bring health as well as the promise of forgiveness, and that to the poor we could grant an earthly, while we make known a heavenly, inheritance. One who has experienced these scruples, and known how hard it is to get rid of them, will know also how to honour the faith of Jacob, by which he assumes the right to bless Pharaoh—though he is himself a mere sojourner by sufferance in Pharaoh's land, and living on his bounty—and by which he gathers his children round him and portions out to them a land which seemed to have been most barren to himself, and which now seemed quite beyond his reach. The enjoyments of it, which he himself had not very deeply tasted, he yet knew were real; and if there were a look of scepticism, or of scorn, on the face of any one of his sons; if the unbelief of any received the prophetic utterances as the ravings of delirium, or the fancies of an imbecile and worn-out mind going back to the scenes of its youth, in Jacob himself there was so simple and unsuspecting a faith in God's promise, that he dealt with the land as if it were the only portion worth bequeathing to his sons, as if every Canaanite were already cast out of it, and as if he knew his sons could never be tempted by the wealth of Egypt to turn with contempt from the land of promise. And if we would attain to this boldness of his, and be able to speak of spiritual and future blessings as very substantial and valuable, we must ourselves learn to make much of God's promise, and leave no taint of unbelief in our reception of it.

And often we are rebuked by finding that when we do offer things spiritual, even those who are wrapped in earthly comforts appreciate and accept the better gifts. So it was in Joseph's case. No doubt the highest posts in Egypt were open to his sons; they might have been naturalised, as he himself had been, and, throwing in their lot with the land of their adoption, might have turned to their advantage the rank their father held, and the reputation he had earned. But Joseph turns from this attractive prospect, brings them to his father, and hands them over to the despised shepherd-life of Israel. One need scarcely point out how great a sacrifice this was on Joseph's part. So universally acknowledged and legitimate a desire is it to pass to one's children the honour achieved by a life of exertion, that states have no higher rewards to confer on their most useful servants than a title which their descendants may wear. But Joseph would not suffer his children to risk the loss of their share in God's peculiar blessing, not for the most promising openings in life, or the highest civil honours. If the thoroughly open identification of them with the shepherds, and their profession of a belief in a distant inheritance, which must have made them appear madmen in the eyes of the Egyptians, if this was to cut them off from worldly advancement, Joseph was not careful of this, for resolved he was that, at any cost, they should be among God's people. And his faith received its reward; the two tribes that sprang from him received about as large a portion of the promised land as fell to the lot of all the other tribes put together.

You will observe that Ephraim and Manasseh were adopted as sons of Jacob. Jacob tells Joseph, "They shall be mine," not my grandsons, but as Reuben and Simeon. No other sons whom Joseph might have were to be received into this honour, but these two were to take their place on a level with their uncles as heads of tribes, so that Joseph is represented through the whole history by the two populous and powerful tribes of Ephraim and Manasseh. No greater honour could have been put on Joseph, nor any more distinct and lasting recognition made of the indebtedness of his family to him, and of how he had been as a father bringing new life to his brethren, than this, that his sons should be raised to the rank of heads of tribes, on a level with the immediate sons of Jacob. And no higher honour could have been put on the two lads themselves than that they should thus be treated as if they were their father Joseph—as if they had his worth and his rank. He is merged in them, and all that he has earned is, throughout the history, to be found, not in his own name, but in theirs. It all proceeds from him; but his enjoyment is found in their enjoyment, his worth acknowledged in their fruitfulness. Thus did God familiarise the Jewish mind through its whole history with the idea, if they chose to think and have ideas, of adoption, and of an adoption of a peculiar kind, of an adoption where already there was an heir who, by this adoption, has his name and worth merged in the persons now received into his place. Ephraim and Manasseh were not received alongside of Joseph, but each received what Joseph himself might have had, and Joseph's name as a tribe was henceforth only to be found in these two. This idea was fixed in such a way, that for centuries it was steeping into the minds of men, so that they might not be astonished if God should in some other case, say the case of His own Son, adopt men into the rank He held, and let His estimate of the worth of His Son, and the honour He puts upon Him, be seen in the adopted. This being so, we need not be alarmed if men tell us that imputation is a mere legal fiction, or human invention; a legal fiction it may be, but in the case before us it was the never-disputed foundation of very substantial blessings to Ephraim and Manasseh; and we plead for nothing more than that God would act with us as here He did act with these two, that He would make us His direct heirs, make us His own sons, and give us what He who presents us to Him to receive His blessing did earn, and merits at the Father's hand.

We meet with these crossed hands of blessing frequently in Scripture; the younger son blessed above the elder—as was needful, lest grace should become confounded with nature, and the belief gradually grow up in men's minds that natural effects could never be overcome by grace, and that in every respect grace waited upon nature. And these crossed hands we meet still; for how often does God quite reverse *our* order, and bless most that about which we had less concern, and seem to put a slight on that which has engrossed our best affection. It is so, often in precisely the way in which Joseph found it so; the son whose youth is most anxiously cared for, to whom the interests of the younger members of the family are sacrificed, and who is commended to God continually to receive His right-hand blessing, this son seems neither to receive nor to dispense much blessing; but the younger, less thought of, left to work his own way, is favoured by God, and becomes the comfort and support of his parents when the elder has failed of his duty. And in the case of much that we hold dear, the same rule is seen; a pursuit we wish to be successful in we can make little of, and are thrown back from continually, while something else into which we have thrown ourselves almost accidentally prospers in our hand and blesses us. Again and again, for years together, we put forward some cherished desire to God's right hand, and are displeased, like Joseph, that still the hand of greater blessing should pass to some other thing. Does God not know what is oldest with us, what has been longest at our hearts, and is dearest to us? Certainly He does: "I know it, My son, I know it," He answers to all our expostulations. It is not because He does not understand or regard your predilections, your natural and excusable preferences, that He sometimes refuses to gratify your whole desire, and pours upon you blessings of a kind somewhat different from these you most earnestly covet. He will give you the whole that Christ hath merited; but for the application and distribution of that grace and blessing you must be content to trust Him. You may be at a loss to know why He does no more to deliver you from some sin, or why He does not make you more successful in your efforts to aid others, or why, while He so liberally prospers you in one part of your condition, you get so much less in another that is far nearer your heart; but God does what He will with His own, and if you do not find in one point the whole blessing and prosperity you think should flow from such a Mediator as you have, you may only conclude that what is lacking there will elsewhere be found more wisely bestowed. And is it not a perpetual encouragement to us that God does not merely crown what nature has successfully begun, that it is not the likely and the naturally good that are most blessed, but that God hath chosen the foolish things of the world to confound the wise, and the weak things of the world to confound the things that are mighty; and base things of the world and things which are despised hath God chosen, yea, and things which are not, to bring to nought things that are?

In Reuben, the first-born, conscience must have been sadly at war with hope as he looked at the blind, but expressive, face of his father. He may have hoped that his sin had not been severely thought of by his father, or that the father's pride in his first-born would prompt him to hide, though it could not make him forget it. Probably the gross offence had not been made known to the family. At least, the words "he went up" may be understood as addressed in explanation to the brethren. It may indeed have been that the blind old man, forcibly recalling the long-past transgression, is here uttering a mournful, regretful soliloquy, rather than addressing any one. It may be that these words were uttered to himself as he went back upon the one deed that had disclosed to him his son's real character, and rudely hurled to the ground all the hopes he had built up for his first-born. Yet there is no reason to suppose, on the other hand, that the sin had been previously known or alluded to in the family. Reuben's hasty, passionate nature could not understand that if Jacob had felt that sin of his deeply, he should not have shown his resentment; he had stunned his father with the heavy blow, and because he did not cry out and strike him in return, he thought him little hurt. So do shallow natures tremble for a night after their sin, and when they find that the sun rises and men greet them as cordially as before, and that no hand lays hold on them from the past, they think little more of their sin—do not understand that fatal calm that precedes the storm. Had the memory of Reuben's sin survived in Jacob's mind all the sad events that had since happened, and all the stirring incidents of the emigration and the new life in Egypt? Could his father at the last hour, and after so many thronged years, and before his brethren, recall the old sin? He is relieved and confirmed in his confidence by the first words of Jacob, words ascribing to him his natural position, a certain conspicuous dignity too, and power such as one may often see produced in men by occupying positions of authority, though in their own character there be weakness. But all the excellence that Jacob ascribes to Reuben serves only to embitter the doom pronounced upon him. Men seem often to expect that a future can be *given* to them irrespective of what they themselves are, that a series of blessings and events might be prepared for them, and made over to them; whereas every man's future must be made by himself, and is already in great part formed by the past. It was a vain expectation of Reuben to expect that he, the impetuous, unstable, superficial son, could have the future of a deep, and earnest, and dutiful nature, or that his children should derive no taint from their parent, but be as the children of Joseph. No man's future need be altogether a doom to him, for God may bless to him the evil fruit his life has borne; but certainly no man need look for a future which has no relation to his own character. His future will always be made up of *his* deeds, *his* feelings, and the circumstances which *his* desires have brought him into.

The future of Reuben was of a negative, blank kind—"Thou shalt *not* excel;" his unstable character must empty it of all great success. And to many a heart since have these words struck a chill, for to many they are as a mirror suddenly held up before them. They see themselves when they look on the tossing sea, rising and pointing to the heavens with much noise, but only to sink back again to the same everlasting level. Men of brilliant parts and great capacity are continually seen to be lost to society by instability of purpose. Would they only pursue one direction, and concentrate their energies on one subject, they might become true heirs of promise, blessed and blessing; but they seem to lose relish for every pursuit on the first taste of success— all their energy seems to have boiled over and evaporated in the first glow, and sinks as the water that has just been noisily boiling when the fire is withdrawn from under it. No impression made upon them is permanent: like water, they are plastic, easily impressible, but utterly incapable of retaining an impression; and therefore, like water, they have a downward tendency, or at the best are but retained in their place by pressure from without, and have no eternal power of growth. And the misery of this character is often increased by the *desire* to excel which commonly accompanies instability. It is generally this very desire which prompts a man to hurry from one aim to another, to give up one path to excellence when he sees that other men are making way upon another: having no internal convictions of his own, he is guided mostly by the successes of other men, the most dangerous of all guides. So that such a man has all the bitterness of an eager desire doomed never to be satisfied. Conscious to himself of capacity for something, feeling in him the excellency of power, and having that "excellency of dignity," or graceful and princely refinement, which the knowledge of many things, and intercourse with many kinds of people, have imparted to him, he feels all the more that pervading weakness, that greedy, lustful craving for all kinds of priority, and for enjoying all the various advantages which other men severally enjoy, which will not let him finally choose and adhere to his own line of things, but distracts him by a thousand purposes which ever defeat one another.[4]

The sin of the next oldest sons was also remembered against them, and remembered apparently for the same reason—because the character was expressed in it. The massacre of the Shechemites was not an accidental outrage that any other of the sons of Jacob might equally have perpetrated, but the most glaring of a number of expressions of a fierce and cruel disposition in these two men. In Jacob's prediction of their future, he seems to shrink with horror from his own progeny—like her who dreamt she would give birth to a firebrand. He sees the possibility of the direst results flowing from such a temper, and, under God, provides against these by scattering the tribes, and thus weakening their power for evil. They had been banded together so as the more easily and securely to accomplish their murderous purposes. "Simeon and Levi are brethren"—showing a close affinity, and seeking one another's society and aid, but it is for bad purposes; and therefore they must be divided in Jacob and scattered in Israel. This was accomplished by the tribe of Levi being distributed over all the other tribes as the ministers of religion. The fiery zeal, the bold independence, and the pride of being a distinct people, which had been displayed in the slaughter of the Shechemites, might be toned down and turned to good account when the sword was taken out of their hand. Qualities such as these, which produce the most disastrous results when fit instruments can be found, and when men of like disposition are suffered to band themselves together, may, when found in the individual and kept in check by circumstances and dissimilar dispositions, be highly beneficial.

In the sin, Levi seems to have been the moving spirit, Simeon the abetting tool, and in the punishment, it is the more dangerous tribe that is scattered, so that the other is left companionless. In the blessings of Moses, the tribe of Simeon is passed over in silence; and that the tribe of Levi should have been so used for God's immediate service stands as evidence that punishments, however severe and desolating, even threatening something bordering on extinction, may yet become blessings to God's people. The sword of murder was displaced in Levi's hand by the knife of sacrifice; their fierce revenge against sinners was converted into hostility against sin; their apparent zeal for the forms of their religion was consecrated to the service of the tabernacle and temple; their fanatical pride, which prompted them to treat all other people as the offscouring of the earth, was informed by a better spirit, and used for the upbuilding and instruction of the people of Israel. In order to understand why this tribe, of all others, should have been chosen for the service of the sanctuary and for the instruction of the people, we must not only recognise how their being scattered in punishment of their sin over all the land fitted them to be the educators of the nation and the representatives of all the tribes, but also we must consider that the sin itself which Levi had committed broke the one command which men had up till this time received from the mouth of God; no law had as yet been published but that which had been given to Noah and his sons regarding bloodshed, and which was given in circumstances so appalling, and with sanctions so emphatic, that it might ever have rung in men's ears, and stayed the hand of the murderer. In saying, "At the hand of every man's brother will I require the life of man," God had shown that human life was to be counted sacred. He Himself had swept the race from the face of the earth, but adding this command immediately after, He showed all the more forcibly that punishment was His own prerogative, and that none but those appointed by Him might shed blood—"Vengeance is Mine, saith the Lord." To take private revenge, as Levi did, was to take the sword out of God's hand, and to say that God was not careful enough of justice, and but a poor guardian of right and wrong in the world; and to destroy human life in the wanton and cruel manner in which Levi had destroyed the Shechemites, and to do it under colour and by the aid of religious zeal, was to God the most hateful of sins. But none can know the hatefulness of a sin so distinctly as he who has fallen into it, and is enduring the punishment of it penitently and graciously, and therefore Levi was of all others the best fitted to be entrusted with those sacrificial symbols which set forth the value of all human life, and especially of the life of God's own Son. Very humbling must it have been for the Levite who remembered the history of his tribe to be used by God as the hand of His justice on the victims that were brought in substitution for that which was so precious in the sight of God.

The blessing of Judah is at once the most important and the most difficult to interpret in the series. There is enough in the history of Judah himself, and there is enough in the subsequent history of the tribe, to justify the ascription to him of all lion-like qualities—a kingly fearlessness, confidence, power, and success; in action a rapidity of movement and might that make him irresistible, and in repose a majestic dignity of bearing. As the serpent is the cognisance of Dan, the wolf of Benjamin, the hind of Naphtali, so is the lion of the tribe of Judah. He scorns to gain his end by a serpentine craft, and is himself easily taken in; he does not ravin like a wolf, merely plundering for the sake of booty, but gives freely and generously, even to the sacrifice of his own person: nor has he the mere graceful and ineffective swiftness of the hind, but the rushing onset of the lion—a character which, more than any other, men reverence and admire—"Judah, *thou* art he whom thy brethren shall praise"—and a character which, more than any other, fits a man to take the lead and rule. If there were to be kings in Israel, there could be little doubt from which tribe they could best be chosen; a wolf of the tribe of Benjamin, like Saul, not only hung on the rear of retreating

Philistines and spoiled them, but made a prey of his own people, and it is in David we find the true king, the man who more than any other satisfies men's ideal of the prince to whom they will pay homage;—falling indeed into grievous error and sin, like his forefather, but, like him also, right at heart, so generous and self-sacrificing that men served him with the most devoted loyalty, and were willing rather to dwell in caves with him than in palaces with any other.

The kingly supremacy of Judah was here spoken of in words which have been the subject of as prolonged and violent contention as any others in the Word of God. "The sceptre shall not depart from Judah, nor a lawgiver from between his feet, until Shiloh come." These words are very generally understood to mean that Judah's supremacy would continue until it culminated or flowered into the personal reign of Shiloh; in other words, that Judah's sovereignty was to be perpetuated in the person of Jesus Christ. So that this prediction is but the first whisper of that which was afterwards so distinctly declared, that David's seed should sit on the throne for ever and ever. It was not accomplished in the letter, any more than the promise to David was; the tribe of Judah cannot in any intelligible sense be said to have had rulers of her own up to the coming of Christ, or for some centuries previous to that date. For those who would quickly judge God and His promise by what they could see in their own day, there was enough to provoke them to challenge God for forgetting His promise. But in due time *the* King of men, He to whom all nations have gathered, did spring from this tribe; and need it be said that the very fact of His appearance proved that the supremacy had not departed from Judah? This prediction, then, partook of the character of very many of the Old Testament prophecies; there was sufficient fulfilment in the letter to seal, as it were, the promise, and give men a token that it was being accomplished, and yet so mysterious a falling short, as to cause men to look beyond the literal fulfilment, on which alone their hopes had at first rested, to some far higher and more perfect spiritual fulfilment.

But not only has it been objected that the sceptre departed from Judah long before Christ came, and that therefore the word Shiloh cannot refer to Him, but also it has been truly said that wherever else the word occurs it is the name of a town—that town, viz., where the ark for a long time was stationed, and from which the allotment of territory was made to the various tribes; and the prediction has been supposed to mean that Judah should be the leading tribe till the land was entered. Many objections to this naturally occur, and need not be stated. But it comes to be an inquiry of some interest, How much information regarding a personal Messiah did the brethren receive from this prophecy? A question very difficult indeed to answer. The word Shiloh means "peace-making," and if they understood this as a proper name, they must have thought of a person such as Isaiah designates as the Prince of Peace—a name it was similar to that wherewith David called his son Solomon, in the expectation that the results of his own lifetime of disorder and battle would be reaped by his successor in a peaceful and prosperous reign. It can scarcely be thought likely, indeed, that this single term "Shiloh," which might be applied to many things besides a person, should give to the sons of Jacob any distinct idea of a personal Deliverer; but it might be sufficient to keep before their eyes, and specially before the tribe of Judah, that the aim and consummation of all lawgiving and ruling was peace. And there was certainly contained in this blessing an assurance that the purpose of Judah would not be accomplished, and therefore that the existence of Judah as a tribe would not terminate, until peace had been through its means brought into the world: thus was the assurance given, that the productive power of Judah should not fail until out of that tribe there had sprung that which should give peace.

But to us who have seen the prediction accomplished, it plainly enough points to *the* Lion of the tribe of Judah, who in His own person combined all kingly qualities. In Him we are taught by this prediction to discover once more the single Person who stands out on the page of this world's history as satisfying men's ideal of what their King should be, and of how the race should be represented;—the One who without any rival stands in the mind's eye as that for which the best hopes of men were waiting, still feeling that the race could do more than it had done, and never satisfied but in Him.

Zebulun, the sixth and last of Leah's sons, was so called because said Leah, "Now will my husband *dwell with me*" (such being the meaning of the name), "for I have borne him six sons." All that is predicted regarding this tribe is that his *dwelling* should be by the sea, and near the Phœnician city Zidon. This is not to be taken as a strict geographical definition of the tract of country occupied by Zebulun, as we see when we compare it with the lot assigned to it and marked out in the Book of Joshua; but though the border of the tribe did not reach to Zidon, and though it can only have been a mere tongue of land belonging to it that ran down to the Mediterranean shore, yet the situation ascribed to it is true to its character as a tribe that had commercial relations with the Phœnicians, and was of a decidedly mercantile turn. We find this same feature indicated in the blessing of Moses: "Rejoice, Zebulun, in thy *going out*, and Issachar in thy tents"— Zebulun having the enterprise of a seafaring community, and Issachar the quiet bucolic contentment of an agricultural or pastoral population: Zebulun always restlessly eager for emigration or commerce, for *going out* of one kind or other; Issachar satisfied to live and die in his own tents. It is still, therefore, character rather than geographical position that is here spoken of—though it is a trait of character that is peculiarly dependent on geographical position: we, for example, because islanders, having become the maritime power and the merchants of the world; not being shut off from other nations by the encompassing sea, but finding paths by it equally in all directions ready provided for every kind of traffic.

Zebulun, then, was to represent the commerce of Israel, its *outgoing* tendency; was to supply a means of communication and bond of connection with the world outside, so that through it might be conveyed to the nations what was saving in Israel, and that what Israel needed from other lands might also find entrance. In the Church also, this is a needful quality: for our well-being there must ever exist among us those who are not afraid to launch on the wide and pathless sea of opinion; those in whose ears its waves have from their childhood sounded with a fascinating invitation, and who at last, as if possessed by some spirit of unrest, loose from the firm earth, and go in quest of lands not yet discovered, or are impelled to see for themselves what till now they have believed on the testimony of others. It is not for all men to quit the shore, and risk themselves in the miseries and disasters of so comfortless and hazardous a life; but happy the people which possesses, from one generation to another, men who must see with their own eyes, and to whose restless nature the discomforts and dangers of an unsettled life have a charm. It is not the instability of Reuben that we have in these men, but the irrepressible longing of the born seaman, who *must* lift the misty veil of the horizon and penetrate its mystery. And we are not to condemn, even when we know we should not imitate, men who cannot rest satisfied with the ground on which we stand, but venture into regions of speculation, of religious thought which we have never trodden, and may deem hazardous. The nourishment we receive is not all native-grown; there are views of truth which may very profitably be imported from strange and distant lands; and there is no land, no province of thought, from which we may not derive what may advantageously be mixed with our own ideas; no direction in which a speculative mind can go in which it may not find something which may give a fresh zest to what we already use, or be a real addition to our knowledge. No doubt men who refuse to confine themselves to one way of viewing truth—men who venture to go close to persons of very different opinions from their own, who determine for themselves to prove all things, who have no very special love for what they were native to and originally taught, who show rather a taste for strange and new opinions—these persons live a life of great hazard, and in the end are generally, like men who have been much at sea, unsettled; they have not fixed opinions, and are in themselves, as individual men, unsatisfactory and unsatisfied; but still they have done good to the community, by bringing to us ideas and knowledge which otherwise we could not have obtained. Such men God gives us to widen our views; to prevent us from thinking that we have the best of everything; to bring us to acknowledge that others, who perhaps in the main are not so favoured as ourselves, are yet possessed of some things we ourselves would be the better of. And though these men must themselves necessarily hang loosely, scarcely attached very firmly to any part of the Church, like a seafaring population, and often even with a border running very close to heathenism, yet let us own that the Church has need of such—that without them the different sections of the Church would know too little of one another, and too little of the facts of this world's life. And as the seafaring population of a country might be expected to show less interest in the soil of their native land than others, and yet we know that in point of fact we are dependent on no class of our population so much for leal patriotism, and for the defence of our country, so one has observed that the Church also must make similar use of her Zebuluns—of men who, by their very habit of restlessly considering all views of truth which are alien to our own ways of thinking, have become familiar with, and better able to defend us against, the error that mingles with these views.

Issachar receives from his father a character which few would be proud of or would envy, but which many are very content to bear. As the strong ass that has its stall and its provender provided can afford to let the free beasts of the forest vaunt their liberty, so there is a very numerous class of men who have no care to assert their dignity as human beings, or to agitate regarding their rights as citizens, so long as their obscurity and servitude provide them with physical comforts, and leave them free of heavy responsibilities. They prefer a life of ease and plenty to a life of hardship and glory. They are not lazy nor idle, but are quite willing to use their strength so long as they are not overdriven out of their sleekness. They have neither ambition nor enterprise, and willingly bow their shoulders to bear, and become the servants of those who will free them from the anxiety of planning and managing, and give them a fair and regular remuneration for their labour. This is not a noble nature, but in a world in which ambition so frequently runs through a thorny and difficult path to a disappointing and shameful end, this disposition has much to say in its own defence. It will often accredit itself with unchallengeable common sense, and will maintain that it alone enjoys life and gets the good of it. They will tell you they are the only true utilitarians, that to be one's own master only brings cares, and that the degradation of servitude is only an idea; that *really* servants are quite as well off as masters. Look at them: the one is as a strong, powerful, well-cared-for animal, his work but a pleasant exercise to him, and when it is over never following him into his rest; he eats the good of the land, and has what all seem to be in vain striving for, rest and contentment: the other, the master, has indeed his position, but that only multiplies his duties; he has wealth, but that proverbially only increases his cares and the mouths that are to consume it; it is *he* who has the air of a bondsman, and never, meet him when you may, seems wholly at ease and free from care.

Yet, after all that can be said in favour of the bargain an Issachar makes, and however he may be satisfied to rest, and in a quiet, peaceful way enjoy life, men feel that at the best there is something despicable about such a character. He gives his labour and is fed, he pays his tribute and is protected; but men feel that they ought to meet the dangers, responsibilities, and difficulties of life in their own persons, and at first hand, and not buy themselves off so from the burden of individual self-control and responsibility. The animal enjoyment of this life and its physical comforts may be a very good ingredient in a national character: it might be well for Israel to have this patient, docile mass of strength in its midst: it may be well for our country that there are among us not only men eager for the highest honours and posts, but a great multitude of men perhaps equally serviceable and capable, but whose desires never rise beyond the ordinary social comforts; the contentedness of such, even though reprehensible, tempers or balances the ambition of the others, and when it comes into personal contact rebukes its feverishness. They, as well as the other parts of society, have amidst their error a truth—the truth that the ideal world in which ambition, and hope, and imagination live is not everything; that the material has also a reality, and that though hope does bless mankind, yet attainment is also something, even though it be a little. Yet this truth is not the whole truth, and is only useful as an ingredient, as a part, not as the whole; and when we fall from any high ideal of human life which we have formed, and begin to find comfort and rest in the mere physical good things of this world, we may well despise ourselves. There is a pleasantness still in the land that appeals to us all; a luxury in observing the risks and struggles of others while ourselves secure and at rest; a desire to make life easy, and to shirk the responsibility and toil that public-spiritedness entails. Yet of what tribe has the Church more cause to complain than of those persons who seem to imagine that they have done enough when they have joined the Church and received their own inheritance to enjoy; who are alive to no emergency, nor awake to the need of others; who have no idea at all of their being a part of the community, for which, as well as for themselves, there are duties to discharge; who couch, like the ass of Issachar, in their comfort without one generous impulse to make common cause against the common evils and foes of the Church, and are unvisited by a single compunction that while they lie there, submitting to whatever fate sends, there are kindred tribes of their own being oppressed and spoiled?

There seems to have been an improvement in this tribe, an infusion of some new life into it. In the time of Deborah, indeed, it is with a note of surprise that, while celebrating the victory of Israel, she names even Issachar as having been roused to action, and as having helped in the common cause—"the princes of Issachar were with Deborah, *even* Issachar;" but we find them again in the days of David wiping out their reproach, and standing by him manfully. And there an apparently new character is given to them—"the children of Issachar, which were men that had understanding of the times, to know what Israel ought to do." This quite accords, however, with the kind of practical philosophy which we have seen to be imbedded in Issachar's character. Men they were not distracted by high thoughts and ambitions, but who judged things according to their substantial value to themselves; and who were, therefore, in a position to give much good advice on practical matters—advice which would always have a tendency to trend too much towards mere utilitarianism and worldliness, and to partake rather of crafty politic diplomacy than of far-seeing statesmanship, yet trustworthy for a certain class of subjects. And here, too, they represent the same class in the Church, already alluded to; for one often finds that men who will not interrupt their own comfort, and who have a kind of stolid indifference as to what comes of the good of the Church, have yet also much shrewd practical wisdom; and were these men, instead of spending their sagacity in cynical denunciation of what the Church does, to throw themselves into the cause of the Church, and heartily advise her what she *ought* to do, and help in the doing of it, their observation of human affairs, and political understanding of the times, would be turned to good account, instead of being a reproach.

Next came the eldest son of Rachel's handmaid, and the eldest son of Leah's handmaid, Dan and Gad. Dan's name, meaning "judge," is the starting point of the prediction—"Dan shall judge his people." This word "judge" we are perhaps somewhat apt to misapprehend; it means rather to defend than to sit in judgment on; it refers to a judgment passed between one's own people and their foes, and an execution of such judgment in the deliverance of the people and the destruction of the foe. We are familiar with this meaning of the word by the constant reference in the Old Testament to God's *judging* His people; this being always a cause of joy as their sure deliverance from their enemies. So also it is used of those men who, when Israel had no king, rose from time to time as the champions of the people, to lead them against the foe, and who are therefore familiarly called "The Judges." From the tribe of Dan the most conspicuous of these arose, Samson, namely, and it is probably mainly with reference to this fact that Jacob so emphatically predicts of *this* tribe, "Dan shall judge his people." And notice the appended clause (as reflecting shame on the sluggish Issachar), "as one of the tribes of Israel," recognising always that his strength was not for himself alone, but for his country; that he was not an isolated people who had to concern himself only with his own affairs, but *one* of the tribes of Israel. The manner, too, in which Dan was to do this was singularly descriptive of the facts subsequently evolved. Dan was a very small and insignificant tribe, whose lot originally lay close to the Philistines on the southern border of the land. It might seem to be no obstacle whatever to the invading Philistines as they passed to the richer portion of Judah, but this little tribe, through Samson, smote these terrors of the Israelites with so sore and alarming a destruction as to cripple them for years and make them harmless. We see, therefore, how aptly Jacob compares them to the venomous snake that lurks in the road and bites the horses' heels; the dust-coloured adder that a man treads on before he is aware, and whose poisonous stroke is more deadly than the foe he is looking for in front. And especially significant did the imagery appear to the Jews, with whom this poisonous adder was indigenous, but to whom the horse was the symbol of foreign armament and invasion. The whole tribe of Dan, too, seems to have partaken of that "grim humour" with which Samson saw his foes walk time after time into the traps he set for them, and give themselves an easy prey to him—a humour which comes out with singular piquancy in the narrative given in the Book of Judges of one of the forays of this tribe, in which they carried off Micah's priest and even his gods.

But why, in the full flow of his eloquent description of the varied virtues of his sons, does the patriarch suddenly check himself, lie back on his pillows, and quietly say, "I have waited for Thy salvation, O God"? Does he feel his strength leave him so that he cannot go on to bless the rest of his sons, and has but time to yield his own spirit to God? Are we here to interpolate one of those scenes we are all fated to witness when some eagerly watched breath seems altogether to fail before the last words have been uttered, when those who have been standing apart, through sorrow and reverence, quickly gather round the bed to catch the last look, and when the dying man again collects himself and finishes his work? Probably Jacob, having, as it were, projected himself forward into those stirring and warlike times he has been speaking of, so realises the danger of his people, and the futility even of such help as Dan's when God does not help, that, as if from the midst of doubtful war, he cries, as with a battle cry, "I have waited for Thy salvation, O God." His longing for victory and blessing to his sons far overshot the deliverance from Philistines accomplished by Samson. That deliverance he thankfully accepts and joyfully predicts, but in the spirit of an Israelite indeed, and a genuine child of the promise, he remains unsatisfied, and sees in all such deliverance only the pledge of God's coming nearer and nearer to His people, bringing with Him *His* eternal salvation. In Dan, therefore, we have not the catholic spirit of Zebulun, nor the practical, though sluggish, temper of Issachar; but we are guided rather to the disposition which ought to be maintained through all Christian life, and which, with special care, needs to be cherished in Church-life—a disposition to accept with gratitude all success and triumph, but still to aim through all at that highest victory which God alone can accomplish for His people. It is to be the battle-cry with which every Christian and every Church is to preserve itself, not merely against external foes, but against the far more disastrous influence of self-confidence, pride, and glorying in man—"For *Thy* salvation, O God, do we wait."

Gad also is a tribe whose history is to be warlike, his very name signifying a marauding, guerilla troop; and his history was to illustrate the victories which God's people gain by tenacious, watchful, ever-renewed warfare. The Church has often prospered by her Dan-like insignificance; the world not troubling itself to make war upon her. But oftener Gad is a better representative of the mode in which her successes are gained. We find that the men of Gad were among the most valuable of David's warriors, when his necessity evoked all the various skill and energy of Israel. "Of the Gadites," we read, "there separated themselves unto David into the hold of the wilderness men of might, and men of war fit for the battle, that could handle shield and buckler, whose faces were like the faces of lions, and were as swift as the roes upon the mountains: one of the least of them was better than an hundred, and the greatest mightier than a thousand." And there is something particularly inspiring to the individual Christian in finding this pronounced as part of the blessing of God's people—"a troop shall overcome him, *but he shall* overcome at the last." It is this that enables us to persevere—that we have God's assurance that present discomfiture does not doom us to final defeat. If you be among the children of promise, among those that gather round God to catch His blessing, you shall overcome at the last. You may now feel as if assaulted by treacherous, murderous foes, irregular troops, that betake themselves to every cruel deceit, and are ruthless in spoiling you; you may be assailed by so many and strange temptations that you are bewildered and cannot lift a hand to resist, scarce seeing where your danger comes from; you may be buffeted by messengers of Satan, distracted by a sudden and tumultuous incursion of a crowd of cares so that you are moved away from the old habits of your life amid which you seem to stand safely; your heart may seem to be the rendezvous of all ungodly and wicked thoughts, you may feel trodden under foot and overrun by sin, but, with the blessing of God, you shall overcome at the last. Only cultivate that dogged pertinacity of Gad, which has no thought of ultimate defeat, but rallies cheerfully and resolutely after every discomfiture.

FOOTNOTES:

[2] Merivale's *Romans under the Empire*, vi. 261.

[3] Plato, *Repub.* i. 5, etc.

[4] The subsequent history of the tribe shows that the character of its father was transmitted. "No judge, no prophet, not one of the tribe of Reuben, is mentioned." (*Vide* Smith's Dictionary, *Reuben*.)